HOUSING WITHOUT H

HOUSING WITHOUT HOUSES

Participation, Flexibility, Enablement

NABEEL HAMDI

INTERMEDIATE TECHNOLOGY PUBLICATIONS 1995

Intermediate Technology Publications Ltd
103–105 Southampton Row, London WC1B 4HH, UK

First published in paperback by
Intermediate Technology Publications 1995

First published by Van Nostrand Reinhold

ISBN 185339 292 8

A CIP catalogue record for this book is available from the British Library.

Printed by SRP, Exeter, UK

To Rachel, Nadia, and Oliver

CONTENTS

Foreword by John F. C. Turner ix
Preface xi

PART I
THEORIES OF PRACTICE: CHANGING PARADIGMS

1   DECIDING ON CONTEXT   3

Worsening Conditions: The Third World, 4   Worsening Conditions:
The First World, 6   Professional Dilemmas, 7   The Issues, 8

2   A TALE OF TWO PARADIGMS   11

Public Interventions: How and Why? 12   Paradigms in Conflict? 26
No Single Solution, 32

3   A TALE OF TWO ARCHITECTS   38

Common Objectives, 39   Differences in Method, 43   Flexibility,
Participation, and Enablement, 46

PART II
THE PRACTICE OF THEORY: ENABLEMENT AND
THE INDETERMINACY OF DESIGN

4   FLEXIBILITY AND BUILDING   51

Getting the Right Fit, 53   Designing Capacities for Change and Fit, 57
Design Principles, 73

5   PARTICIPATION AND COMMUNITY   75

The Beginnings in Britain, 76   The Beginnings in the United States, 77
The Beginnings in the Developing Countries, 78   Why We Need
Participation, 80   Conditions and Objections, 83   Participation:
The Means or the Ends? 85

6   ENABLEMENT AND DESIGN   88

Making Plans with Minimal Planning: An Example, 89   Design
Thinking, 102   Designing, 104

7   LOOKING, LISTENING, AND MEASURING   109

Knowing the Actors, 110   Getting Organized, 111   Looking and
Listening, 114   Measuring, 123   Examining the Information, 126

8   BUILDING A PROGRAM   129

Identifying and Positioning Problems, 131   Identifying Options and
Establishing a Plan of Action, 140   Evaluating Linkages, 144
Methods and Assumptions, 147

9   DECIDING INTERVENTIONS: METHODS AND MODELS   151

Making Strategic Choices, 152   GamePAK, 153   Cognitive
Maps, 154   Planning for Real, 156   A Pro Forma Attempt at
Public Participation, 160   A Metaphorical Model, 161

10   ARCHITECTS AND HOUSING: CHANGING PROFESSIONAL
     RESPONSIBILITIES AND TRAINING   168

Architects and Housing in History, 169   Implications of the Support
Paradigm for Teaching, 172   Operational Implications, 175   A New
Agenda, 179

ADDITIONAL READINGS   182

General Readings, 182   History, 184   Ideas, Approaches,
and Critiques, 185   Public and Private: Policies and Interventions, 188
Financial Management, 188   Building Technology, 189   Methods
and Tools, 190

Index   *192*

FOREWORD

Nabeel Hamdi has written that this book "is a primer for practitioners and a resource for teachers." He is too modest. *Housing Without Houses* raises issues that transcend home and neighborhood design and building. For readers who see what I see through Hamdi's original and correct understanding of architecture ("the action or process of building" as the *Oxford English Dictionary* defines it), he throws light on the roots of genuine architecture and on its present context of a threatened world.

The encouraging paradigms Hamdi extracts (in Chapters 2 and 3) partly from John Habraken's work and from my own indicate the third, community-based system and the complementary roles of architects in the sustainable society that all responsible citizens must build.

This primer and resource is a tool for building or rebuilding the community base socially and economically as well as environmentally and architecturally.

The failures of the market- and state-based housing provision and the relative success of community-based home and neighborhood building (especially the so-called third world and supposedly developing countries) highlight the complementarities of these three essentially different "sectors." In local architectural terms, Hamdi identifies and illustrates the nongovernmental and not-for-profit sectors as a distinct subsystem generally confused with the private and predominantly commercial sector. He breaks the habit of confrontational argument, insisting on the complementarities of what are, in fact, three different kinds of social and political energy: state powers, market forces, and people power manifested mainly through local, community-based initiatives.

Chapter 7, "Looking, Listening, and Measuring," and Chapter 8, "Building a Program," explain the third power or energy base: the unique and vital personal and local knowledge that we all have of our own situations and priorities. Hamdi deals with the sometimes justified complaint that "community architects" abdicate their professional responsibilities by uncritical acceptance of their clients' opinions (a weakness often observed in buildings designed for corporate employers). It is clear in these and other parts of the book that the knowledge of the "inperts," as Charles Abrams called them, is both different from and complementary to that of the experts—the supralocal authorities and professionals.

To the extent that power depends on knowledge, it also depends on what can be seen and from where.

The necessary administrative distance adopted by those from above reduces local details that are often too complex and variable for central management. On the other hand, supralocal and introlocal connections cannot be seen directly from the insiders' viewpoint—and most will have much less interest in them than in their own situations. When local groups are aware of or interested in others' experience, it is usually less accessible to them than it is to professionals.

There is plenty of evidence for the often unavoidable costs of unilateral decision making, whether top down or bottom up. Centrally administered and therefore necessarily standardized and imposed "solutions" to "housing problems" (which are generally misstated by authorities and professionals) cannot match the great variety of personal and local demands. Mismatches of microdemand with macrosupply generate frictions that burn up additional financial, human, and material resources (sometimes literally) inflating social, economic, and environmental costs of the kinds illustrated by Hamdi's examples. Conversely, unauthorized and/or unplanned "microsupply" can generate costly conflicts with the "macrodemands" of orderly development, as both uncontrolled speculative development and large-scale squatting demonstrate.

Hamdi's repeated emphasis on political convergence and partnerships between complementary powers reinforces an emerging trend and growing recognition of the new paradigm of change and development. Competitive industry and commerce, which have played an important role in Habraken's work, are accepted, rightly I now believe, as an essential source of "tools for building community," as I call them. The legislative and executive authority of government is accepted, as all but primitive anarchists acknowledge, for setting the limits on what may be done locally in order to protect neighbors' rights and the environment—the "software" that ensures people's freedom to build within those limits by guaranteeing access to resources, a central theme in my own work. Both themes coincide on the necessity of personal and local autonomy (interdependent self-management) and its enablement by professionals and supralocal authorities—cooperation, in other words, without which there can be no productive competition or liberating authority.

In the view that Hamdi presents in *Housing Without Houses,* three complementary enabling roles for professionals can be clearly seen: working directly for and with the actual or future users or residents; working for and with supralocal authorities or suppliers who control access to resources on which local initiative depends; and acting as an intermediary in negotiations between local and central organizations. This focus on enabling roles and community architecture is clearly intended to be seen as a complement to civic and commercial architecture, which provides greater scope for individual statement ("arquitectos de author" as the current debaters in Spain put it).

If what I was referring to in my first paragraph as a genuine architecture is rooted in everyday life and the vernacular, if culture is indeed a process of refinement from the grass roots, then the new global civilization must return control over personal and local life to people in their own homes and neighborhoods, however long the recovery may take.

Books like *Housing Without Houses* are essential contributions to the regeneration of genuine culture and great architecture, which must be the expression of sustainable, global civilization.

John F. C. Turner
Hastings, England

PREFACE

This book constructs its theories of practice based on a hypothesis: Building lots of houses for people and places one does not know, where money is scarce and statistical information is unreliable, is neither an efficient nor an equitable way of solving housing problems, nor is it good design practice. This hypothesis is especially true when confronting economic, political, and social climates that are always changing, and in contexts where a vast number of vested interests are always in conflict.

The book started as a primer for practitioners—a sort of "if this is the way things are, then these are things we need to do, and this might be a way of doing them." A rather complicated number of lists and matrices appeared of differences in clients, client demand, context and countries, points of departure for design, and all the implications these people and things have on the services and modus operandi of architects. The results looked misleadingly comprehensive, even analytical, and yet could never be complete. The whole was prescriptive and sectoralized. It looked impressive but was not very useful.

Instead, I have attempted to identify themes that run throughout my own teaching and practice and have enabled me to understand design practice in housing across conventional disciplinary demarcations, at the margins between public and private, between projects and policies, first world and third world, architecture and planning. And as conventional demarcations continue to shift and change, ever more unpredictably and to become sometimes indistinguishable except for convenience and expediency, I attempt to understand the impact these changes have on practice—what theories of practice emerge given these changes that underpin designing and the actions of designers.

First, I consider designing to be a process of enablement (the process of rendering able, competent, or powerful—*Oxford English Dictionary*). In the absence of detailed client programs in the context of mass housing, and if we are to avoid working with "optimums," we need methods for designing without detailed programs—a way of making plans without a preponderance of planning and social surveying. We need methods for deciding about the structure of our design interventions—the choice of physical and nonphysical elements, their size, position, configuration and hierarchies—that encourage rather than inhibit pluralism in built form and that are tolerant of all the inventive surprises and improvisations that are a daily and productive part of informal building.

Second is the theme of participatory design. Its premise is by now commonly accepted: that the involvement of users and community clients in design is an important part of decision making and of guaranteeing the efficiency of building in use. I consider the participation of nonprofessionals an important part of rigorous inquiry into the form of building and into the needs, habits, and social institutions that produce some 80 percent of the world's built residential environment. I do not believe that participation undermines the discipline of architecture or the role of architects, nor need it turn architects into political activists or social workers, as some would have it. I have spent much time understanding the skills and tools we need to explore with community groups' alternative design strategies, assessing their trade-offs and learning how to package an integrated design response.

Third, I have sought to understand emerging professional roles and responsibilities in view of the first two themes, both in the context of the design activity itself and in the field of practice. What kinds of new tools for design are demanded? What alternative partnerships are implied with client groups, and with public and private institutions? What new skills may be required of architects, and what additional services and resources do architects bring to local organizations? What principles of practice are common to both first and third world countries?

Fourth, I practice and teach that what housing is as shelter and what housing environments are as formal expressions of social and political systems are as important as what housing does to improve health, generate income, and provide security. The objective is to describe housing as a multidisciplinary and nonsectorially bound system of activities that are likely to expand the services of architects without losing the specificity of architecture.

Fifth, I introduce the element of time as a critical component of design and teach methods for judging appropriate design interventions that get things started, adopting principles of action science and planning. Incremental development and speed are priorities in the design activity where housing cannot be viewed as an act of finished building.

Finally, I have sought to extrapolate principles and paradigms that are common in housing in both first and third world contexts and that are unbound regionally and culturally. I seek to craft tools that enable architects and students of architecture to work in any context, but not irrespective of context, and to be precise about their interventions.

This book, then, is about design, design practice, and housing set specifically in contexts where resources are minimal, demand is high, urgency is acute, and uncertainty is a way of life. It demonstrates that under these conditions, efficient practice depends on methods that promote rather than hinder spontaneity, improvisation, and incremental development. The book develops its theories and demonstrates its methods in the face of progressive changes witnessed internationally in housing policy. It explores what these changes are, why and how they have emerged, and what impact they have on design and on the attitudes, skills, methods, and tools of designers.

Part I traces the histories of various disparate ideas and strategies for housing the poor and offers an understanding of design practice built on three themes: participation, flexibility, and enablement. Part II draws on examples from a variety of countries and locations to demonstrate how these themes and indeterminacy work in practice. It demonstrates how plans can emerge in action without a preponderance of master planning and how participation, flexibility, and enablement together can improve the efficiency of practice and promote an architecture of cooperation.

To do this, I have opted for a reflective account of my own research and practice. I do not propose anything new—only to sharpen what we already know, to bring into focus ideas, issues, and methods that have become an integral part of our intellectual and practical setting to give these some historical context.

My choice of heroes and villians—people, places, and projects—is based on their place and influence on my own work, as much as on any other criteria. My critique and evaluations are mostly intuitive convictions based on personal experience rather than on scholarship—sometimes modified, sometimes qualified, and always supplemented by friends and colleagues whom I have encountered along the way in academia and in practice. I am indebted to all these people who, in different ways, have shaped my career so far.

I would particularly like to acknowledge John Habraken for his encouragement, support, ideas, and guidance over twenty years of development work, and for believing that I now had enough to say of interest to others to warrant a book. My gratitude is extended to Reinhard Goethert for his creatively skeptical critiques, filling in gaps in my thinking, and providing examples in the text. Many of the examples in this book are based on projects and programs that we have worked on together over the past nine years.

Thanks go to Edward Robbins for his incessant desire to understand what, if anything, was new or different about what I was saying.

I offer acknowledgments to John Habraken, Reinhard Goethert, Moustafa Mourad, Sandra Howell, Brad Edgerly, John Turner, and Colin Ward for reading bits of early text and providing their comments and ideas. I thank Jeannie Winner for her help in structuring my ideas at a formative stage.

I am especially grateful to Jonathan Teicher for editing critical chapters and for his guidance in preparing the initial proposal, as well as for his insights into what it takes to get anything published these days.

Thanks also to Paula Maute and Betty Lou McClanahan who typed manuscripts and provided invaluable editorial commentary, and to the Department of Architecture at MIT for giving me the time and resources to complete my work satisfactorily.

Finally, I am indebted to my students at MIT who have helped shape my thinking, and who have provided points of departure to many of my arguments.

PART I

Theories of Practice:
Changing Paradigms

CHAPTER 1

Deciding on Context

If you ask me what it takes to be a member of a party exploring the continent called design, you will get a description of the strange creatures one encounters on the way and the strange geographies one has to feel at home: a story about the hostile regions of regulatory processes, the frightening herds of other people's values, the shifting sands of time, the weird animal called change, and finally, the unknown tribes of users. It is enough to decide that architecture should leave housing alone, as it generally has done in the past.

John Habraken, "Notes of a Traveler"

Almost everyone reasonably familiar with housing issues agrees on the most pressing problem facing the industry today insofar as housing the poor: the shortfall in supply to demand, in both first and third world countries, is getting worse, not better (it has never been good), despite all the innovations and investment so far. Most also agree that old paradigms are unworkable, formal supply channels hopelessly inadequate, and most conventional approaches largely irrelevant given the magnitude of demand. There is no such unanimity regarding solutions.

If we ask what kind of professionals and professional interventions are demanded to meet this problem or what methods, tools, skills, knowledge, attitudes, and theories of practice might help, the answers, from even the most eminent "housing experts," will be much less confident and much more muddled. The answers will vary according to how the problems are perceived, which in turn will vary according to who provides the definition.

Different people will put forth different sorts of theories explaining the shortfall of supply. We will be told, for example, of the inequitable distribution of resources, and yet we will see no evidence of redistribution on either national or international scales. Some will point to a crude surplus of housing units to households in the first world, yet the rate of homelessness there is increasing at an alarming rate and waiting lists for public housing continue to grow. Others will cite a lack of land for new development in the inner city, and yet others show a plethora of available small sites and sound but derelict houses. There is enough land but not enough incentives or federal subsidy to build on it. And there is a surplus of units but a mismatch between needs and price and the existing housing stock.

This debate becomes even more complicated in the developing world where high political aspirations are often coupled with scarce resources; where equity is sometimes sacrificed for efficiency; where export production is seen as more important to national development than local use of essential building materials; where uncertainty is intrinsic to practice rather than just a passing condition; and where housing deficits miraculously become surpluses, depending largely on what one counts, how one counts, and who counts. Is available stock, for example, counted in dwelling units, in building permits issued, in total cost of construction, or by floor area? Do these physical yardsticks tell enough about quality to enable comparisons of acceptable standards from one area to another, from one country to another?

It is not surprising that most formal housing over the past few decades has consisted of isolated interventions, temporarily relieving local conditions but making little significant impact on national or even urban need. Few programs have succeeded in matching supply with demand in terms of either sheer numbers or social acceptability.

The numbers are revealing. An estimated 53,000 new houses a day are needed globally to keep pace with demand (Miles and Parkes 1984). And the cost is enormous. Providing a 30 sq m finished house for every poor family would consume 25–50 percent of the gross national product (GNP) in most countries (Wheaton 1983). Yet most nations spend only 3–6 percent of their GNP on all forms of shelter, and the poorest spend as little as 0.5 percent. Worldwide, about 100 million people remain without shelter.

WORSENING CONDITIONS: THE THIRD WORLD

The problem has not gone unnoticed. In the past few decades, billions of dollars have been spent on housing and urban improvement projects, there has developed an abundance of data, information, expertise, technology, and even political goodwill, architects, planners, engineers, economists, and sociologists from every corner of the globe have traveled to every other corner of the globe. Think of all the books and learned articles, all the schools of archi-

tecture and planning, all the aid agencies with their money and wisdom, all the good intentions and good ideas.

The World Bank spent $3,500 million to assist housing and urban projects between 1972 and 1981 in thirty-five countries (Williams 1984); it spent $14.1 billion for 127 projects of all kinds in its 1987 financial year; the United States spent $14.4 million alone in various aid programs in 1988 (Kidder 1988); and Great Britain invested 1,770 pounds sterling 1986–1987 (although for both Britain and the United States, the percentage of investment of the GNP is low and diminishing: 0.45 percent for the United States in 1985, 0.35 percent by Britain, and 0.48 percent by Canada, Australia, and New Zealand) (Clark 1986). On June 11, 1976, 132 governments, sitting together, endorsed sixty-four "recommendations for national action," all demanding "radical changes in the way governments approached their citizens' housing problems" and calling for "greater political and financial commitment to be directed to helping the poor, and emphasized the importance of working with and through people (Miles and Parkes 1984, 1). In 1987, the Year of Shelter, there were numerous conferences and demonstration projects aimed at developing new ideas and an awareness of the disparity in standards between communities and countries.

Debates within housing circles have examined whether the public or private sectors have been effective in delivering housing to low-income people; whether standards should be lowered, increased, or abandoned altogether; whether the participation of users makes any difference to productivity, user satisfaction, or economies in building; whether cooperatives, sites and services or integrated upgrading projects, or rent control and subsidies or zoning have worked to control speculation, regulate densities, ensure affordability, create jobs, and provide security of tenure.

Yet despite this commitment and effort, this talk and study, the housing situation has worsened since

1976. According to the 1989 United Nations Conference on Trade and Development (Bollag 1989), all of the austerity measures imposed by agencies like the International Monetary Fund in the interests of economic development and prosperity have produced the opposite results. "I guess you could say the sacrifices have been in vain," said one official of the United Nations.

After all the investment of time, money, and energy, who is better off? Why has not a single country "graduated from less developed to developed status in the past twenty years" (Woods 1989, 16)? Which national housing authority has ever met its housing targets, and when not, why not? Why do El Salvador and Guatemala have only 25 percent of their housing stock serviced with piped water and Indonesia only 3.3 percent? Why is electricity in Pakistan available only to 17.9 percent of households and only to 9 percent in Sri Lanka (Global Report 1987)?

Again, many explanations are offered. Some say that conditions are getting worse because urban populations are growing at unprecedented rates and urban systems cannot keep up. Some say it is because of the decrease in the purchasing power of households, and not just poor ones, because of rapid migration from the villages, high inflation, or high interest rates. Others suggest that it is largely due to reductions in international aid so far as poor countries are concerned and federal aid in the case of rich ones. The United States, for example, reduced its total aid budget from $9.6 billion in 1986 to $9.2 billion in 1988.

Yet others challenge this view and propose that it is not so much reduction in aid as the manner in which it is offered that is harmful. Thirty-eight percent of all U.S. aid and 46.5 percent of British aid, for example, is tied—that is, the recipient countries are required to spend the money on lender country goods and services (Sancton 1988).

Moreover, international aid is targeted to developing countries according to the political influence and commercial interests of the donor, not according to need. "Hence, in 1985, in spite of massive public and media concern about famine in Africa, Gibraltar with a population of 27,000 received almost as much United Kingdom aid as Ethiopia, with 40 million people, mostly extremely poor. In 1985, the Falkland Islands received the equivalent of £5500 per person of the United Kingdom aid, while India received 15 p per person" (Clark 1986, 19).

Some experts remind us that, irrespective of aid, the population of developing countries is growing at rates varying between 2 and 3½ percent each year, and the population of their major cities grows at roughly double this rate; that people of third world cities are poor in both relative and absolute terms; that if people are poor, then their governments are even poorer because collecting taxes from the very poor costs more than one could possibly collect, one reason for the failure of welfare policies in a number of countries: the failure of government to provide enough housing for their fast-growing cities has driven people to various forms of self-help both in terms of illegal subdivision and squatting; and that cities of the poor are largely self-help cities—their growth is unplanned and usually follows lines of least resistance. Forty percent of Mexico City, for example, is occupied by squatters and other informal settlements, 60 percent of Bogota in Colombia, 85 percent of Addis Ababa in Ethiopia, and 70 percent of Dar es Salaam (Global Report 1987).

The picture for planners is grim. In 1984 A. W. Clausen, then president of the World Bank, said that

rapid population growth is creating urban economic and social problems that risk becoming wholly unmanageable. Cities in developing countries are growing to a size for which there is no prior experience anywhere. Between 1950 and 1980, the proportion of urban dwellers in developing countries in cities of more than 5 million increased from 2% to 14%, growing at a rate of 15% a year. Brazil's Sao Paulo, which by the year 2000 could well be the world's second largest city after Mexico City, was smaller in 1950 than either Manchester, Detroit, or

Naples. London, the world's second largest city in 1950, will not even be ranked among the twenty-five largest by the end of the century. The rise in urban population, 60 percent of which is due to natural increase, poses unprecedented problems of management even to maintain, let alone improve, the living conditions of city dwellers. (Clausen 1984, 11)

Perhaps the most contentious explanation for the poverty of third world nations comes from those who say that conditions have been made worse by the very agencies whose public intention was to eradicate poverty. Worse still is the contention that foreign intervention, "far from helping countries develop, has produced underdevelopment" in the interest of world economic dominance by the rich industrialized countries.[1]

The largest single contributor to the poverty of nations in recent times has been debt. Julius Nyerere, president of Tanzania, asked, "Should we really let our people starve so that we can pay our debts?"[2] The current debt problem originated in 1973 when oil prices increased fourfold, producing large sums of money that the oil producers invested in the banks of first world nations, signaling enormous profits for the banks and significant growth for the economies of the industrial nations. "A new mood of liberal lending emerged. Bankers positively courted the finance ministers of developing countries. . . . As interest rates soared in the late 1970s, the burden of debt payment became heavier and commodities' export prices fell" (Clark 1986, 60). Countries like Tanzania, Bangladesh, and Indonesia saw their foreign earnings through exports fall by more than half. "Growth and prosperity failed to materialize; instead, developing countries fell deeper into debt" (Clark 1986, 60). A perverse form of aid began, aptly called reverse aid.

In 1983, the poor countries contributed $11 billion in net transfer to rich countries. By 1985, this reverse aid amounted to $16–25 billion per year. From 1981 to 1986, Africa's debt payment tripled from $4 billion to an estimated $11.7 billion. "For every £1 put in a charity tin, the West's financial institutions was taking out £9" (Clark 1986).

WORSENING CONDITIONS: THE FIRST WORLD

Poverty is not a third world phenomenon. Millions are homeless in the United States and Britain; decay is found in and around nearly every major city in the world; houses throughout the world lay vacant; projects, even those that have won design awards, have been systematically dismantled; the waiting lists for public housing are long; millions of people are sheltered in temporary accommodations. (Massachusetts, for example, pays $35,000 a night to keep 644 of its homeless families in hotels. Local authorities in England put up 11,250 people in "temporary" bed and breakfast accommodations.)[3]

In the United States, poverty increased by an average of 14 percent between 1980 and 1987, and "the proportion of poor people in metropolitan areas grew from 62% in 1979 to 70% in 1985—an increase of 7.6 million people, with most living in central cities." In 1970, 16 percent of low-income people living in poor, isolated, urban neighborhoods were below the poverty level. In 1980, this figure was an astonishing 40 percent (*New York Times,* March 12, 1989). In 1982, 40 percent of New York City's children lived in poverty. Today in the same city, 28,000 people are homeless and living in emergency shelter, with 40,000 people unsheltered. In 1983 in New York, 17,000 families were illegally doubled up in public housing; the number jumped to 35,000 in 1986. In the United States as a whole, 3–4 million people are homeless,

---

1. See, for example, Teresa Hayter, *The Creation of World Poverty—An Alternative View to the Brandt Report* (London: Pluto Press in association with Third World Now, 1981).
2. *Guardian*, March 3, 1985.

3. See, for example; No place like home, *Economist,* December 26, 1987.

and up to 10 million live near and even closer to the edge of homelessness (Kozol 1988).

In Britain, the numbers are just as dramatic: 60,000 households were homeless in 1978 and over 130,000 in 1987 (*Economist*, December 26, 1987). In 1985, there were 123,859 empty houses in England and Wales and 123,140 households accepted as homeless, figures that confirm that houses built are only one piece of a much larger equation in matching demand, which includes location, standards, costs, and timing.

Here again, explanations for why poverty and homelessness are on the increase are numerous. Conventional wisdom suggests that worsening circumstances are the direct result of federal cutbacks in financial assistance—the 70 percent cut in assistance programs in the United States since 1980, for example, and the 50 percent cut in the same period in Britain on capital expenditures by local government. Closely related is the affordability issue: dwindling buying power coupled with rising prices. Some are forced out of houses through defaulting on mortgage payments (accounting for about 15 percent of homeless people in Britain). Renters can no longer keep up with rent increases. "Between 1978 and 1980, median rents [in the United States] climbed 30 percent for those in the lowest income sector. Half of those people paid nearly three quarters of their income for housing" (Kozol 1988, 11).

Another theory might be called the vagrancy argument; it suggests that most figures on shortfall are in fact grossly overstated because most who do not have housing could if they gave up drink and drugs, made up with their families, got themselves a job, and generally improved their moral well-being. More recently, the Manhattan Institute for Policy Research found a direct correlation between homelessness and rent controls: "We infer that only where rent control has been imposed do vacancies become pathologically low, pushing homelessness to abnormal heights." Builders stop building, despite exemptions on new property, older housing deteriorates, people stop moving, the filter clogs, and cheap housing dries up (Tucher 1987).

PROFESSIONAL DILEMMAS

Think of a site typical of any in a country where the demand for housing is acute; where engineers, community builders, politicians, international funders, and slum dwellers all want their ideas to be dominant in planning and design; where there is very little information, time, or money; and where everyone knows that none of the old models or ideas—like public housing, sites and services, industrialized building systems, large estates, "pavilions in the park," "streets in the air"—is in favor with funders, with the political party in office, or even with planners or architects.

It is worth remembering that 1½ million new buildings are constructed annually in countries like the United States and that there are more than five architects on average to every 10,000 urban residents (Gutman 1988). How many of the 90,000 architects in the United States have anything to do with the 900,000 houses built every year? Which of these five architects had anything to do with at least half of the 10,000 residents who cannot afford his or her services and most others who are bewildered by them, even when they can?

How can one possibly serve the demands of this massive client body and yet respect the needs of individuals? How can one possibly learn all that one was told to learn before one could act? How can one teach all that there is to teach to leave behind a cadre of skilled, informed people who must go to scale with all these initiatives, knowing that even the little experience built around the old projects and those to come will disappear with those who will leave their country for richer countries? How can one program and design in the short time one has, without the rigor one was taught at school, without all the data, the systems analysis, without the rationale of flowcharts and precise schedules, with very few standards or optimums, with all the guesswork it will entail. How can one convince anyone to agree on even the smallest detail to develop priorities, strategies, programs, and plans?

Imagine a new wave of architects and planners

confronting this site calling themselves all sorts of curious new names—community architects, reflective practitioners, urban managers, enablers—dropping in and out of slums and shanties, bent on solving the housing problem once and for all, bringing with them their new paradigms, confronting hordes of ordinary people and all the ordinary things they build that for years others had not noticed or cared much about. Ask why all these ordinary people should be puzzled by all this extraordinary coming and going. Then wonder about the tenacity of all these architects and ask: What is so new about what they say—about self-help, self-management, upgrading, incremental development, learning by doing, reflecting in action—which ordinary people, ordinary craftsmen, and small builders have been practicing for centuries, which they have known about all along. What is so new about architects and planners or any other professional body today talking and dealing with their real clients? How can all these professionals better serve their public?

In his book *Urban Planning in Rich and Poor Countries,* Hugh Stretton (1978, 4) suggested to planners that the profession has been "troubled by chronic disagreement about its ends and means, its theories and methods, and even about the need for it to exist at all." If this is true for planners, then it is equally true for architects, working in a complex field where limited resources and the scarcity of money can barely sustain rudimentary shelter, let alone architecture as we know it in the industrialized world, and where the severity and immediacy of conditions demand swift professional and governmental action rather than a preponderance of study and master planning.

What J. M. Richards said in 1972 about architects holds true today: "Their persistent search for novelty has helped to prevent the growth of an informed body of public opinion—something on which a healthy profession very much depends. The public has been bewildered when it needs to be reassured. The result has been the architect's habit of only looking to each other for approbation—the

profession has turned in on itself. Above all, they will need to realize that the world is in the process of deciding that the environment is too important to be left to the mercy of architects." In 1987 many American educators, writing in the *Journal of Architectural Education* cited similar concerns:

It remains very difficult to determine how vast and deep the schism is today in architecture. That void between what we think and what we say, what we teach and what they observe, and what we hope and what we feel. Architectural education in particular, but the profession generally is very willing to accept these polarities as social indices. It is both a defensive mechanism and an issue of furious debate. The result, however, is public uncertainty over what we do, not to mention the value of it. (Lambla 1987, 38)

These issues continue to generate substantial debate within the profession about the kind of contribution it can make. It is a debate about the precarious and shifting balance between interlocking and always jibing professional responsibilities; the designer as supplier of design methods, building techniques, and first world models and styling, a teacher in the field; as project maker or as maker of tools, methods, and procedures for use by others in making projects; as advocate or as public servant; as strategist or as technical expert; as initiator or as respondent. These are only a few of the more common dichotomies.

THE ISSUES

By now you have some picture of the issues at stake today, some general picture of the muddle architectural students face, and some general idea of the context in which this book is set. Some say that most housing and urban problems can be resolved without professional help and with much less government intervention. Whether they are ideologically right or wrong is one thing. In practice, antiprofessionalists cloud their thinking with romantic illusion.

As long as there is government, there will be international aid. And as long as there are both, there will be experts who will be in the technical, social, political, and economic business of shaping local, national, and international reputations. The question is not whether architects, planners, engineers, economists, and sociologists have a role in shelter and in urban policy making. The question is how and with what.

The architectural profession is hopelessly out of touch with the realities of shelter, if indeed these realities fit the general schema of architecture as it is currently taught and practiced and currently confined within the art and the politics of the special and the monumental rather than the ordinary. You might agree that these issues about supply, poverty, homelessness, and aid are relevant for planners, public administrators, students of government, economics, and international affairs but dismiss them as beyond the bounds of architecture. What have they to do with design, building, and form making? After all, architecture has little influence over the plight of the poor or the inequalities of political and social life. It has little to do with the ideological debate in favor of self-determination or the political debate about decentralized versus centralized decision making, equity versus efficiency, export production versus domestic consumption, and so on. Nor is it centrally about public sector or private sector interventions or formal or informal systems of production, employment, and building. Indeed, architecture, some legitimately suggest, has little or nothing to do with solving housing problems, in which case it may be "enough to decide that architecture should leave housing alone, as it generally has done in the past" (Habraken 1979).

As Lisa Peattie has suggested, there are usually two ways of dealing with this issue. One is to do as the profession has always done: engage in discussion as to the "nature and bounds of architecture." The other, for people who want to work in housing and be part of the history of urban development, is to ignore the question (Peattie 1985).

The fact is that most bilateral and multilateral agencies and most governments are the same organizations that will be either clients of architects or their employers. They will be doing most of the hiring in the housing and urban development business. Architects should know who these organizations are, the context in which they operate, and the context in which they will demand architects operate. We as architects should know this context in order to decide where and how we fit, if indeed we fit at all. We should know this context in order to decide the breadth of knowledge now demanded of those working in housing so that they can be effective, rather than peripheral, without losing necessarily the specificity of their trade. We should know these things not only so that our responses can be technically proficient but also, and more fundamentally, so that we can be ethically correct, rather than ethically naive, in our responses.

Housers, whatever their disciplinary allegiances, face a terrible shortfall in the supply of good housing alternatives for the poor. In this context, how should our efforts be directed? What kinds of skills can best respond? What alternative paradigms are worth contemplating? Why do seemingly good ideas, theories and designs regularly fail? What are the causes of some of these failures? How can performance be improved? What are the implications for designers and their activities? Can the experience in industrialized nations be of assistance in third world countries or vice versa? These are pressing questions, inducing responses that so far have been sketchy and uncertain.

REFERENCES

Bollag, Burton. 1989. UN critical of IMF austerity plan. *New York Times,* September 6, Sec. D7.

Clark, John. 1986. *For Richer For Poorer: An Oxfam Report on Western Connections with World Hunger.* Oxford: Oxfam.

Clausen, S. W. 1984. Population growth and economic and social development. Address to the National

Leaders Seminar on Population and Development, Nairobi, Kenya, July 11, and to the International Population Conference, Mexico City, August 7.

Global Report on Human Settlements 1986. 1987. Oxford: Oxford University Press for the United Nations Centre for Human Settlements (HABITAT).

Gutman, Robert. 1988. *Architectural Practice—A Critical View.* Princeton, N.J.: Princeton Architectural Press.

Habraken, John. 1979. Notes of a traveler. *Journal of Architectural Education* 32(4).

Kidder, Rushworth M. 1988. U.S. foreign aid goals focus on literacy and global poverty. *Christian Science Monitor,* August 22, p.17.

Kozol, Jonathan. 1988. *Rachel and Her Children—Homeless Families in America.* New York: Fawcett.

Lambla, Ken. 1987. Two-faced. *Journal of Architectural Education* 40(2):38–39.

Miles, Derek, and Parkes, Michael. 1984. Housing for the poor. *Appropriate Technology* 11(3) (December):1–4.

New study finds the poor getting poorer, younger, and more urban. 1989. *New York Times,* March 12.

Peattie, Lisa. 1985. Design, building and the quality of life. Paper presented at the CAA/JIA Conference, Ocho Rios, Jamaica, June 8.

Richards, J. M. 1972. The hollow victory: 1932–1972. Paper presented at the Royal Institute of British Architects Annual Discourse, London, March 14.

Sancton, Thomas A. 1988. From the land of the rising sun—Tokyo steps up its foreign aid. Reported by Barry Hillenbrand in *Time,* May 19, p. 55

Stretton, Hugh. 1978. *Urban Planning in Rich and Poor Countries.* Oxford: Oxford University Press.

Tucher, William. 1987. Where do the homeless come from? Memo, Manhattan Institute for Policy Research.

Wheaton, William C. 1983. Housing policies in developing countries. *Open House* 8(4):11–14.

Williams, David G. 1984. The role of international agencies: The World Bank. In *Low-Income Housing in the Developing World,* pp. 173–85. Edited by G. K. Payne. New York: Wiley.

Woods, Alan. 1989. *Boston Globe,* Feb. 21, p. 16.

CHAPTER 2

A Tale of Two Paradigms

No, the housing problem as we know it, with its causes and effects reaching into every department of economics, politics, science, and sociology, owes its majestic scale to the developments of the last century. It must always remain one of the great historic ironies that the century which invented the notion of material Progress, which unfolded more scientific possibility than all the preceding years of western civilization put together, was also the century which debased human environment to about its lowest known level.

Catherine Bauer, *Modern Housing*

A healthy growing society will always have a housing problem. If I ever met a society that claimed to have solved all its housing problems, I would look at it with great suspicion and conclude that it must be in a worrying state of decline.

Otto Koenigsberger, "Intentions of Housing Policy Alternatives"

Public housing, with its policy of building directly for the poor, has failed to provide adequate numbers of houses for all sorts of reasons, including high standards and high costs. Even when it did, the housing fell largely into the hands of middle-income families who could afford to pay for it and on whose votes politicians counted. There are also examples of empty public housing, too expensive for the poor but undesirable for those who might afford them.

The more that governments built houses, the less they seemed to achieve because the more they built, the more demand they created—and the more they needed to build, the larger they grew, so the more they had to build to balance their books and legitimize their purpose both socially and politically. The larger they grew, the more energy and money they consumed, until they progressively ran out of both.

In the late 50s, and early 60s, practically all public housing policies, whether urban or rural, ran out of steam. Except for the island city states of Singapore and Hong Kong, there was no country or city that could hope to produce public housing in sufficient numbers to cope with a steadily worsening situation. (Koenigsberger 1987)

Those who persisted, either because of their political and ideological objectives or because it was what they knew how to do best, had their money supply cut off by the funding agencies or by unsympathetic political foes and had to search for alternatives. That search has traditionally led to shifting the business of providing to the private sector and equivalently shifting toward a trickle-down policy in which housing is built for those who can afford to pay; as those houses age and become less desirable to the better off, they theoretically become accessible to the less well off. There is no evidence however, that the private sector has been effective in providing housing to the poor or that trickle-down policies have worked. As Jackson (1976) and others point out, "the filter always clogs."[1]

Privatization is the panacea and trend of party politics, not some new theory of housing. What the *London Times* reported in 1846 holds true today: "A town of manufacturers and speculators is apt to leave the poor to shift for themselves, to stew in cellars and garrets, nor are landlords and farmers apt to care much for cottages. . . . something of a central authority is necessary to wrestle with the selfishness of wealth" (Burnett 1978,92)—to which one builder replied, albeit in Texas and in 1988, "Don't blame us for not building more low-income housing. People don't really want it. They don't want to see it and they don't want to live next to it. Remember, we're just businessmen, so we have to go where the profit is" (McManamy 1988, 8). If the pragmatism of providing has been brought to question, so increasingly has its claim to benevolence.

PUBLIC INTERVENTIONS: HOW AND WHY?

Most public interventions in housing were and still are in response to crises that appear to threaten the structure of society and therefore the people and institutions that govern it. For all the laudable efforts of the early reformers in Europe, for example, few interventions were designed out of a concern for improving the living conditions of the poor. It was the cholera epidemic in England in 1831, for example, that led to the Cholera Act of 1832, which gave the authorities "power to enter into any home for the purpose of cleansing, fumigating and white-washing," largely to protect "the rights and

privileges of the dominant classes in society who were threatened by conditions" (Bristow 1981, 7).

In addition, the growth of "commercial imperialism" as well as the constant threat of war inspired concern for national defenses in France, Germany, and Britain. "The birth rate, the death rate, and the general stamina of the nation became objects of serious internal *Realpolitik*. When health statistics resolved themselves into the necessity, on two occasions before 1900, of reducing the standard height of men entering the British army, even generals and bankers began to take interest in sanitary conditions" (Bauer 1934, 21).

In the United States, events were largely similar. The appalling living conditions of migrants—some 300,000 people crammed into 3,000 tenements in New York that had been constructed quickly and badly by corrupt speculative builders, poorly lit, and ventilated—led to the health bill of 1864 and the Health Act of 1866. Epidemics such as smallpox and tuberculosis and riots in 1863 panicked the middle class into reforms that would make cities safe for ordinary people: "Better housing was needed not only to protect the health of the entire community, but to Americanize the immigrant working class population, to impose upon it the middle class code of manners and morals" (Lubove 1962). Unless conditions improved, "the poor would overrun the city as thieves and beggars—endanger public peace and security of property and life—tax the community for support and entail upon it an inheritance of vice and pauperism" (Lubove 1962, 7). Thus, it was that the Tenement Act of 1867 in New York mobilized the government to improve standards of fire fighting, sanitation, and other environmental controls.

Many have concluded that few, if any, public responses to poor housing conditions have been benevolent; their purpose was to prevent disturbance, create jobs, and fuel industry and therefore eco-

---

1. For a simple explanation of the filtering concept, see D. A. Kirby, *Slum Housing and Renewal—The Case in Urban Britain* (London and New York: Longman, 1979), pp. 29–33.

nomic growth.[2] "Instead of arising out of benevolent concern for the poor, housing efforts were more closely related to the manufacture of war supplies to support American efforts in World War I and II, with concern to appease the discontent of returning veterans of that war, and finally with the provision of employment following the Great Depression" (Marcuse 1986, 253). This was paralleled with the Houses for Heroes campaign in Britain during the same period, which itself was preceded almost 100 years earlier, in 1816, with much the same concern for the embattled peasantry returning from Waterloo.

Housing policy, then, has been more an instrument of political and social reform than a way to increase the supply of houses. Providing housing enables reformers to control and direct the impact of what is provided as much as to decide the performance, quality, and quantity of the product. Measured against intentions, it has arguably worked very well and may well be a legitimate form of intervention under conditions of crisis.

Whether it is a house, a school, or a town plan, these products become instruments of political power and social class differentiations—an expression of cultural dominance, a means to control standards of safety, hygiene, construction, and even moral well—being. It is, indeed, the tacit belief in this professionalization of knowledge, and of most design and planning solutions that first created and now continues to emphasize the divisions between thinkers and doers and between professionals and the public. Most significant, it emphasizes divisions between the contrivances of projects and town plans that represent systems of management and governance rather than the realities of community life.

2. See, for example, Charles Abrams, Housing policy—1937 to 1967, in *Shaping an Urban Future: Essays in Memory of Catherine Bauer Wurster,* ed. Bernard Frieden and William W. Nash (Cambridge, Mass.: MIT Press, 1969).

It is indeed the issues of control, professional methods, attitudes, and responsibilities that are most hotly debated among housing theorists and practitioners, particularly in the case of complex social, economic, and political networks of informal settlements. There, entrepreneurs—money lenders, materials manufacturers and suppliers, water vendors, milkmen, recycling garbage collectors, and builders—emerge to provide necessary services ad hoc. "Systems" or linkages develop for purchasing and exchanging commodities, exerting influence, buying into services, securing employment, and sometimes levering a stake in the general body politic of the urban or regional districts in which they are placed. As Benjamin (n.d.) explains,

The neighborhood is a complex bundle of activities, relating market and non-market and political issues towards increasing its "productivity." This happens in three ways. First, the grouping of such enterprises creates a local market. Secondly, this grouping provides enterprises with security of tenure which helps prevent demolition by public authorities. Finally, public authorities are pressurized to make interventions that have welfare effects to the mass of the poor, even those who have not been able to directly participate in political activities. Productive environments as Bhogal (a housing block in Delhi, India) generate economic stability and social purpose for the residents in a process of physical transformation.

In time, people build a substantial body of experience about how best to build, to connect to utility lines, to profit from or to dodge the authorities. It is a process of doing and learning built up through individual experiences and passed on to others in a variety of formal and informal ways. If things go wrong or do not work as well as expected, no one need step in with elaborate explanations. People will usually know, or will have a theory about what works and why and what does not or what they need and what they do not need.

If it was a land invasion—squatters—that got a development started, someone will have prepared plans setting out a few simple rules for who will get

Incremental informal growth of cities: Imbaba, Cairo (below) and . . .

(Source: Reinhard Goethert)

200 Meters

PROPERTY LINES 1940's
AGRICULTURE LAND

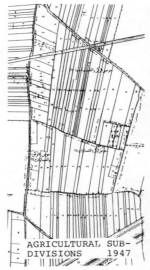

AGRICULTURAL SUB-
DIVISIONS   1947

BUILT-UP LAYOUT
1976

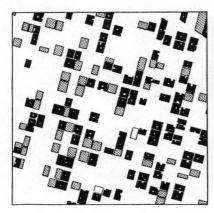

1957

1966

1977

14

. . .Santa Ursula, Mexico City.
(Source: Jorge Andrade-Narvaez)

1959

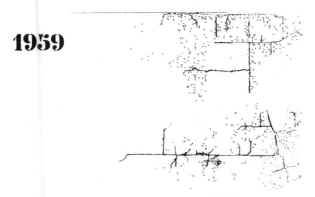

1966

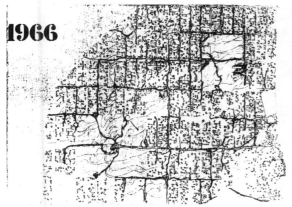

1972

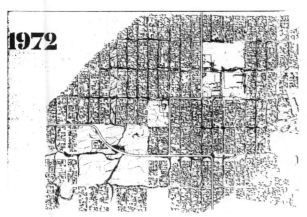

what and where, reserving lines of access and circulation, and establishing lines of least resistance for invasion and building. Otherwise these rules may have been set through the sale of agricultural subdivisions, which will regulate the pace and form of development. With this general framework, which itself will consolidate and become specific over time, people will devise rules and improvise services as they go tailored to needs, aspirations, income, and profit. The marketplace, both formal and informal, will have much to say about what happens, as will respected elders and rituals.

Those who believe these processes are the sole domain of developing countries forget that vast tracts of land, some of the most alluring suburbs of England and the United States, developed in much the same way. They grew and acquired services through the same incremental connectivity between formal and informal systems.

Even today, community-initiated self-help housing action—rent strikes, tent cities, building squats, sweat equity, homesteading, and various forms of cooperatives—is dominant among the range of formal alternatives available to the poor. "This combination of pressure and opportunity has provoked self-help as a means of preserving both the housing stock and community profits of low-income neighborhoods" (Schuman 1986, 464).

A shadow market in the United States, like its informal counterpart in the developing world, supplies the market with substantial numbers of low-cost houses (accounting for 21 percent of the increase in total stock between 1973 and 1980) that are not usually counted in the official census (Baer 1986). It does this largely through conversions of nonresidential structures and through incremental transformations of existing housing—adding rooms, converting attics, subdividing larger houses, and so on. All of these initiatives are taken in spite of legislation and by individuals and small builders. Most of the shadow market's units are low-cost rental accommodations that are unsubsidized and therefore unaffected by federal or state shifts in policy.

In England, places like Canvey Island, Rye Bay, and Jaywick Sand on the east coast and Laindon and Pitsea in the hinterland of London started with shacks, unpaved roads, and few services or utilities (Ward 1983, 84). There are remarkable parallels between the informal and squatter developments in developing countries and those in areas like Pitsea-Laindon—similarities in the way people turn their labor into capital over time. Colin Ward's descriptions are enlightening. In Pitsea-Laindon, Ward (1983, 84) showed one resident a description of his area as a "vast pastoral slum." His respondent "denied this of course, remarking that most people came down here precisely to get away from the slums."

"But what was it like before the road was made up?"
    "Well, you had to order your coal in the summer as the lorry could never get down the road in wintertime."
    "But there was a pavement."
    "People used to get together with their neighbors to buy cement and sand to make the pavement all the way along the road."
    "Street lighting?"
    "No, there was none. Old Granny Chapple used to take a hurricane lamp when she went to the Radiant Cinema in Laindon."
    "Transport?"
    "Well, a character called Old Tom used to run a bus to Laindon Station to the Fortune of War Public House. . . . On the same road lived Mr. Budd. . . . He was a bricklayer by trade, and every time he had a new grandchild, he would add a room to his house."

Sometimes the entire settlement process occurred outside the law, as in Canvey Island at the turn of the century: "Very often people did not even bother to purchase a plot of land; they just pitched a tent and became squatters. . . . It became possible to erect any form of structure, and if you were not a permanent resident, it was all the more difficult for you to be traced" (Ward 1984, 124).

Such processes of informal, incremental, and sometimes illegal development have traditionally been considered a blight in urban planning and design. Although they are resourceful, in many ways

they are problematic (Mangin 1967). They are resourceful because they are fast, ingenious, full of inventive surprises, and highly productive. Partnerships and organizations emerge if and when they are needed and, as important, disappear when they are not. In contrast to conventional wisdom, at least until recently, these settlements are evidence of healthy, working cities.

As early as 1944, Sir Patrick Abercrombie (Ward 1983, 85) was pointing out: "It is possible to point with horror to the jumble of shanties and bungalows on the Laindon Hills and Pitsea. This is a narrow-minded appreciation of what was as genuine a desire as created the groups of lovely gardens and houses at Frensham and Bramshott." Thinkers such as Ward, John Turner, William Mangin, Lisa Peattie, and C. J. Stokes have led us to redefine the vast urban shanties, historically depicted as the despair of cities, as "slums of hope."[3] Shanties are no longer housing in deterioration but alternatively viewed as housing in the process of improvement.

Why these ideas should have become increasingly accepted through the 1960s and 1970s is probably best explained by social historians. But accepted they did become, at least to some who had influence over public policy. Gradually burgeoning informal settlements of the poor became an unavoidable urban fact. Yet they emerged in perception less as a problem than as an opportunity for efficient, even equitable, housing.

Nevertheless, these settlements are problematic because governments pay a price for these unregulated processes. Cities develop unpredictably and are therefore strained in terms of services, utilities, and government. These squatter settlements suffer acute poverty, disease, and political unrest.

Upgrading rather than redevelopment was a natural policy consequence of the view that vast shan-

---

3. See, for example, Lisa Peattie, Social issues in housing, in *Shaping an Urban Future: Essays in Memory of Catherine Bauer Wurster*, ed. Bernard Frieden and William Nash, Jr., (Cambridge, Mass.: MIT Press, 1969), pp. 15–34.

ties and squatter settlements are mainstream rather than marginal—a part of the new paradigm for housing development. Upgrading was supported widely by the World Bank and others in the mid–1970s so that public authorities could "restore formal control over land subdivision and house building processes, while seeking to mobilize the energies and resources of low-income groups for either the improvement or creation of shelter" (Global Report on Human Settlements 1987, 174).

Most upgrading programs entailed the provision of sanitation, electricity, water, and drainage, the paving of streets and footpaths, the legalization of tenure rights to land (a policy designed to control the growth of illegal settlements), and the provision for improving community facilities such as schools, clinics, and community centers. A large number of projects involved land regularization to establish legal boundaries to properties (the basis to issuing titles) and to get services into these settlements. And most programs, inevitably and out of necessity rather than desire, confronted the interests and demands of local residents.

Despite criticism that they tend to serve the most able, physically and politically, and the most enterprising, that they were often overly planned, that their rate of cost recovery was far worse than sites-and-services projects, that they had failed to turn the tide of illegal occupations—indeed in some cases had encouraged it—the implications of this approach were profound. All of the established standards for design, all of the instruments of town planning, and all of the established work habits of

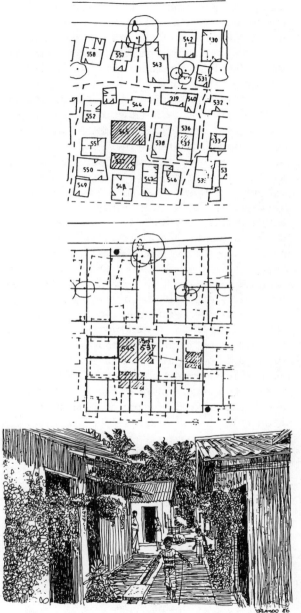

Palahimi Mawatha, Colombo, Sri Lanka.
(Sources: National Housing Development Authority of Sri Lanka (top) and Orlando Mingo (bottom)

Slum upgrading typically entails blocking out to regularize land, control settlement, and deliver services and utilities.

planners, engineers, and architects were brought to question and challenged. Professional freedoms that once enabled wide boulevards, pavilions in the park, ceremonial public gardens, garden cities, and systems building were largely usurped. Public protest inspired these shifts in policy. Participatory design, advocacy planning, and public consultation usually followed as a consequence of policy.

Changes in attitude and approach came slowly and not altogether satisfactorily. They came not because these ideas were growing more acceptable but because governments were running out of money and public confidence. At the same time housing programs were falling short of their targets, because neither policies nor the institutions that provide houses and manage policies were effective in sustaining adequate supply. Agencies such as the World Bank and the United Nations Development Program, recognizing this, changed their lending policies. Instead of making large transfers of financial resources to project building, the World Bank directed its funds more toward the reform of policies and institutions: to public administration, to local banks, and to providing technical assistance. Its terms of reference for borrowers encouraged programs to be designed more on the basis of effective user demand and less on preconceived notions of adequate housing (Williams 1984).

Governments were becoming poor (not richer, as had been predicted), and programs of public housing and new towns came to a standstill. Few governments—in rich or poor countries—had the institutional capacity, skilled management, technical staff, materials, or the money to sustain traditional building activity. The government provision of mass housing, a process historically argued as being fast and cheap due to economies of scale, became slow, expensive, and with little significant impact on what was perceived as a housing shortage.

National governments in developing countries, moreover, were no longer willing to accept international solutions to their problems. Their growing sense of national identity mingled with a growing

Redevelopment versus . . .

sense of disillusionment with Western ideals as exemplified in public housing or city planning. Western rationalists marketed modernist notions of garden cities, tower blocks, and streets in the air, coupled with mechanization, as the salvation to what was seen as public serfdom. Yet alluring as they were, these visions could not deliver what they promised.

The ends, more often than not "restructured to fit the requirements of techniques of performance and measurement (Winner 1977, 235) in the West, have atrophied the means. Having been disillusioned with ends so alien to the cultures in which they were applied, developing nation governments increasingly sought to disentangle means from ends. They sought methods and tools rather than projects

. . . upgrading.

Street improvements in slums typical of many developing countries.

Tenement rehabilitation in Glasgow.

and city plans, which they already had in abundance.

In this context, the old instruments of efficient planning and building—plan types, master plans, building systems, statistical models—no longer apply. Instead we find a new breed of tools emerging—more open, more adaptable, more skeletal in character, more thematic, bent on information, improvisation, and dialogue, less certain, less precise, less prescriptive, and less deterministic.

The move away from designed solutions and toward technical and organizational support passed through various transitional phases. In countries like Britain, France, Sweden, Holland, and, in a different way, the United States, one could observe significant shifts in thinking, policy, and projects. From 1969 on, for example, clearance and redevelopment began to give way to infill and rehabilitation. High-rise, high-density projects with their preoccupation with the public domain (freeing the land, light, and air for all) and with production gave way to low-rise, high-density development emphasizing privacy, community, and identity, which the early projects had seemed to ignore.

The trend toward "People's Participation in Housing," albeit patronizing as a slogan (after all, housing as a historical process was preeminently under people's control for millennia before the invention of professional intervention) began to question existing relationships among people, professionals, industry, and government authorities. In the United States, advocacy planning got underway during the 1960s with architects and planners working through design centers. In Britain, the Skeffington Report, published in 1969, represented the first official government inquiry in the world into public participation in planning (Wates and Knevitt 1987). Also around the same time, projects like Shelters Neighborhood Action Project (SNAP) and Ralph Erskine's Byker project in Newcastle saw architects installed locally in project offices, involving inhabitants in planning and design and using innovative, unorthodox techniques. Initiated by Strathclyde University in Scotland during 1972, Project Assist involved residents in the rehabilitation of old tenements, signaling the attempt by a number of academic establishments to connect to fieldwork through project offices and other extension services. Around 1974, various nonstatutory neighborhood councils were set up, the first and perhaps most workable being in Covent Garden in London. And in 1976, the community architecture movement officially got under way with the community architecture working group formed at the Royal Institute of British Architects "to examine the relationship between the profession and the community" (Wates and Knevitt 1987, 165). This was also the year of the United Nations Habitat conference in Vancouver, which many consider a watershed in international housing development policy.

Other shifts in thinking and practice were also occurring. Flexibility of buildings to adapt to changing user needs was becoming popular among architects, who were recognizing the futility of trying to pin down the average family and the fact that change, and therefore building obsolescence, was occurring rapidly. The renaissance of cooperatives in many public housing projects gave recognition to the understanding that tenant self-management was not only the potentially most equitable system; it could also save the authorities money. Scattered self-build projects in inner cities gave recognition to the fact that small sites owned by local authorities, which littered cities like London, were too expensive when developed by large public authorities. Politicized students of planning and design raised questions about old precedents while holding sit-ins to save old neighborhoods. Ultimately these changes led to looser standards and a shift toward a more "loose-fit" arrangement between form and function. All of these ideas and expressions of ideas, whether in policy or in projects, were and still are transitional stages of progressively emerging support policies for housing and urban improvement.

For the developing countries, the watershed in policy change from providing to supporting came

Community activism emerged as . . .

community participation in design and planning.

Using design tools. *(Source: Greater London Council, Department of Architecture and Civic Design)*

Designing house plans. *(Photo copyrighted by Greater London Council, Department of Architecture and Civic Design)*

Making programs. *(Photo by Rita Sampat)*

Sites and services: Investment in land, services, and utilities rather than in building houses.

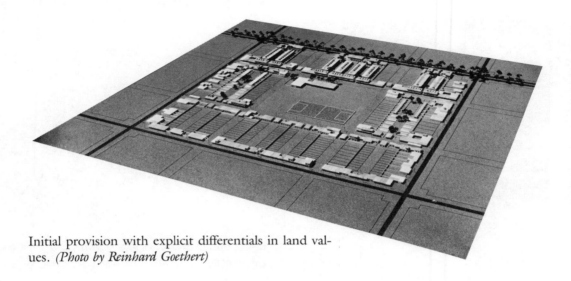

Initial provision with explicit differentials in land values. *(Photo by Reinhard Goethert)*

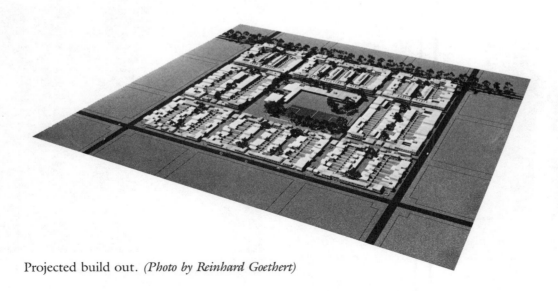

Projected build out. *(Photo by Reinhard Goethert)*

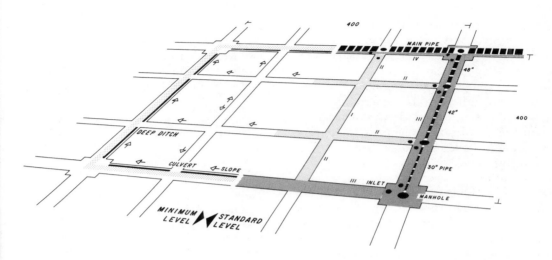

Progressive development: Storm drainage and circulation. *(Photo by Reinhard Goethert)*

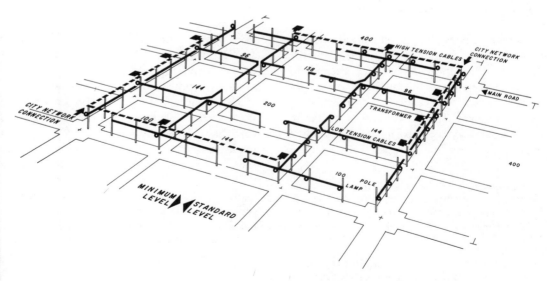

Progressive development: Electrical provisions. *(Photo by Reinhard Goethert)*

more explicitly with legitimization of sites and services projects, coupled, as they usually were, with various self-help and aided self-help programs. Such programs, inspired by Charles Abrams and John Turner, crafted as a means to lever affordable housing for the poor by Horacio Caminos and Reinhard Goethert, and progressively legitimized by the World Bank and others, today remain the single most practiced option to new development. Their proponents argued for governments to stop putting their money into building houses. Instead efforts and investments were focused on delivering land, services, and utilities.

Critics viewed with alarm the high level of investment in infrastructure. This was coupled with the demand placed on governments by lending agencies to recover their costs and with the desire of governments to see these sites consolidate with permanent materials and to standards set by municipal authorities. As detractors correctly argued, the resulting projects were in fact little more than public housing projects but without the houses. Nevertheless, such sites-and-services projects did recognize, perhaps officially for the first time, that making housing might better be achieved without governments' building houses.

The benefits of sites-and-services projects could not be confidently identified. Did they reach the lowest-income population? Were they cheaper to build and manage? Were they any more socially appropriate than their three-, four-, and five-story walk-up counterparts? The World Bank's own evaluation of sites-and-services projects and upgrading was positive:

The conclusions of the detailed evaluation have confirmed that the experiment embodied in the first generation of bank supported urban shelter projects has been remarkably successful. The validity of the progressive development model has been established. Self-help construction methods have been relatively efficient. The impacts of projects on the housing stock have been generally greater than anticipated. The projects have been affordable—and generally accessible—to the target populations. Those measurements which have been concluded indicate that the projects' impacts on the socio-economic conditions of participants have been in the directions expected. And, notably, the projects have not had negative impacts on expenditures for food and other basic necessities. Notwithstanding this general record of success, the projects have encountered some problems and produced some unexpected results. For example, most projects have experienced delays in implementation; materials and loan components have not been as successful as expected; support packages for small businesses have encountered problems; and two of the first three projects have experienced cost recovery problems. In addition, the use of family labor in construction has been less than expected. An analysis of projects' successes and shortcomings supports recommendations that future projects endeavor to push standards and costs still lower, include explicit provisions and opportunities for rental arrangements and incorporate credit provisions more nearly tailored to the needs of targeted families—about which we also know much more as a result of this program. (Keane and Parris 1982, abstract)

Criticism of the projects grew, however, as they were completed and as their impacts were measured, despite the bank's recommendations. Architects and planners were worried by their technically rational design emphasis, their use of coefficients of efficiency as the only determinants of design decisions. These projects lacked art and lacked design as an artistic endeavor. They more or less followed the cookie cutter approach, the international style, ignorant of context and resentful of culture.

Others argued that these projects required the same level of planning as public housing projects, that they displaced people who depended for their work on inner cities to the periphery of cities, that the cost of their administration was high, and that they would polarize classes and present far fewer economic opportunities than in the mixed economies of informal settlements (Peattie 1982). Families would sell out when they had finished building and would return to their shanties. There were few guarantees that people would repay their loans, which made them unattractive to private loan institutions. And in this sense, they favored people with steady incomes, which most poor do not have. In short, they would fail to reach those in most need unless governments continued their heavy subsidies for land and infrastructure, which they were advised by the funders to halt.

Because they relied heavily on self-help construction, they were criticized as being exploitive of labor. Marxists argued that the lowered housing costs made possible by self-help benefited capitalists rather than workers because it provided the opportunity to lower wages and therefore increase the extraction of surplus value (Burgess 1982).

If these arguments and counterarguments were puzzling to the professional world, they were even more puzzling to the self-helpers. First, self-helpers were legitimately skeptical. For years they had been helping themselves despite government policies. Now they were helping themselves because of government policies. Second, these policies encumbered the freedoms they had had before: to build as they wished, where they wished, and with whatever they could afford. Now there were loans, titles, repayments, standards, rules, and regulations. Most puzzling, the public housing projects—finished, permanent, well-serviced—were far more expensive than the sites and services offered to self-helpers. Yet the people who lived in public housing paid little or nothing. Sites-and-services occupants were paying more for less.

While some argued that enormous resources would be conserved when people built and managed their own housing, others pointed out that building one's own house within the confines of formal regulatory processes had little to do with controlling one's own destiny. In any event, few people actually built their own homes, preferring to hire small builders and masons. Poor people, up to 75 percent of whom may derive their income from informal activities, were not prepared to divert their time and energy away from the business of earning an income.

While theorists were busy arguing whether self-help was capitalist or socialist, a good thing or a bad thing, they forgot to consider that for lack of alternatives, it will go on happening anyway as an inevitable part of the way cities grow.

If the politics of benevolent pragmatism earned poor standing and accusations of paternalism among colleagues, the more popular advocacy approach gained a tarnished image for its romantic idealism. The "let's do it all with the people, because people are always right" approach drew (and continues to draw) much criticism both within and without their ranks. Participatory processes were time-consuming in the face of huge housing deficits and out of touch with the real world of global politics and international monetary systems.

Some people attracted criticism because of their radical belief that nothing could be done without first changing the whole system by dismantling existing political and legal structures that get in the way of constructing effective "support policies."[4] Radical populists believed that professionals were in a conspiracy against the public and that "the only going thing in the professions is to keep the professions going" (Miller 1987). "As the disciplines have expanded," they argued, "they have become only less illuminating, dealing less with common problems, and resorting more and more to such obscurantist devices as cliomentrics, mathematical models, and more jargon. The purpose of such professionalization has been not to enlighten non-professionals but to make them feel stupid, while generating new opportunities for the advancement of careers" (Miller 1987).

Populists emphasized community empowerment as the way to effective planning and design and proceeded to busy themselves more with social work than with planning. They emphasized the grass-roots technologies for building—small in scale, indigenous, and using locally sustainable means of production—even when it came to outmoded tech-

---

4. See Colin Ward, *When We Build Again* (London: Pluto Press, 1985), pp. 109–10.

nologies that the grass-roots itself resented. About the time some were discovering self-help (and before others had discovered that it was unfeasible), populists were arguing for technologies that were intermediate and indigenous. Such ideologies purported "production by the masses rather than mass production" and "small is beautiful." This too became a movement, resonating the ideals of those evangelists who got public housing underway.

Schumacker's ideas that provided the theoretical foundation to intermediate or appropriate technologies (AT) were nevertheless a direct challenge to advocates of "technology transfer." AT's emphasis on low capital costs, local materials, grassroots decision making, collective rather than individual efforts, user control, community empowerment and economic self-sufficiency, contrast starkly with the big business and large capital that fuel the transfer of technologies, usually from first world countries to the third world.

The perpetuation of dependency inherent in technology transfer allows bankers, engineers and business people—the modern conquistadors—to ensure continued control of developing nations while at the same time presenting themselves as altruists. Their assistance is usually channeled through elite institutions in the underdeveloped countries, thereby creating a development bureaucracy that is narrowly controlled, urban-based, and dependent. (OVITT 1989, 24)

And yet appropriate technology is limited by its own claims to self-sufficiency, limitations not easily accepted by some of its practitioners.

It is fine to prescribe windmills as an energy resource to poor people as long as it is clear that by doing so the AT expert is imposing a limit on the degree to which the windmill-powered economy can grow, on the types of products it can produce, and on the extent to which its people will emerge from poverty. . . . AT cannot, by definition, solve national economic problems except insofar as these problems are the sum of local needs. (OVITT 1989, 26, 27)

This claim probably fits the support paradigm in more general terms as well.

The trouble was that governments were not so much interested in technologies that were indigenous or appropriate as in those that contributed to their national economies and earned foreign currency, which locally sustainable technologies never did. Quite the contrary, they were considered by economists to consume capital and contribute little to national production in terms that contribute to the growth of the gross national product. Nor were the people to whom the "appropriate technology" arguments directed that interested either. Their concern was with earning status, and no amount of mud bricks, thatched roofs, or beer cans for walls was going to do that. What people had and did was because there were no other alternatives. "Small is beautiful" was to become "small is difficult."[5]

PARADIGMS IN CONFLICT?

Clearly, then, insofar as what government can do to scale up the supply of affordable housing to low-income people, two distinct paradigms have been operative. The first, which we may refer to as the *provider paradigm* is the one that had been dominant in housing history. It remains the one most practiced. In its simplest form, providing holds that if the goal is to reduce housing deficits and improve the quality of houses, then public authorities and/or formal or private developers have to control the production of houses. It is the paradigm most governments and most housing managers continue to advocate privately. It has, however, been growing progressively out of favor with most funders and academics and thus is widely discounted in the policy statements of public agencies, if not in practice.

The second, or *support,* paradigm is the one most talked about, if not implemented, and the one most encouraged now by multilateral agencies. It

---

5. Pierre Gillet, *Small Is Difficult: The Pangs and Success of Small Boat Technology* (London: Intermediate Technology Press, 1985).

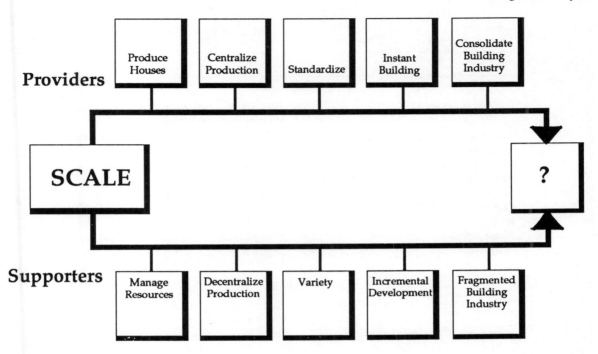

Supporters and providers. *(Drawing by Sevag Pogharian)*

holds that controlling the production of housing, even building lots of houses, in the capital-intensive way in which governments and private industry usually do has not worked. A better approach is to be more realistic in defining adequate housing in assessing existing stock and in the management of resources, including land, labor, skills, services, utilities, materials, and money. Supporting is a paradigm that has been around for years in books and journals but has only recently come to the fore in housing practice. It has become believable not because of benevolence but out of necessity.[6] Both

paradigms establish significantly different intellectual, physical, political, and economic settings for the work of architects and planners (Table 1).

In politics, providing and supporting each tend to find backing among both the left and the right but for very different reasons. The left may like the providing paradigm depending on who is doing the providing. If it is government, that means welfare, which the left likes but the right does not. If the provider is private, then it is speculative and profit motivated, which finds strong advocacy on the political right.

Today the support paradigm is also liked by the left and right but in a way that converges rather than diverges the interests of both poles. It does this by shifting the discussion away from public *or* private, and therefore away from leftist or rightist

6. John F. C. Turner, From central provision to local enablement, in *The Courier*. Reprinted in *Open House International* 8(4) (1983):6–10.

Table 1
Theories of Practice: Key Characteristics

Providing	*Supporting*
Objectives	
Build houses for people	Allocate resources for people to organize their own house building
Use house building to fuel economy	Use the economy to fuel house building
Centralize resources to facilitate management and control standards	Decentralize resources to support local enterprise and home building
Build organizations that facilitate central initiatives	Build regulations to support and give structure to local initiatives
Consolidate and centralize building production	Fragment building production and support small builders
Sectoralize development activities for ease of management, single-function projects	Integrate development activities and link housing to larger urban systems of employment and production
Methods	
Build large projects to achieve scale	Build programs and allocate resources for many small projects
Manufacture housing to speed production	Manage resources to increase volume
Build fast by building instantly	Build fast by building incrementally
Standardize project and operations Clearance and redevelopment	Promote variety, improvisation, infill, sites, and services
Tell what to do	Tell how to find out what to do, then how to find out how to do it

politics. It speaks instead to partnerships *between* public and private, *between* center and periphery. For the left it is a means toward greater community autonomy. Because it builds cooperation, it is a means to empowerment through the transfer and distribution of resources from central to local levels. The right likes it because it relieves the burden of housing from the public purse—a process that privatizes the business of housing (and urban development)—something it has been arguing all along as both more equitable and more efficient.

For countries that have always been too poor to match supply with demand in the provider mode, the support paradigm comes as a blessing in dis-guise. As an illustrative case in point, consider Sri Lanka, which elected candidates pledged to build 1 million houses. With only 3–4 percent of gross public expenditures usually allocated to housing, such attempts are impossible to achieve without a new paradigm, without changing the measure of success from how many houses built (provider) to how many families benefit.

Providers (those who believe in the provider paradigm) argue that large numbers of houses can best be delivered by speeding up the construction of houses and that big industry knows best how to do this. As such, the paradigm gives legitimacy to various forms of mechanization and Taylorization, no-

Table 1
(Continued)

Providing	*Supporting*
Products/Component	
Projects	Interventions
Behaviorally deterministic planning	Technical aid centers
Industrialized building systems	Training
Master plan	Housing options and loan packages
	Guidebooks, guidelines, tools, and methods
	Appropriate technologies
	Structure plans
Key Actors	
Consultants	Families
Government agencies	Community groups, tenant organizations, nongovernmental organizations
Funders	Nonprofit and voluntary organizations
Large contractors/developers	Government agencies
	Small contractors
	Funders
	Formal and informal private community developers
	Consultants

tably the prefabrication of houses, the industrial production of housing components—the Henry Ford syndrome of standard parts and mass production that typically demands large plants, sophisticated organization, large amounts of up-front capital, and large markets to guarantee economies of scale. Scale through mechanization, argue providers, is best achieved if production is brought to the center, where resources can be concentrated and properly managed. And when they are, it becomes easier to control centralized production processes in ways that facilitate the management of supply, which control quality and cost. Providers go on to argue that if production is to be increased, then housing types (tightly defined packages of space and material) should be rationalized to represent a careful balance of technical feasibility, building regulations, and planning controls—the very things that supporters argue have raised costs beyond the reach of those with the lowest income, especially in developing countries.[7]

Providers argue that to mass produce effectively is to mechanize, to mechanize effectively is to standardize, to standardize effectively enables better control of quality, quantity, and cost. For provid-

---

7. See, for example, ibid., 6–10.

ers, to build fast is to build instantly; to solve problems of housing is to build a large number of houses. This kind of thinking is designed to target whatever land, labor, and capital to encourage consumption rather than to satisfy human needs. This, we are told, fuels the economy, creates employment, generates profit, and generally improves the standard of living of even the poorest.

As might be expected, supporters challenge this narrow conception of production and its intrinsic consumerist economic stance. While the provider argument, they suggest, may be valid in large scale abstract national terms, it does little to improve the conditions of poor communities—indeed, it has more often quite the opposite effect.

Schumacher (1973, 47, 48) emphasizes the point eloquently. He argued that most modern economists are accustomed to "measuring the 'standard of living' by the amount of annual consumption, assuming all the time that a man who consumes more is 'better off' than a man who consumes less." He contrasts this attitude with the Buddhist economist, whose ideals may seem closer to those of supporter than those of modern economists. "A Buddhist economist would consider this approach excessively irrational: Since consumption is merely a means to human well being, the aim should be to obtain the maximum of well being with the minimum of consumption."

To supporters, minimizing the consumption of scarce resources is an important ideological tenet of their policies, particularly with respect to mass production of housing. Indeed, in their view and rightly, the ecology of production is likely to receive increasing attention in the decades to come.

The support paradigm holds assumptions about supply that appear to be in stark contrast to those of providers. First, supporters question the measure of deficit. In the developed world, the count of what is actually produced is based on formal building approvals. In most developing countries, these are insignificant compared to the average 80 percent of stock built informally and not usually counted as adequate housing. In one rapidly developing nation, huge housing deficits existed according to all surveys. Gearing up to build mass housing also happened to bring staggering benefits: billions of dollars in aid and low-cost loans, imported steel, cement, trucks, dumpsters, buses, and prestigious international consultants. Discovering that the figures provided to him were based on building permits, one consultant decided to fine tune the estimate by including housing stock produced informally. When he did, the housing deficit disappeared. Government officials were unhappy to learn that they did not in fact have a house production problem at all; rather they had an unrealistic definition of housing. Having geared up with industrialized building systems, heavy plant infrastructure, materials, borrowed money, and so on, there was no time to waste. The consultant was fired on the spot and then escorted to a jet bound for home.

The allocation of building materials is always influenced by regional politics and the political economics of production. Cement, for example, a key material for construction in cities, had been readily available throughout the Middle East. Yet within Iraq, a major producer in the region, it became scarce locally because it was expedient to export the material to neighboring countries in return for political favors. Large plants for prefabricating building systems that the Iraqis had purchased from France and that depended for output on steady supplies ground to a halt. Similarly, in Egypt, cement is in short supply to the vast majority (who build informally and buy it on the black market) because the government appropriates most of what it can and distributes it according to its own national priorities.

Other countries control and allocate essential materials to sectors that help build the industrial core of their economies. For them, housing is a "durable form of investment, requiring substantial outlay to create, but paying little per year. Building houses generates no foreign exchange, competes with industry and agriculture for capital, draws off needed labor, and materials, and may even be inflationary'' (Abrams 1964). The Soviet Union, which in the early 1930s envisioned building ''socialist collective cities as symphonies of steel, concrete and glass'' organized on the basis of the ''most radical standardizations and modular coordination of the whole building process'' (Stein 1931, 201), reverted to more flexible, more modest, small-scale timber construction, which was much faster and much cheaper to build.

Supporters like Strassman (1975, 100) point out that ''once construction enterprises exist, the annual volume of building depends less on a rapid rate of output from each enterprise, than on the volume of resources devoted to building . . . . If dwellings are expensive and built with imported molds and cranes as they usually are in the developing world, a country may not be able to afford to build at less volume, or to close the housing deficit very fast, regardless of saving in months or houses per [more expensive] dwelling.'' Removing housing shortages quickly therefore constitutes an economic policy question, not a technical problem. And, as he goes on to observe, ''within a radius of about 50 kilometers of the component factory, 1,000 to 8,000 almost identical dwelling units must have a market over five years, depending on the type of ISB [Industrial Systems Building] or the investment will be a waste.''

Supporters conclude that the management of resources is more critical to increasing supply and that rather than worry about the means of building production, it may be better instead to improve the means by which hundreds of small builders, manufacturers, and suppliers, both formal and informal, gain access to essential building materials, cheap credit, better utilities, larger markets, and easier transportation.

The large-scale production of houses, in other words, can best be achieved by increasing the participation of small builders and ordinary people—by building their capacity to deliver houses, services,

and even some utilities located close to their market. For supporters, the question is not how government and industry can produce more houses but what help their organizations can give so that those who already produce and others who want to but cannot can produce more effectively. For supporters, deciding interventions is far more crucial to building projects. Building houses, whether through government or formal market channels, has little to do with solving housing problems.

To providers, fragmentation gauges the weakness of the building industry as evidenced in both formal and informal markets in developed and developing countries. Yet supporters, faced with such inevitable fine-grained diversity, look upon it opportunistically as necessary to efficiency, quantity, and cost-effective production and not, as providers might argue, its antithesis. They tell us that a fragmented rather than consolidated building industry is better equipped to respond to market demands, it is more resilient to fluctuations in building activity as it has been throughout history. As Gwendolyn Wright (1981) explains, a speculator often sold several lots to a housewright or an independent building tradesman, who put up one or two new houses within a year. Rather than controlling standards or quality or normalizing production processes, supporters tell us that the more ways that are developed to achieve objectives, then the more likely it will be that one will fit the needs and budget. Small builders with low overheads and very little physical plant can adjust their work load far more flexibly than can their industrialized counterparts.

In contrast to the instant delivery of houses, supporters argue that scaling up the supply of housing without risking bankruptcy and without displacing entire populations means building incrementally, precisely as people in informal developments do. It means cultivating an environment in which housing, small businesses, and communities will grow, consolidate, and change and where production and building can provide opportunities for employment, for accumulating wealth, and for improving health. To supporters, housing becomes an integral part of a larger system of urban development.

Outside politics and production, such differences in a paradigm trigger fundamental differences in professional attitudes and self-image, especially when set in a historical context. Providers present themselves as benevolent pragmatists whose prime interest is getting the job done quickly, efficiently, cleanly, and with some social grace. They recognize that political parties are often short-lived and seek the fruits of their policies quickly and visibly. Elected politicians, for instance, must seek the greatest visible impact in the shortest period of time, often irrespective of the resources that may be consumed and the implications this may have in the long term. Most professionals working in housing and urban development usually have these governments as their principal clients and are therefore bound to frame solutions within the paradigm of the stated need.

For providers, slums represent a national failure, a threat to political and social stability, something to be eradicated. Providers are generally party to one of two approaches. The first is the *technological fix*, with a heavy emphasis on professional and managerial expertise. The second, or *one-shot fix* approach, is to "bring in the consultants, sort out priorities, put a figure and a time limit to the job and then throw in the task force."[8] This is by no means a quick fix. The standards are generally high and result in a terrific technological accomplishment—one that is, however, not replicable. To supporters, such practices are technically inappropriate and hopelessly impractical on any significant scale, whether the providing is done publicly through government agencies or privately through formal speculative builders.

---

8. From Ray Pahls's six contrasting approaches to urban issues, as reported by Ward, *When We Build Again*.

NO SINGLE SOLUTION

What has experience taught us in the housing field, and what are we left with? Is the support paradigm workable as an alternative? What does it mean for design and planning of housing and neighborhoods? Is it any more likely to deliver affordable housing services and utilities to the poor?

There are, unfortunately, few certainties in response to these questions. But we have learned that users are indispensable to making more efficient the practice of design and planning and the production of houses because they are more conversant with and knowledgeable about local needs and conditions and because they bring a resourcefulness not easily replicated by formal institutions. If they are to be a part of deciding, building, and managing project work, they need both the reason and the capacity to act—both denied in the old days of public housing and city planning.

We have learned that public housing was not as public as we had thought, since most construction in this sector is done by private contractors; that self-help was less an ideal and more a necessity because most poor people prefer finished houses but cannot afford them; that the informal sector was not as informal as we had thought; and that the distinction drawn between it and the formal sector was somewhat arbitrary, particularly in the ways land, materials, and labor are often acquired across formal-informal boundaries.

In the end, deficits of adequate shelter were growing and not diminishing—not just because not enough houses were being produced or because governments were corrupt, bankrupt, or both, but because expectations were rising; because we had not allowed adequately for the reduction in household size; because we had failed to uncover concealed households that came into being as soon as housing was available; because the age of marriage had become unexpectedly lower; because there were more people living as independent households

**Centrally planned projects versus locally managed
progressive development.**

Cairo. *(Source: Reinhard Goethert)*

Boston. *(Source: Boston Housing Authority)*

Instant building versus . . .

Boston. *(Source: Boston Housing Authority)*

. . . incremental and differential growth.

Ottawa, Canada: Two identical houses in transformation.

Colombo, Sri Lanka: As the permanent structure consolidates, the temporary structure will disappear. *(Photo by National Housing Development of Sri Lanka)*

Alexandria, Egypt: An informal settlement showing construction at different stages fifteen years after initial settlement.

for a longer period; because larger families were an economic necessity; because of increased migration to cities; and so on.

We have also discovered the ubiquitous irony: what puzzles supporters, whose explicit intention is to serve people, is that people secretly prefer providers. They like finished homes, offered under heavy subsidy, built to much higher standards than they could ever hope to achieve in any other way. Who wouldn't, particularly when defaulting on government-subsidized loan payments is unlikely to lose you your house? And what puzzles providers, whose intentions historically have been to serve government and industry in the interests of the national economy, is that governments and industry increasingly prefer supporters. It turns out that supporting is as profitable for industry as providing. As puzzled economists working for Mexico's enormous producer of Blue Circle Cement discovered, when the formal construction industry crashed, the combined informal market of thousands of home owners and squatters continued to edge up the price of bags of concrete. (They subsequently distributed free manuals on self-building.)

Most important, we have learned that public housing, self-help, sites and services, new towns, streets in the air, and the rest "have not been pushed aside by more up-to-date solutions. Instead, they have been superseded by the belief that no such solutions exist."[9] They have been superseded by the knowledge that so many housing problems that experts have been pursuing with arrogant confidence for decades have been created in the minds of those industriously pursuing solutions, which in turn have fueled the "housing problems industry." In his preface to Turner's book *Housing by People,* Ward said, "The moment that housing, a universal human activity, becomes defined as a

problem, a housing problems industry is born, with an army of experts, bureaucrats and researchers, whose existence is a guarantee that the problem won't go away."

The shift away from the problem-solving ethic and away from providers who depend on it is at the core of the support paradigm. It is a shift that requires new professional attitudes and habits, new relationships among people, organizations, and experts, and new responsibilities. All of this is reflected in three key tenets that, albeit sometimes begrudgingly, are becoming an intrinsic part of design and planning practice: participation, flexibility, and enablement. All three themes emerged during the transitional phases, all three were first articulated as theories of practice in contrasting yet synergistic ways by two architects, John Turner and John Habraken.

Supporters differ from providers primarily insofar as they believe that most solutions to problems exist in everyday practice; they only need to be recognized and then built on. They exist not as government and professionals might like and might not be working as effectively as we would need them, but they exist nevertheless.

REFERENCES

Abrams, Charles. 1964. *Man's Struggle for Shelter in an Urbanizing World.* Cambridge, Mass.: MIT Press.

Baer, William C. 1986. The shadow market in housing. *Scientific American* 255(5): 29–35.

Bauer, Catherine. 1934. *Modern Housing.* Boston: Houghton Mifflin Company. Reprinted 1974 by Arno Press Inc., New York.

Benjamin, Solomon J. n.d. Income and housing: Understanding household productivity within the framework of urban structuring. Unpublished paper. MIT, Cambridge, Mass.

Bristow, David. 1981. The legal framework, the role of the lawyer. In *Participation in Housing,* pp. 1–38. Working Paper 58. Edited by Nabeel Hamdi and Robert Greenstreet. Oxford: Oxford Polytechnic Department of Town Planning.

Burgess, Rod. 1982. Self-help housing advocacy: A curi-

---

9. This was a phrase used by Robert Fishman in reference to the ideal cities of Howard, Wright, and le Coubusier in *Urban Utopias in the Twentieth Century* (Cambridge, Mass.: MIT Press, 1987), pp. 267.

ous form of radicalism. A critique of the work of John F. C. Turner. In *Self-Help Housing: A Critique,* pp. 56–97. Edited by Peter M. Ward, London: Mansell Publishing Ltd.

Burnett, John. 1978. *A Social History of Housing, 1815–1970.* London: Methuen.

Global Report on Human Settlements. 1986. 1987. New York: Oxford University Press, for the United Nations Centre for Human Settlements (HABITAT)

Jackson, Anthony. 1976. *A Place Called Home: A History of Low-Cost Housing in Manhattan.* Cambridge, Mass.: MIT Press.

Keane, Douglas H., and Parris, Scott. 1982. *Evaluation of Shelter Programs for the Urban Poor: Principal Findings.* World Bank Staff Working Paper 547. Washington, D. C.: World Bank.

Koenigsberger, Otto. 1987. The intentions of housing policy alternatives, their development and impact in the third world since the 1950s. Paper presented to the International Symposium on the Implications of a Support Policy for Housing Provision, Development Planning Unit, University College, London, December 9–11.

Lubove, R. 1962. *The Progressives and the Slums: Tenement House Reform in New York City, 1890–1917.* Pittsburgh: University of Pittsburgh Press.

McManamy, Rob. 1988. Affordable housing: needed but unattractive. *Engineering News-Record,* April 7.

Mangin, William. 1967. Latin American squatter settlements: A problem and a solution. *Latin American Research Review* 2(3):65–98.

Marcuse, Peter. 1986. Housing policy and the myth of the benevolent state. In *Critical Perspectives on Housing,* pp. 248–63. Edited by Rachel G.Bratt, Chester Hartman, Ann Meyerson.

Miller, Mark Crispin. 1987. Out of mind. *Atlantic* (October):104–6.

Ovitt, George. 1989. Appropriate technology: Development and social change. *Monthly Review* 40(9) :22–32.

Peattie, Lisa R. 1982. Some second thoughts on sites and services. *Habitat International* 6(1–2):131–39.

Schumacher, E. F. 1973. *Small Is Beautiful. A Study of Economics as If People Mattered.* London: Abacus.

Schuman, Tony. 1986. The agony and the equity: A critique of self-help housing. In *Critical Perspectives on Housing,* pp. 463–73. Edited by Rachel G. Bratt, Chester Hartman, Ann Meyerson.

Stein, Wilm. 1931. Experiment: "Socialist cities." In *Russia: An Architecture for World Revolution,* pp. 184–203. Edited by El Lissitzky. Cambridge, Mass.: MIT Press.

Strassman, W. P. 1975. Industrialized systems building for developing countries: A discouraging prognosis. *International Technical Cooperation Centre Review.* 55(January):99–113.

Ward, Colin. 1983. *Housing: An Anarchist Approach.* London: Freedom Press.

Ward, Colin. 1984. *Arcadia for All: The Legacy of a Makeshift Landscape.* London and New York: Mansell.

Wates, Nick, and Knevitt, Charles. 1987. *Community Architecture: How People Are Creating Their Own Environment.* London: Penguin Books.

Williams, David G. 1984. The role of international agencies: The World Bank. In *Low-Income Housing in the Developing World,* pp. 173–85. Edited by Geoffrey K. Payne, Chichester: John Wiley & Sons.

Winner, Langdon. 1977. *Autonomous Technology: Technics-out-of-control as a Theme in Political Thought.* Cambridge, Mass.: MIT Press.

Wright, Gwendolyn. 1981. *Building the Dream.* Cambridge, Mass.: MIT Press.

CHAPTER 3

A Tale of Two Architects

To my mind, we should quietly and humbly re-think our housing policy from first principles, and then consider how the circumstances we have inherited can be re-shaped to fit the principles of housing. Fortunately, we have two excellent guides to the discovery of a viable philosophy of housing. One is the Dutch architect N. J. Habraken and the other is the English architect, John F. C. Turner.

Colin Ward, "Self-Help and Mutual Aid in Housing"

Housing by People by John Turner (1976) and *Supports* by John Habraken (1972) challenged the very definition of housing and set new precedents for the production of houses. The importance of these books was widely felt by academics and by practitioners and, later, by the bilateral and multilateral funding agencies. Habraken and Turner were influential in at least two generally significant ways. First, the form of their work—their relative positions, their points of departure, their methods and conclusions—represents a ubiquitous and still troublesome division of responsibilities for architects in housing. On the one hand are the politics and economics of housing and housing delivery systems, the management of technology and resources (including the proper distribution of land, materials, and money), and the proper organization of institutions and the training of their personnel to deliver and manage affordable housing. Few of these traditionally have little or anything to do with architecture, but most are fundamental to housing reform and production. On the other hand is the contention that these kinds of issues and those advocated by Turner dilute the fundamental tenets of architecture by diverting attention away from its fundamental business of design and building. This camp has traditionally preferred to exercise its influence in challenging the confines of its discipline rather than that of the political context in which it is set. The concern of those interested in making architecture relevant in housing, like Habraken, is with built form and not with the form of the institutions that govern it.

For students deciding on careers, these two seemingly exclusionary positions, encouraged by schools and by the profession itself, present a dilemma: rigor for design and for architecture as defined usually in modernist terms versus relevance in a field where these terms are hopelessly irrelevant. Can these two positions be compatible? If so, do they demand new professional attitudes, new methods, new tools, new curricula for teaching, new pedagogy, new theories of practice?

The second significant influence of both Habraken and Turner was with respect to the content of their work. Habraken was working and writing in Holland and Turner in Peru, yet both drew similar conclusions about the failings and inequities of housing, suggesting principles that seem appropriate across first world–third world boundaries. Their ideas expanded the housing debate beyond ideology and technique and put design, designing, and the role of architects firmly and squarely in a social and political arena. Both offered a comprehensive definition of the support paradigm and its three tenets for design: flexibility, participation, and enablement.

COMMON OBJECTIVES

Turner and Harbraken were able to articulate for the 1960s what Patrick Geddes had done in the first decade of the twentieth century and which Mumford described as "fresh thought, fresh observation and fresh experiment." Their work had "no finalities of dogma and doctrine," a philosophy that "provided for its own correction and its own replacement."[1]

Turner and Habraken brought new empirical evidence to discredit the preponderance of public building and built an attractive alternative theoretical basis on which to rethink housing as a flexible, dynamic, incremental activity. More important, they fundamentally rethought the tired and increasingly unworkable relationships of people, professionals, and public authorities, seeking more flexible linkages among these actors and more mediation between public authority responsibilities and those of users.

Both Habraken and Turner are supporters. They argue that housing dominated by public authorities is not an equitable way to solve housing problems,

nor is it economic or efficient. Both argue against standard solutions, public dominance of housing supply, and the ubiquitous, simplistic, and ponderous cycle of public versus formal private polarization of housing, between the left and the right of the political spectrum, neither of which had delivered what it promised. Nevertheless, their objectives differ markedly. Turner is more concerned with supports for structuring government policy and directing professional interventions, and Habraken's prime concern is for structuring the physical environment.

For Habraken (1982, 59,60,61), "a support structure is a construction which allows the provision of dwellings which can be built, altered and taken down independently of the others." Unlike a skeletal frame, it is a piece of complete building embodying the needs and aspirations of community and enabling a wide variety of dwelling types. Unlike the skeletal frame, which is, he says, "entirely tied to the single project of which it forms a part," supports are designed on the basis of uncertainty in form and function of dwelling and with the intent therefore, that it would "grow, develop and change with what goes on inside."

For Turner (1989, 182), "the most important supports are those that increase access to affordable and well located land, to secure tenure, basic services, appropriate technologies, affordable standards and procedures and credit." What Turner calls the "supportive shack" (versus the "oppressive house") (1976, 54,56) has much less to do with its physical organization and much more with its location, its low cost, its form of tenancy, its security, and the freedom it offers to move at short notice. The shack for most poor people, especially in developing countries, despite its relatively poor construction, is therefore "an admirable support for their actual situation and a vehicle for the realization of their expectations."

These observations, which he first made in Arequila, Peru, led Turner (1976, 102) to understand that "what matters in housing is what it *does* for

---

1. Introduction to Patrick Geddes, *Patrick Geddes in India* (London: Lund Humphries, 1947).

people rather than what it is. . . . Only when housing is determined by households and local institutions and the enterprises that they control, can the requisite variety in dwelling environments be achieved. Only then can supply and demand be properly matched and consequently satisfied. And only then will people invest their own relatively plentiful and generally renewable resources."

In the face of the extremes of public versus private, left versus right, central versus local, top versus bottom—extremes hotly debated among housers that seemed to dominate the supply of housing—Turner and Habraken instead articulated the need for some measure of balance to be restored between state organizations and community groups if there was to be any progress in improving the quality and quantity of housing. Turner did this with considerable thought for the structure of organizations and introduced the idea of the community sector in which both state and family would have their interests directly represented, albeit through the mediation of nongovernment organizations (NGOs): "As the development and implementation of supportive and enabling policies involve changes of relationship between people and government, NGOs as third parties are essential as mediators as well as in their roles as community developers, innovators, and motivators" (Turner 1989, 182). Habraken did it by splitting decision making into two realms—the communal and the individual—and then explicitly associating with each modes of building, production, and design as supports in the realm of community, to be deliberated by state organizations and others responsible for cities and detachable units in the realm of the individual. In both cases, his intent was to exploit the potential of "modern factory-based mass production," an intent that was an anathema to Turner.

These concerns were remarkably coincidental with and indeed substantiated by those of their counterparts in the field of political science. Berger and Neuhaus (1977, 2,3), for example, put it this way:

For the individual in modern society, life is an ongoing migration between two spheres, public and private. The megastructures are typically alienating, that is, they are not helpful in providing meaning and identity for individual existence. . . . While the two spheres interact in many ways, in private life, the individual is left very much to his own devices, and thus is uncertain and anxious. . . . The dichotomy poses a double crisis. It is a crisis for the individual who must carry on a balancing act between the demands of the two spheres. It is a political crisis because the megastructures (notably the state), come to be devoid of personal meaning and are therefore viewed as unreal, or even malignant.

These, then, were the issues that led Schumacher (1973, 53,54), among others, to conclude:

In the affairs of men there always appears to be a need for at least two things simultaneously, which on the face of it seem to be incompatible and to exclude one another. We always need both freedom and order. We need the freedom of lots of small autonomous units, at the same time, the orderliness of large scale, possibly global unity and coordination. . . . What I wish to emphasize is the duality of the human requirement when it comes to the question of size: There is no single answer. For his different purposes, many needs [require] many different structures. . . . for constructive work, the principle task is always the restoration of some kind of balance.

Turner and Habraken saw design and the activities of designers as measures that would cultivate a balanced, equitable environment for habitation or restore the balance where it had been upset. But they recognized that professional interventions had to be applied carefully and that the actions of professionals had to be made accountable to the public if the public were to be informed rather than bewildered, as Ravetz (1986, 105) suggests: "For between the professionals' expertise and the councilors' prerogative, the one impregnable by mystique and the other by representative democracy, the lay person had no platform to stand on" and therefore no place in the production of housing. It was indeed the lack of place for the lay public that Turner and Habraken saw as the root cause of the imbalance and therefore a priority in formulating new policy.

Too many interventions disable the very organism it is intended to help, not enough will not be helpful; and if they are the wrong kind, all sorts of other problems are created. "At worst, like medicine, [poorly judged interventions] could create 'iatrogenic' disease, or problems that were provoked or even invented by the treatment" (Ravetz 1986, 105). In Turner's words (1972, 133), "As I came to realize the perverse nature of the premises on which professionalism and institutionalization of services (and values) are based, I began to understand how and why the established system is so often counterproductive and so rarely enjoyable. . . . When the house becomes a commodity supplied through paternalistic agencies, there is no room for the enjoyment of the process itself."

But like any other interventionary measure, successes rely heavily on careful diagnosis and an understanding of the conditions, systems, habits, and relationship of the context. When these conditions and its constituents are changing rapidly, as they are in housing, we need to understand the dynamics of systems that induce these changes so that they can be prevented if deemed malignant (poverty, disease, and deterioration, for example) or enhanced if they are not.

Turner's and Habraken's ideas were not new, nor was much of their terminology. What was different were their means more than their intentions. Both, after all, were grounding their visions on insightful observations of the everyday and resourceful way in which people housed themselves, and both recalled the observations and philosophies of others, among them Ebenezer Howard, Peter Kropotkin, Lewis Mumford, and Patrick Geddes. It was Howard, after all, who in 1898 sought to reconcile freedom and order in his garden cities and to "discover the minimum of organization that would secure the benefits of planning while leaving to individuals the greatest possible control over their own lives." As Fishman tells us (1982, 51), he "hated

bureaucratic paternalism . . . [and] realized that planning must stay with self-imposed limits," something that for Turner was to become ideologically rooted as a basic principle of housing—the principle of planning for housing through limits (Turner 1976, 103): "Only if there are centrally guaranteed limits to private action can equitable access to resources be maintained and exploitation avoided. As long as planning is confused with design and lays down lines that people and organizations must follow, enterprise will be inhibited, resources will be lost, and only the rich will benefit."

The Russian anarchist Peter Kropotkin argued in his articles between 1888 and 1890 for small-scale units of society, for cooperation, and for decentralization.[2] Kropotkin had articulated similar concerns in his formulation of anarchist-communist principles.[3] The basic features of his future society were "the abolition of hierarchical authority . . . the end of all state systems regardless of their form." While Kropotkin was thinking of cooperative forms of organization or a kind of socialist anarchy, Turner's writings have shown him to favor individual anarchy—that is, a form of organization that "emphasizes individual liberty, the sovereignty of the individual, the importance of private property or possession, and the inequity of all monopolies" (Bottomore et al. [1983, 18] in Pezzoli, 1986).

Even Frank Lloyd Wright in his discussions of Broadacre used the term and the concept of support to explain an idea about "factories and other economic institutions . . . cast explicitly as 'support units' for the family" (Fishman 1982, 131). For Habraken, the Arsene-Henri brothers in 1955 introduced movable partitions within an open plan setting in Rheims, and Reitolds Schroeder's house consisted largely of open floor plans with a fixed sanitary core and access and sliding partitions.

---

2. I have adopted these notes from Purnima Kapur, Ideas to practice: Self-help housing (master's thesis, MIT, 1989).

3. See, for example; P. A. Kropotkin, *Selected Writings on Architecture and Revolution* (Cambridge, Mass.: MIT Press, 1970).

The fact that Turner's and Habraken's ideas and proposals had the impact they did was probably more a function of timing than anything else. Turner wrote about his observations in Lima, Peru, in architectural design as early as 1963, and Habraken had his work first published in Dutch in 1961. What had changed to make the ideas palatable in 1967 was a growing social consciousness that produced a fresh opportunity for professionals and public authorities and was therefore politically palatable and economically affordable.

Habraken and Turner were received at first with considerable skepticism by public authorities and professional institutions. When Turner presented his principles of self-help to the Greater London Council shortly after his return from Lima, his ideas were more puzzling than enlightening. None of those who crowded the room to hear him could quite figure out what Lima had to teach London or how self-help or self-determination could improve the job lot of GLC architects. No one could figure out what his ideas had to do with architecture. In fact, many who were present found his arguments threatening, serving to undermine the discipline of architecture and even do architects out of a job. The idea of hordes of self-organized self-builders all over London smacked of anarchy. In an already complicated process of planning approvals, the last thing that public authority architects wanted was another layer of approvals—and by a public body whose response could not be easily predicted, modeled, or relied on for good taste.

Inasmuch as Turner was seen to provide little method or structure to his ideas, so Habraken was seen to provide too much. In summing up Habraken's lecture to the Royal Institute of British Architects in April 1972, Geoffrey Darbourne expressed concerns about an approach that seemed to rationalize the art of architecture and the process of design into systems of grids and zones that perhaps were technically rigorous but lacked the creative and artistic spirit that transcends building and makes architecture. He was like others, intimidated by the

SAR methodology, the idea of user involvement in housing design, and the hard-edged deductive thinking that went behind it.[4] He, like others, was intimidated because it showed mistrust of the inductive or intuitive way most architects worked. It seemed to undermine the control that architects would have (and had been taught to have) and left too much open to individual whim. Habraken openly admitted that his methods and ideologies challenged conventional professional roles, as well as methods of finance, building and management. But he never abandoned architecture as a mode of formal artistic expression, something that had never interested Turner that much.

Darbourne's comments represented a gross misunderstanding of Habraken's methods, and they persist today in the minds of many of his critics. Habraken's methods were never a substitute for good design or creative inductive thinking. They were never intended to induce good ideas but rather were aimed at ordering ideas and building production so that they could be communicated to and so inclusive of others. The means of achieving this were perhaps less important than his intentions: if users were to be involved in decision making by being included on design coalition teams, then communication among team members would have to be improved, and there would have to be an effective way of coordinating design and building production and of managing decisions. There would have to be a way of improving communication about options available within any given set of constraints and of formally structuring these constraints in ways that liberate individual freedoms.

Habraken's calls for more flexibility, for adaptability, and for greater user involvement as well as his assumption that "the more variety housing can assume in the support structure, the better," (Habraken 1982, 61) were skeptically (and sometimes

---

4. Stichten Architecten Research (SAR) was founded in 1965 to study decision-making tools for designers to bring about greater user control in housing, based on Habraken's work.

angrily) received in England, where his ideas were first heard at the RIBA and later reviewed when his book was published in English in 1972. Douglas Frank, for example, wrote in the *Architects' Journal* in April 1972 following the RIBA speech:

When asked what were the social criteria upon which his philosophy and design principles were based, Habraken referred the audience to his book but appeared, surprisingly, to miss the point. At the meeting and in his book he seems to think that the arguments for providing more choice are overriding and self-evident. Rightly or wrongly my impression is that he has not considered that people, the dwellers, might prefer the extra money and design time which are involved in his approach, to be devoted to an improvement in other aspects of housing quality.

Some critics were intimidated by what seemed to be another comprehensive and global solution to the housing problem, the sort of thing that had never worked in the past.[5] Gordon Redfern, chief architect to one development corporation, said, "I fear that we might be jumping off one technological tiger's back onto another. For Habraken opens up a vista of such scale and sheer commitment that it makes Ville Radieuse sound like a box of kids' building blocks. . . . One feels that the whole operation belongs within a future society with great wealth at its disposal" (Redfern 1972, 69,70). This skepticism about the realities of support and its underlying assumptions pervaded much of the critique. "Families living in mass housing are inherently conservative, neither wishing for the flexibility we believe essential, nor suffering from the problems posed in the book." Others retorted that "the major factor in good housing is not adaptability, but the environment it creates. Surely the Georgian speculative house builder has taught us how people will adapt and thus defer obsolescence indefinitely if the general environment is good enough" (Trenton 1972).

Even Habraken's assumptions about the natural

relationship, which he argued was the involvement of the individual in deciding on building and "possessing" his own house was brought to question. Some suggested that this relationship existed only for a small minority in history and that the vernacular building from which Habraken draws reference "housed the superior artisan class rather than the poor of the pre-industrial society, while as we all know, the individual poor of the 19th century lived in grossly overcrowded slums. They had nothing to contribute except in exorbitant rent" (Ward 1981, 6). Then there were those who thought supports had all been done before, like the designers of Park Hill in Sheffield, and that therefore it was nothing to get too excited about. Finally, there were others, like Eric Lyons, who wrote it all off as "simplistic illusion" and who was sure it would all go away sooner or later.

In the end, both Turner and Habraken suffered the malaise that befalls all visionaries who have something practical to say and who get something built. The image of their ideas—self-build and self-manage in Turner's case, support in Habraken's—was to become more powerful than their social and technical purpose. And later, ironically, the more acceptable their ideas became to public authorities, the less acceptable they were to those who saw themselves as radicals. If public authorities were unhealthy, which radicals assumed, then any ideas acceptable to the authorities must themselves be unhealthy.

DIFFERENCES IN METHOD

Inasmuch as there were profound similarities between the intentions of Turner and Habraken, so their major preoccupations differed significantly.

Turner was preoccupied with the politics of housing—with systems of organization, financing, and management and with better use of global resources. He argued for the use of income resources as much as possible and capital resources as little as

---

5. The *Architects' Journal* invited various responses to Habraken's book, *Supports—An Alternative to Mass Housing,* from prominent British architects. See *Architects Journal* 12(July 1972).

possible, and he sought to dismantle the division between housing production and consumption. He sought to promote self-management, self-help, and even self-build.

He saw user participation as a means to make the housing delivery system more efficient, not in ways that fueled capitalist modes of production (although Burgess has argued that that is precisely what they do) but that stimulated "individual and social well being. . . . When people have no control over, nor responsibility for key decisions in the housing process . . . dwelling environments may[6] instead become a barrier to personal fulfillment and a burden on the economy" (Turner 1972). He considered centralized large industrial systems as wasteful, counterproductive, and spurred by professional self-interest and greed.

Turner's anarchist principles were rooted in his early work with Pat Cooke, Colin Ward, and Giancarlo Di Carlo and were no surprise to those who knew him. They had published their ideas on participatory housing in the anarchist newspaper *Freedom* and the Italian anarchist journal *Volonta* as early as 1952.

His most ardent critic, Rod Burgess (1982, 57) has written that much of the way in which Turner and others like him have argued his case is "very similar to Victorian ideas of self-improvement." Arguments against state intervention in the economy and for the reduction in scale of economic activities and the drastic deindustrialization of society can be seen as part of the antiurban, antiindustrial bias that has been an important undercurrent of Western social science. It has also constituted an important element in anarchist thought.

Burgess was critical of the "merits of private property," which he read into Turner's definition of security of tenure, much as Engels (1975) had argued before him: that stability, which house ownership

offered poor people, ran against their interest insofar as it undermined badly needed reforms in income and class that would challenge the cause of bad housing.

Worse, Turner's call for performance concerning the specification of standards of space, materials, and construction so that housing could be affordable to the poor met with accusations of inequity, and critics charged that differential standards would reinforce divisions of class. As Burgess suggests (1982, 84), "What is in effect needed is a set of provisions that apply equally to all, precisely because all groups in society have equal right to adequate housing."

All of these ideas came to the fore of the debate in the late 1960s. Their anarchist undertones struck a chord with young intellectuals and grass-roots organizers in search of more autonomy for the growing number of self-styled community organizations that were taking to the streets and demanding more say about the future of their housing and neighborhoods. They also struck a chord with students of architecture, some of whom had turned to activism and away from modernist formalism as an expression of their mistrust with systems of state. These students were intent on finding better connections between the truths of their art and the realities of city politics.

While Turner was driven by a concern for people, politics, and global resources, Habraken looked to improve the efficiency of design, designer, and building. He never abandoned his love for architecture, which Turner seemed to consider irrelevant to housing. Habraken saw the involvement of users in housing as indispensable to making design more efficient—to ensuring a healthy physical environment—but not to the spiritual and moral well-being of people, which he saw best left to others. Involving users in design decision making, he knew, was helpful to designers. It was not a charitable act on their part, nor need it involve architects in social work, politics, or economics.

On the progressive involvement of architects in

6. Turner changed "*may* instead become" to "*will* instead become" in 1987. See *Journal of Architecture and Planning Research* 4(4) (1987):273–80.

social and political issues—community development, political activism, resource management, and the management of technology—Habraken (1983, 4, 5) stated his convictions bluntly:

I believe that the architect's business is built form. He must understand built form as both the means and the result of inhabitation. All these other fields I mentioned a moment ago have their impact on form and built forms relate to all of them. The architect must be able to understand these relations to all other fields of human endeavor but his own field is built form. It is the deployment of materials in space; the organization of space itself as a vehicle for behavior, for power, for territorial organization, for self-expression and for collective coherence among people. If we do not understand what built form is about in this multi-faceted way, what could we contribute that other experts cannot do better?

He was less interested in direct dialogue between architects and users and more interested that the form of building be a basis for direct communication between people and their physical surroundings.

This may have sounded like a spiritual quest in its own right—the sort of idealism that earned early reformers like Howard and Fourier their utopian label. But Habraken was not in search of ideal communities nor was he a reformer. He was describing an architecture of the everyday environment that was responsive to change, dynamic, easily readable, additive, resilient, and reliable. He envisions a public architecture complete in its own right and yet inviting of private transformation. He saw architects "engaged in the cultivation of exactly that everyday environment that was taken for granted in the past. There the result, if not to be static, must change and grow over time. It is not an exception but reality itself. It is full of meaning but not a symbol for society. This alternative model of the professional role is based on the awareness that monuments will eventually grow in a healthy built environment, but that a healthy built environment can never be made out of monuments" (Habraken 1983, 9).

Habraken faced two areas of criticism at the time when he was arguing his methods and probably still

does to this day. First, he did not denounce central systems of technological production or the industrialization of housing. Like Howard, who had "confident faith in industrialization" and saw "a place in which industrialization could be kept in its proper [subordinate] place" (Fishman 1982, 70), Habraken saw it all as inevitable and instead sought ways and means of reshuffling these systems to serve public authorities and users better. But unlike his predecessors, he wanted to disentangle building production (supports) from industrial production (detachable units) and have all products over which users would have control in the planning and finishing of dwellings manufactured like furniture or self-assembled kitchens. He was not seeking to change the institutions of industry or those of government, at least not initially, but to organize them so that they would better serve the vested interest of industrialists, government authorities, and individual consumers. In this sense he was not explicitly an advocate of small scale or a party to the camp who thought that small was necessarily beautiful. And while he was disdainful of architects and managers who ran these institutions, he did not, like Ivan Illich (1973), have any intentions of turning these institutions "upside down and inside out," nor has he gone as far as suggesting that "such an inversion of society is beyond the managers of present institutions" (Illich 1973, 16). Habraken was, after all, developing his ideas in those early days in close collaboration with some of the big captains of industry, at least in Holland, like Philips, Bruynzeel, and Nuijhuis, and got much of his funding from those and others whose prime interest was to maintain the status quo but who were enlightened enough to encourage cautious experimentation.

For these reasons, Habraken has been called (Rabeneck, Sheppard, and Town 1973, 700,701) one of those libertarians whose proposals to tackle the inadequacies of mass housing usually focus in the first place on reorganizing the product and the technology of the product. Their "objectives seldom find more positive expression than antithesis of the present products of Mass Housing, in other words, more space, better amenities, and freedom of choice. This form of libertarian proposal tends to be too technical and overcomplicated to have any political potential." On the other hand, Habraken was also considered by his students as at once a reactionary and a visionary. These students took issue with his ideas that seemed to them to play into the hands of big industry and big industrial systems, which people like Galbraith (1985, 345) were arguing "generally ignore and hold unimportant those services of the state which are not closely related to the system's needs." Those were the very industrial systems and industrial tools that many considered the root cause of public alienation and public servitude. His critics viewed the supports idea at best with skepticism and at worst as a palliative seeking little or no change where it was most required—among those "radical authoritarians" who had joined public agencies as servants of change rather than instigators of it.

The second area of criticism centered around the continuing dominance of professionals, with public authorities, as central to housing design and production. That the environment for habitation (supports) should remain the prerogative of the professional elite and central authorities was out of step with the times. That individual users, the lowest level in the hierarchy of powers, should be responsible only for the internal layout of dwellings and not participate in major decisions affecting the communal environment or the institutions that govern and produce it frustrated matters even more. Illich (1973, 12) captures the spirit of these critics: "At present, people tend to relinquish the task of envisaging the future to a professional elite. They transfer power to politicians who promise to build up the machinery to deliver this future. They accept a growing range of power levels in society (about which Habraken is very explicit) when inequality is needed to maintain high outputs. Political institutions themselves become draft mechanisms to press people into complicity with output goals. What is right comes to be subordinated to what is good for

institutions. Justice is debased to mean the equal distribution of institutional wares." Later, in his chapter on convivial reconstruction (1973, 41), he concludes, "Professional goal setting produces goods for an environment produced by other professionals. Life that depends on high speed and apartment houses makes hospitals inevitable. By definition all these are scarce, and get even scarcer as they approach the standards set more recently by an ever evolving profession; thereby each unit or quantum appearing on the market frustrates more people than it satisfies."

Turner's own critique of Habraken centered more around what was done rather than what Habraken said or wrote. While Habraken said that his ideas and methods were intended to develop more equitable relationships between individuals and authority, to restore the "natural relationship" between people and the built environment (supports and infill), what was done seemed to many to pull the other way. "The purely formal and technological separation of support and infill," said Turner (1984, 61), "strengthens the separation of local and central powers. The added use of industrially-supplied components, coordinated to match the centrally determined modular design of the support structures, increases the division of labor and the separation of production and use. . . . If central planners and authorities decide on the installation of the support systems or infrastructures, then they either tie uses down to specific sites, or society must carry the costs of underused infrastructures in order to provide an adequate range of choice."

FLEXIBILITY, PARTICIPATION, AND ENABLEMENT

How, then, did these two architects influence design thinking, design policy, and design practice? In summary, three themes dominated their work, offered an understanding of the support paradigm, and were to become important new theories of design practice: flexibility, participation, and enablement. Given Turner's and Habraken's relative positions, their definitions of these themes are at once different yet synergistic.

For Habraken, flexibility is a quality by which to measure the capacity of physical settings to be easily modified, which could undergo a series of incremental transformations in order to ensure good fit through time. For him it is directed equally at housing management in deciding dwelling sizes, dwelling types, and dwelling mix as to families. It is a basis on which to rationalize the production of houses, to reconcile both standardization and variety, on which a healthy industry depends.

For Turner, flexibility has to do with ranges of possible courses of action available to people when organizing financing, planning, building, and maintaining buildings and for sorting out tenure and materials. Flexibility is a quality by which to "measure the opportunities available to people to locally self-manage programs." To Turner, the physical setting is secondary to the organizational one. Both positions contrast starkly in their preoccupations. Both are inseparable and synergistic.

For both Turner and Habraken, user participation is an essential part of repairing the natural relationship between people and place, however that is defined. Habraken believes that user participation helps designers better serve their public; it enables the design and the production of buildings to be made more efficient and more dynamic so that architecture can be made relevant. Turner's definition is far broader (1989, 180). His search for better participation is directed at "the ways and means by which governments, NGO's and the building industry can enable people to do well what so many do in any case: the planning, building and management of their own houses and neighborhoods at costs both they and society can afford." He put the onus firmly and squarely on government and professionals to participate in the action of people, not the other way around. His interest is to make housing and the supply of housing more efficient and more dynamic. Both positions contrast starkly in their preoccupations. Both are inseparable and synergistic.

The third theme both architects share is enablement. For Habraken, the concept is very much akin to cultivation. In his analogy to horticulture, he suggests that horticulturalists do not make flowers or trees. Instead they cultivate an environment for plants to grow, preparing the soil with nutrients, water, and correct drainage and positioning the site to attract the right amount of sunlight, shade, and so on. As the plants begin to grow, further interventions may be required to support their growth during the early stages and later with pruning and fertilization so that they can continue to bear fruit. And so it is, he suggests, with housing. In contrast to building houses, enablement is a process by which to cultivate physically and gradually the conditions that enable habitation, that enable neighborhoods to grow and change in response to prevailing conditions. Architects must be part of these processes, which go on despite the infertile settings. "They have to be able to design for change and incremental growth. They must see the user as an indispensable agent in the process. They must understand their work as part of a living process, in short they must be cultivators of environments, rather than makers of projects" (1983, 9).

Habraken's preoccupation is with the structure rather than the content of housing, less interested in deciding its form but more interested in the way changing conditions and functions shape the form. He therefore sees design as a process of enablement in housing, which could change radically not only the process by which housing is produced but also the form of housing itself. Turner, on the other hand, defines enablement relative to government policy and relative to the role and services of professionals. Enablement policies and enabler professionals are those that support locally self-managed programs. They deliver the money and resources to enable local organizations to build and manage their own housing. Both positions contrast sharply in their preoccupations. Both are inseparable and synergistic.

Finally, Habraken developed methods with which to design with generalizations about form and space, without optimums, without modeling the average family, without losing the specificity of architecture. He taught us how to describe and understand the thematic and nonthematic compositions of the built environment as systems of organization that were at one cohesive but unplanned, standard but infinitely variable. His freedom to improvise avoided both the ad hocism of modernist interventions and the reductionist and Cartesian thinking of master planning. He taught us how to be rationalists without being determinists, how to provide structure without being structuralists, and how to avoid doing the kind of research that would deliver the ubiquitous recipe for doing right what researchers thought to be wrong.

Turner delivered a philosophy on user participation that was attractive to international funding agencies because through it they saw economies to their own organization and political favors for their government counterparts and because they could do both with some social grace. He delivered a legitimization of sites and services as a palliative to direct construction through his academic writings and growing international reputation. This was an important first step to his support policies, which he argued at the U.N. Conference in Pittsburgh in October 1966, a watershed in international housing policy. Most important "he was, perhaps to his surprise, expressing universal truths about housing" (Ward 1976, 5) that helped reshape attitudes and policies and rendered most housing that previously most authorities had considered marginal and illegitimate both legitimate and productive.

REFERENCES

Berger, Peter L., and Neuhaus, Richard John. 1977. *To Empower People—The Role of Mediating Structures in Public Policy*. Washington, D.C.: American Enterprise Institute for Public Policy Research.

Burgess, Rod. 1982. Self-help housing advocacy: A curious form of radicalism: A critique of the work of John F. C. Turner. In *Self-Help Housing, a Critique,* pp. 56–97. Edited by C. Ward. London: Mansell Publishing.

Engels, Frederick. 1975. *The Housing Question*. Moscow: Progress Publishers.

Fishman, Robert. 1982. *Urban Utopias in the Twentieth Century: Ebenezer Howard, Frank Lloyd Wright, Le Corbusier.* Cambridge, Mass.: MIT Press.

Frank, Douglas. 1972. Habraken at the RIBA: Supports and social criteria. *Architects Journal*, April 26, pp. 69–72.

Galbraith, John K. 1978; 1985. *The New Industrial State*. Boston; Houghton Mifflin.

Habraken, N. John. 1972. *Supports: An Alternative to Mass Housing*. London: Architecture Press.

Habraken, N. John. 1983. The general from the specific. Address to the Eighth International Forum of the European Association for Architectural Education, Newcastle-upon-Tyne, England, April 13.

Illich, Ivan. 1973. *Tools for Conviviality*. London: Calder and Boyars.

Pezzoli, Keith. 1986. The Development of Mainstream Housing Policies in the Third World. (1940s–1980). Unpublished paper, University of California, Los Angeles.

Rabeneck, Andrew; Sheppard, David; and Town, Peter. 1973. Housing flexibility. *Architectural Design* 43(11). Special issue.

Ravetz, Alison. 1986. *The Government of Space- Town Planning in Modern Society*. London: Faber and Faber.

Redfern, Gordon. 1972. One grows wary of ultimate solutions. *Architects' Journal*, July 12.

Schumacher, E. F. 1973. *Small Is Beautiful: A Study of Economics as If People Mattered*. London: Abacus.

Trenton, H. P. 1972. Complete freedom neither realistic nor wanted. *Architects' Journal*, July 12.

Turner, John F. C. 1972. Reeducation of a professional. In *Freedom to Build*. Edited by John F. C. Turner and Robert Fichter. New York: Macmillan.

Turner, John F. C. 1976. *Housing by People: Towards Autonomy in Building Environments*. London: Marion Boyers; New York: Pantheon Books (1977).

Turner, John F. C. 1984. Commentary on SAR. In *The Scope of Social Architecture*, pp. 61–62. Edited by C. R. Hatch. New York: Van Nostrand Reinhold.

Turner, John F. C. 1989. Barriers, channels and community control. In *The Living City*, pp. 179–89. Edited by David Cadman and Geoffrey Payne. London: Routledge.

Ward, Colin. 1981. Self-help and mutual aid in housing. In *Participation in Housing*, pp. 1–15. Edited by Nabeel Hamdi and Bob Greenstreet. Oxford: Oxford Polytechnic Department of Town Planning.

Ward, Colin. 1983. *Housing, An Anarchist Approach*. London: Freedom Press.

PART II

The Practice of Theory: Enablement and the Indeterminacy of Design

CHAPTER 4

Flexibility and Building

We have indeed been betrayed by the mysterious word Architecture away from reality into a pretence about styles and orders and proportions and periods and conception and composition. If we had no other words than *building* we might have been living in sound, water-tight dwellings. . . . Architecture is human skill and feeling shown in the great necessary activity of building; it must be a living, progressive, structural art, always readjusting itself to changing conditions of time and place.

William Richard Lethaby (in Ward 1983)

Flexibility expresses freedom to choose among options or devise programs that fit individual needs and aspirations, whether for building, finance, ownership, or management. Beyond that, and usually for architects, it describes the capacity designed into buildings, building programs, or building technologies to ensure an initial good fit and to enable them to respond to subsequent change. Such designed capacity has come to influence the size and spatial configuration of built environments, services, and/or the technology of building components themselves.

Flexibility became a widespread design buzzword in the 1960s in response to new demands placed on buildings, particularly in housing. Rapid changes were occurring in family size, composition, and structure and in expectations of comfort and efficiency. Between revolving waiting lists, new programs, and obsolete housing stock, getting the right fit between people and place and among standards, subsidies, and costs became a complex juggling act.

Architects and planners responded to a client body whose demands had previously featured only marginally in surveys and postoccupancy evaluations and were now demanding more participation in housing and urban improvement programs. Socially, politically, technically, and even with respect to the management of local authority waiting lists, housing was undergoing a profound transformation.

The 1960s were not unique because of the change occurring in the built environment. But capacity for change for the first time became accepted as a legitimate goal of architecture and planning. This was largely due to the accelerating rate at which change had begun to occur and, correspondingly, the far shorter period of time it took for buildings to become socially or technically obsolete. Perceptions of change and growth were reinforced by observations in the developing countries of a highly productive informal sector in which building was done on a vast scale but through a series of increments and over substantial periods of time.

51

Informal, locally negotiated additions, extensions, and improvisations to public housing blocks.

Bhogal: Interior court.
(Photo by Soloman J. Benjamin)

Helwan, Egypt.
(Photo by Wilkinson and Tipple)

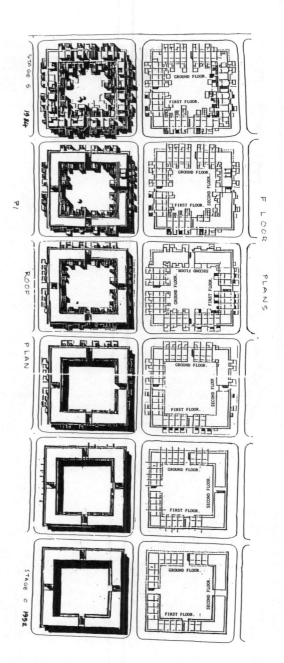

Bhogal, India, transformations: 1952–1984.
(Drawing by Soloman J. Benjamin)

Social effects of obsolescence included long waiting lists, abandoned buildings, high vacancy rates, and blighted neighborhoods. In a climate of increasing social consciousness, architecture was considered peripheral to fundamental social and economic issues. Architects, especially architectural students, were disillusioned with Le Corbusier, Mies, and Wright. The Congrès Internationaux d'Architecture Moderne had lost favor with young architects, as had massive projects, megastructures, and big organizations.

An architectural response was also prompted by rapidly depreciating public investments. Obsolescence affected not only buildings. It also affected *sites* with inadequate amenities or parking; *location,* where population trends made existing schools, churches, or commerce outmoded; *mechanical systems,* with changing standards of heating and sanitation; and *function* where day care facilities were obviated when the population structure changed (Heath 1984).

In Britain, the issue of change in housing was formally recognized by Parker Morris in the Parker-Morris Committee's recommendations to the minister in 1961 (paragraph 28):

It is thus not to be wondered at that the adaptable house—the house which could easily be altered as circumstances changed—is a recurring theme in the evidence we received and in our own thoughts. At the present stage of development, such a dwelling is some way from practical reality, because of the high cost and other difficulties. With the greatly increased rate of social and economic change, the adaptable house is becoming a national necessity. Not only would it be valuable for the family staying in one house for most of its life: it would allow much easier and perhaps more satisfactory adaptation to the changing general needs. We see the investigation of the practical possibilities of doing it easily and at reasonable cost as one of the most important lines of future research into the development of design and structure. The sooner it is started the better.

By the mid–1970s, one London paper reported 6000 flats in London earmarked for renovation at a cost to the public of £34 million.

What strategies have emerged for flexibility in housing practice? How much designed capacity is appropriate before it sacrifices basic freedoms? What form should it take to be achieved and yet remain affordable? Is flexibility the planner's way of controlling freedoms—of professionalizing choice—or can it signal alternatives that otherwise would remain hidden?

GETTING THE RIGHT FIT

Response to change and to obsolescence was the main priority of flexibility advocates; the longstanding desire to enable a fit initially more suitable for management and for families ran a close second. Achieving that fit required flexibility in managing the relationship of standards, costs, and user demand when making programs; and for many it meant flexibility in the spatial and physical organization and construction of buildings, a notion compatible with experiments in prefabrication and the industrialization of building.

Frank Lloyd Wright, in pursuit of his ideal for individualism and with his belief in industrial production, envisioned mass-produced components that were " 'sufficiently flexible to enable everyone to put them together in his own way. 'The house,' he was suggesting, 'should grow as the trees around the man himself grow.' Its shape would be determined by the individual's resources, the needs of his family and his understanding of his own land" (Fishman 1982, 130).

As early as 1938, the Philadelphia architect O. Stonorov wrote to the Public Works Administration's Housing Division, responding to the unit plans produced by the division in 1935, which set precise standards for the size of units and rooms and also provided architects who knew little about housing with ready-made designs. What began as recommendations and minimum standards wound up as determinant factors for the entire United States and continues to influence design and planning to this day (Sprague and Testa 1983). In 1938 Stonorov (Pommer 1978, 242) wrote: "The very purpose of housing is at stake. . . . I mean that a certain trivial standardization has taken hold of the interior arrangement and the exterior appearance which will definitely class those buildings once they are erected as 'those buildings which the government built to house the poor people.'"

In both the first and third worlds, the essence of the debate about fit has centered around standards and standardization. In one camp in both worlds were those (providers) who argued that, given the complexity and density of urban life, carefully packaged and centrally controlled standards were essential to maintain efficiencies of production and maintenance, reduce costs, and ensure equal or similar privileges between the well-off and the not-so-well-off. The other camp (supporters) argued that the inflexible way in which standards are prescribed achieves precisely the opposite results. The following statements exemplify the two positions. The first is from the preface of the Greater London Council's (GLC) "preferred dwelling plans," the basis to all GLC housing design:

They [should] avoid the need for detailed planning considerations, save duplication of design work and waste of manpower, serve to speed up and simplify the preparation of scheme estimates, and it means the layout of services and other components can be standardized for each, cutting needless repetition. . . . It should be noted then the plans represent a difficult compromise involving a large number of requirements of a technical, economic, mandatory and policy nature, many of which are in conflict. If a plan is modified, it will seldom satisfy all of these requirements, with the same balance of priorities. . . . A type plan is a standard solution for a dwelling having a particular set of characteristics which distinguish it as a basic type. All type plans are designed to meet the requirements of the housing committee, the D.O.E. [Department of the Environment], statutory controls, and as far as possible, existing codes of practice.

This precarious balancing act contrasts markedly with those objectives advocated in the Peterbor-

ough Master Plan, which proposed that "each prospective tenant and owner occupier will not only need a dwelling with the number of rooms appropriate to the size and composition of his household, he will want one that comes as close as he thinks he can afford to what rent suits him and his family in terms of type, quality, tenure, garden size, outlook and environment—social as well as physical."[1] As John Worthington (1971, 518) concludes, "It is the opportunity for the prospective householder to decide how best to spend his income which is advocated. Housing becomes a subtle balancing of a great variety of requirements, the balance sheet varying for each household according to its values."

The tight fit of space, quality (standards), and cost as exemplified in many public housing projects throughout the world wound up raising costs to levels usually unaffordable to low-income people without heavy subsidies. This tight fit also imposed an unmistakable, institutional, and resented stigma. The question for many was to what extent change could be predicted and correspondingly, what, if any thing, could be provided or designed into the planning of sites or buildings. Heath (1984, 158) suggests that predicting change itself was unlikely to be fruitful; rather the likelihood, rate, and degree of such changes might give clues to what provisions should be made:

It makes possible, *a "sensitivity analysis:" which will indicate the need for investment to mitigate the effects of change.* Thus, if a proposed building houses activities which are especially sensitive to environmental factors which make intensive use of the surrounding site area; which are highly dependent on characteristics of the population served which are known to fluctuate, such as average age, or on good access; which require intensive and modern services; and which are the subject of much social concern and conflict and are highly valued; then we are entitled to conclude that the building is extremely sensitive to change. Hospitals and airports meet most of these

---

1. Quoted in J. Worthington, Housing—The economics of choice, *Official Architecture and Planning* (July 1971).

conditions; so do some types of university building and some factories. Other buildings can be arranged on a descending scale of sensitivity; though it is important to look at each case on its merits, and not to assume that a given "building type" will always have the same character.

In Britain in 1961, Parker Morris published his committee's recommendations for a range of space minimums in housing based on careful evaluation of activity patterns around the home. This was a progressive document when compared to its forerunners, the Tudor Walters Report of 1918 and the Dudley recommendations of 1944, both of which set standards for minimum room sizes. In 1967, however, the Ministry of Housing and Local Government turned these into mandatory standards. By linking them to subsidy and costing procedures, the minister was attempting "to bring all authorities up to this standard, and the Parker Morris house is a very good house indeed—we just can not afford to let other authorities build to even higher standards." Variations were permitted but only within strict limits. A maximum minus variation of 1.5 percent was permitted, to allow for planning on a modular grid, with the maximum deviation determined by a 10 percent limit on expenditure, inclusive of all other facilities beyond which schemes would not receive loan approval.

No sooner had these procedures begun to bear fruit than they began to sour. While maintaining the new space standards to attract subsidy, local authorities reduced others. By 1969, the housing minister advised against economies that entailed reducing standards of finish and quality of materials when likely consequences included increasing maintenance costs. Two years later, the Royal Institute of British Architects dispatched a memorandum to Julian Amory, then minister of housing, pointing out that standards of both finishes and the external fabric of buildings were being reduced to meet yardstick requirements. For similar reasons, housing programs were being distorted by manipulating

densities to boost subsidy allocation. The RIBA identified two new design strategies, density boosting (selecting house types that offered the maximum density of persons per acre) and mix beating (selecting the cheapest combination of house sizes for any one project that afforded the best subsidy). They also expressed concern that standards for play spaces, privacy, and noise abatement, among others, were falling. Some two-thirds of the projects analyzed at the time were affected in these ways. Ten years later, the government's June 1977 green paper recommended relaxing central government control over local authorities and abandoning the cost yardstick and the Parker Morris standards.

One explanation for this vicious circle of events came from John Worthington (1971, 519): "We may have created too many standards and criteria for what we can or are prepared to afford. Possibly we should be prepared to vary our standards according to particular conditions, and search for forms that will easily allow us to upgrade and adapt as finances become available in the future." This opened public housing to advocates of flexibility.

Flexibility to achieve good fit that can change over time was argued not only on grounds of cost and standards but also on grounds of good design with a strong social and user bias—"to provide a private domain that will fulfill each occupant's expectations" (Rabeneck, Sheppard, and Town, 1973, 701). Fictitious, statistically modeled average families had provided normative spatial requirements for all tenants. Flexible buildings could offer choices to occupants, "where everyone should be able to fit out his house as he wishes, including the right to make mistakes as part of that freedom" (Arséne-Henri in Rabeneck, Sheppard, and Town 1973, 703), an invitation by professionals to people to *participate* in planning their own houses. This theme became increasingly popular during the 1960s and 1970s, argued on grounds of political expediency, social necessity, and even building and design efficiency.

Planners, architects, and sociologists who advocated flexibility with user participation were critical of behavioral determinists who figured out activities, functions, and equipment and then designed around their needs. They were critical of behavioralist-formalist architects, planners, and public authorities unprepared to relinquish housing from the ties of professional determinism or from public authority control.

If housing lacked individuality, if it lacked the personality acquired in the private owner–occupied house over years of incremental additions and adaptation, then architects could provide this as well. Architects spent endless hours and a great deal of money zig-zagging terrace row housing or pitching roofs in every direction to give an impression of individuality. Thus emerged the deliberate randomness exemplified in the tower blocks of London County Council's Canada Estate, at Lillington Street, at Thames Mead, at Safdie's Habitat, at Erskine's Byker, and at Kroll's student facility in Louvain, whose inhabitation concerns became submerged in an obfuscating deluge of architectural debate over style.

Criticism of behavioralists also brought to question user surveys, which frequently were structured to justify design intentions rather than to generate them. Behaviorally determined plans, irrespective of user needs surveys, exhibited all the traits of tight fit. They were neither easily adapted nor universal. One cannot assume, as the standard dwelling types did, that the spatial requirements of a family of four with three young children are the same for a family of four with two working adults or that an elderly mother and her daughter should be allocated the same arrangement as a young couple. Inherent in the establishment of universal standards—what Maureen Taylor (1973) called "normative needs"— is getting a wrong fit between standardized dwellings and nonnormative households.

Dimensions and proportions designed for one function only or for function-specific furniture and fittings and built-ins are difficult to adapt to other uses. Lighting and electrical outlets similarly rein-force predetermined usages, and window positioning and sizing in bedrooms, such as small windows and high sills, may preclude their functioning as living rooms. Hallways and corridors designed to minimal circulation specifications cannot satisfy the other uses of entryways (reception, storing bicycles, strollers, etc.). The functional distribution of rooms is invariably determined by linking desirability related functions and by placing bedrooms adjacent across party walls and floors to reduce the likelihood of noise traveling between dwellings.[2]

Critique of such layouts was not limited to the research of architects and behavioralists. Standard plans were becoming increasingly difficult to let and an embarrassment to managers and politicians. In Britain, the lack of flexibility in the existing housing stock contributed to high vacancy rates. The structure of waiting lists was also changing more rapidly. Housing commitees were concerned that many projects in progress reflected poorly the actual needs of those on housing authority lists. The initial programs had not been badly worked out, but during the three to five years it took from program siting to completion, few projects remained even reasonably matched to the demands of waiting lists. Project adjustments would require significant redesign, delays, and additional costs. The result was a housing stock out of synch with demand even before occupancy. Explanations for difficult-to-let public housing came in 1973 from the minister of housing and again in 1978 from the Housing Centre Trust. Both pointed out that "difficult to let housing is not necessarily a question of household surplus, but a reflection of the fact that hard-up applicants, who know they have a high priority for housing, are now a good deal more choosy."

Lessons were also filtering through from both

---

2. See, for example, Andrew Rabeneck, David Sheppard, and Peter Town, The structure of space in family housing—An alternative to present design practice, *Progressive Architecture* (November 1974): 100–107.

Change by increments ensures good fit and durability.

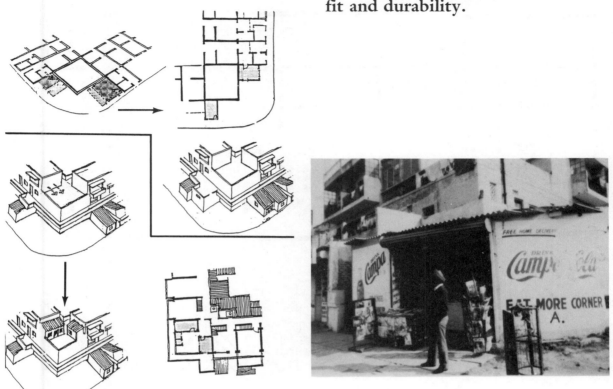

Bhogal, India. *(Drawings and photos by Soloman J. Benjamin)*

59

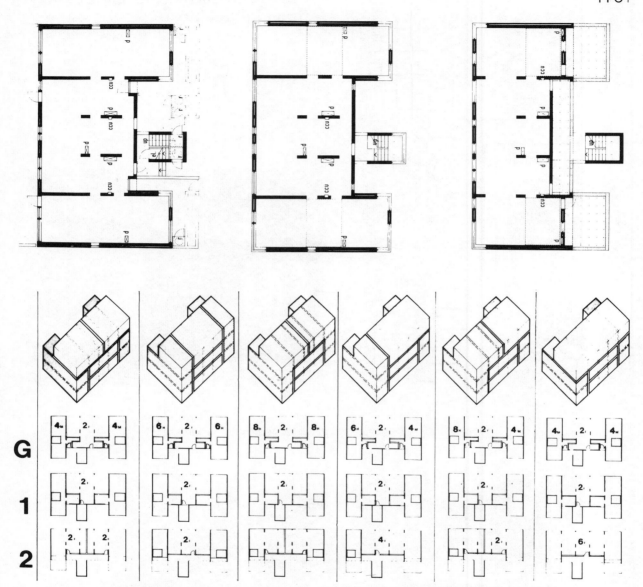

The GLC's PSSHAK project at Adelaide Road, London. The structure included optimum positions for windows, front entrances, ducts, radiators, and electricity meters. To cope with a variety of dwelling types and sizes, none of these needs to be decided until after the structure is built. Adaptions could easily be made to suit changes in structure of waiting lists and to changing family needs. Different sizes of flats could be made by combining bays horizontally. Different-size houses can be made by combining bays vertically.

60

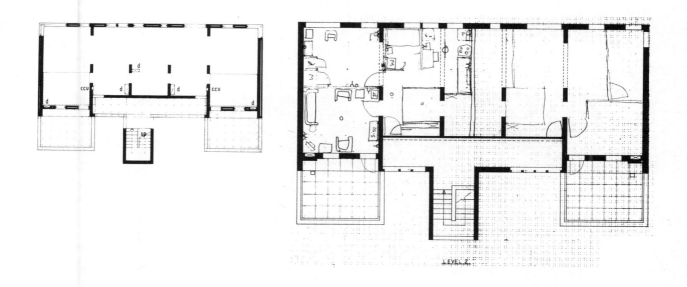

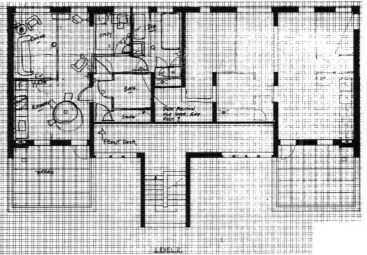

Families were invited to plan their own dwellings.

The size and positions of structural elements, windows, and utilities enable a number of plan variations.

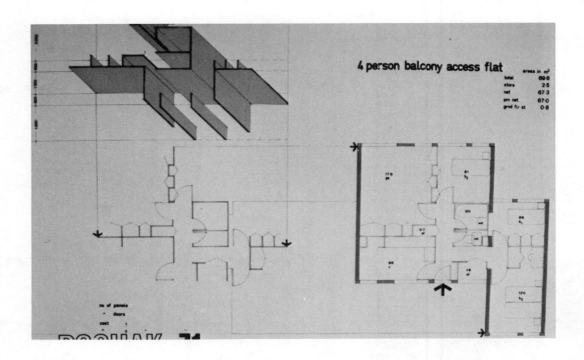

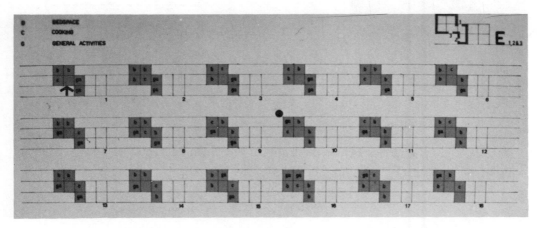

Early schematics of the GLC's PSSHAK project at Stamford Hill.

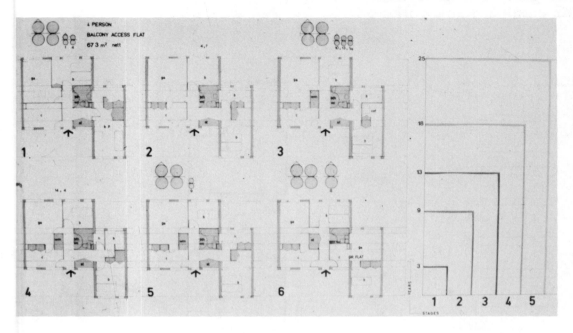

Plan variations.

same way that it is possible to design a system for building without knowing the specific context for it. More important, most flexible projects or systems for projects have built-in capacities for change and pay a price for it and for their indeterminacy in either energy or aesthetic compromise. They do this in order to increase the range of initial options and to meet future demands for adaptation—in both cases, to cope with uncertainty by increasing capacity in one or more ways.[5]

By careful and systematic arrangement, dimensional systems enable a significant variety of special combinations. The capacity in this case is not in extra space but in space that can be used in different ways, whose functional and symbolic value is left uncertain at the programmatic stage of design. At the scale of the shell itself, this enables parcels of space or bays to be combined laterally or vertically to form smaller or larger apartments or houses. And similarly, for each dwelling, a smaller system of di-

5. For an assessment of the PSSHAK project, which I have chosen to illustrate the issues, see PSSHAK 18 months on, *Architects' Journal* (February 27, 1980) 425–439. PSSHAK was based on the thinking of Habraken and was developed in England by Nabeel Hamdi and Nicholas Wilkinson. Two support structures were built in London by the GLC, the first at Stamford Hill in 1972, the second at Adelaide Road completed in 1978. The support at Adelaide Road is constructed of load-bearing brick cross-

walls supporting reinforced concrete floor slabs. Each of eight structures is designed to accommodate from 4 to 8 dwellings ranging from two-person apartments to eight-person houses. The assembly kit of internal doors, partitions, closets, bathrooms, kitchens, and service ducts was supplied by the Bruynzeel Company of Holland. The projects were built by the Greater London Council's direct labor department. Most of the original families helped design their own house layouts.

Change as an objective of the design program: Dimensional frameworks.

1	ENTRY
2	VESTIBULE
3	DININGROOM
4	HALL
5	PUBLIC TOILET
6	KITCHEN
7	BREAKFAST RM
8	ELEVATOR
9	COURTYARD
10	SHOWER ROOM
11	DWELLING ONE
12	PARLOR/DINING
13	DWELLING TWO
14	VESTIBULE
15	ENTRY

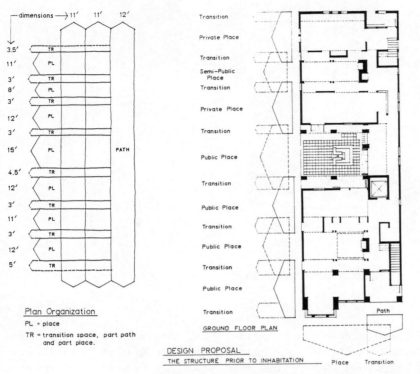

—dimensions→ 11' 11' 12'

3.5'	TR
11'	PL
3'	TR
8'	PL
3'	TR
12'	PL
3'	TR
15'	PL
4.5'	TR
12'	PL
3'	TR
11'	PL
3'	TR
12'	PL
5'	TR

PATH

Transition
Private Place
Transition
Semi-Public Place
Transition
Private Place
Transition
Public Place
Transition
Public Place
Transition
Public Place
Transition
Public Place
Transition

GROUND FLOOR PLAN

Path

Place   Transition

Plan Organization

PL = place

TR = transition space, part path and part place.

DESIGN PROPOSAL
THE STRUCTURE PRIOR TO INHABITATION

Design for the elderly. *(Drawings by Brad Edgerly)*

64

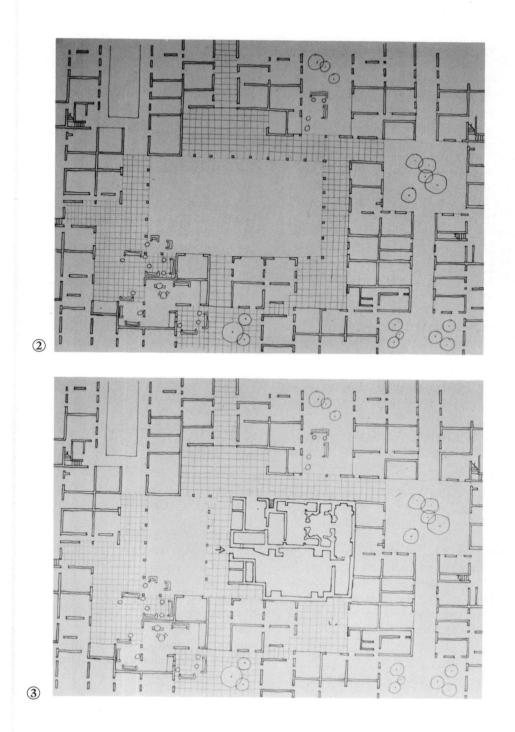

②

③

mensions enables a variety of alternative room sizes and arrangements.

What emerged was a dimensional framework—a system of dimensional rules for deciding the fit, location, arrangement, and rearrangement of structural elements, party walls, services, windows, and doors, many of which can be arranged and rearranged independently of the shell. Designing the rule system took on a far greater significance than designing the dwelling plan itself. The best example is the SAR methodology devised in Holland. Like a chess game, the rules were written to facilitate all kinds of moves as well as strategies to be discovered, and a new board was not needed for each new strategy. A standard framework could therefore be used for a variety of plans; standardization and variety no longer seemed incompatible.

Dimensional frameworks, however, were less favored by long-life, loose-fit advocates. Their bias toward incorporating extra space was closely allied to the definition of flexibility provided by Cowan, Simon Nicholson, and Alex Gordon:[6]

If the majority of activities can be carried on in rooms of a certain rather limited range of sizes, why not simply provide rather more such rooms than appear to be needed immediately, and rely on adaptation? There is over provision, but quite possibly no more than is required to make a modular system work and the costs of providing and designing for demountability are avoided. (Heath 1984, 160)

And if your space needs and aspirational wants were still unmet, then you moved.

Andrew Rabeneck, Cowan, Gordon, and others advocated *extra space* as "an approach which avoids the architect inventors' devices of moveable walls, convertible furniture, and multifunctional spaces (which the frameworks approach implied) in favour of simple planning, more space and ambiguities of

use, which were once familiar in the domestic architecture of most cultures" (Rabeneck, Sheppard, and Town 1974, 100). The Victorian terraces in London, the traditional Japanese house, the courtyard houses of the Middle East, and the infinitely flexible stick and timber framed houses of the United States immediately come to mind:

The New England dwelling evolved out of unpartitioned wooden cottages with undifferentiated use. These easily transformed post-and-beam colonial prototypes perched tentatively on fieldstone foundations, held in place by gravity. As late as the beginning of the twentieth century, one of the part-time jobs in any small village was that of housemover. As Myron Meserve, an octogenarian New Hampshireman recalled: ". . . they used to move them around constantly, like so many checkers on a board." Given the relative lightness and tensile strength of their construction system and its minimal connection to foundation, it represented a practical and efficient system for adaptive reuse, at a time when spatial types were less use-specific. (Teicher 1989, 27)

Arguments in favor of dimensional reserve, particularly of the kind advocated by the loose-fit camp, were further substantiated on grounds of cost. Research on the cost implications of increasing standards in finishes, equipment, and space showed that prices rose considerably less for size, indicating that more space could be provided relatively cheaply: "The greater the floor area, the lower the price per square foot, so the cost per square foot of a dwelling of 500 square feet is only just over 80% of the cost of a dwelling unit of 300 square feet" (Stone in Worthington 1971, 518).

The second kind of capacity I will call a *design reserve*. In this case a number of provisions are physically designed into projects so that last-minute decisions about dwelling size, dwelling mix, and dwelling plans can be made and further adaptation facilitated. Such provisions have as much to do with the organization of building parts and services as with careful detailing and frequently have significant implications for cost and contract management. A case in point in detailing and positioning ductwork

---

6. See, for example, Alex Gordon, Architects and resource conservation: The long life, loose fit, low energy study, *RIBA Journal* (January 1974): 9–12.

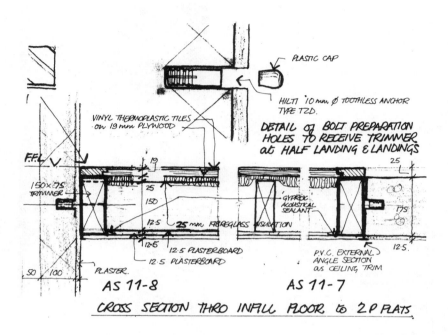

PLASTIC CAP

HILTI `10 mm Ø TOOTHLESS ANCHOR TYPE T2D.

DETAIL of BOLT PREPARATION HOLES TO RECEIVE TRIMMER a6 HALF LANDING & LANDINGS

VINYL THERMOPLASTIC TILES on 19 mm PLYWOOD

F.F.L

150 x 75 TRIMMER

GYPROC ACOUSTICAL SEALANT

25 mm FIBREGLASS INSULATION

12.5 PLASTERBOARD
12.5 PLASTERBOARD

P.V.C. EXTERNAL ANGLE SECTION a/s CEILING TRIM

PLASTER.

AS 11-8   AS 11-7

CROSS SECTION THRO INFILL FLOOR to 2P FLATS

Detail of floor section for Adelaide Road structure showing provisions for removeable floor section.

to enable easy and multiple connections to plumbing. Other examples are the careful positioning of structural walls, entries, windows, heating radiators, and electrical outlets or carefully choosing profiles to the dwelling envelope and the building components themselves. All of these considerations jointly establish opportunities to maximize the range of possible plan arrangements and in some cases to give reference to these through careful sizing and positioning of structural and nonstructural building elements.

As Richard Rogers (Rowe 1987, 33) points out, such design was to be an architecture of possibilities in which "flexibility should be communicated by the legibility of the building." He concludes, however, that "an enormous amount of effort had to be invested in order to release this architecture of possibilities." The usual search for finite and specific solutions was avoided; for whom one was designing or how requirements might change remained unknown.

The question was less whether these approaches were more expensive than conventional design—a difficult comparison, given the differences in objectives—but whether in fact, given their argued advantages, they offered good value for capital outlay. While some of these design provisions required additional materials, others implied differences in de-

Party wall system, Adelaide Road, London.

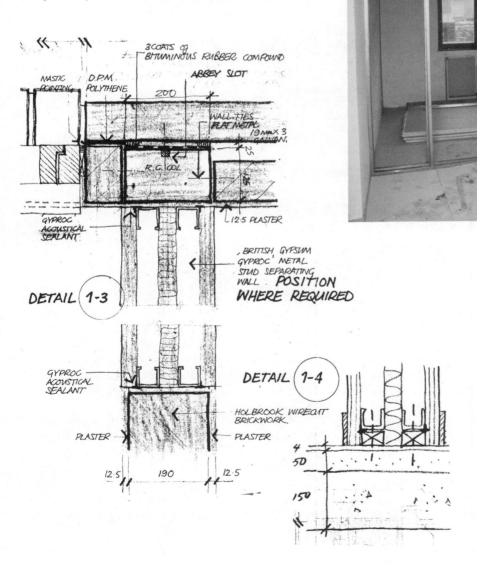

3 COATS of BITUMINOUS RUBBER COMPOUND

ABBEY SLOT

MASTIC POINTING

D.P.M. POLYTHENE

200

WALL TIES FLAT METAL 19mm X 3 GALVAN.

R.C. COL

25

12.5

12.5 PLASTER

GYPROC ACOUSTICAL SEALANT

BRITISH GYPSUM 'GYPROC' METAL STUD SEPARATING WALL · POSITION WHERE REQUIRED

DETAIL 1-3

GYPROC ACOUSTICAL SEALANT

DETAIL 1-4

HOLBROOK WIRECUT BRICKWORK

PLASTER

PLASTER

12.5   190   12.5

4
50
150

sign procedure and, later, in the sequence of site operations. For example, the project at Adelaide Road (see illustrations) had allowed openings in the concrete floor slabs that could either receive a stair in the case of a two-story dwelling or joists and optional finishes if it was to be a party floor between two flats. The stairwell was oversized to allow for various stair positions and therefore various plan arrangements. After stair installation, the remaining part of the stairwell was filled in with timber joists. The sequence of site operations necessitated that carpenters, plasterers, flooring contractors, and decorators all return to an otherwise finished dwelling to work on an area about 18 sq ft.

In a similar way, party walls were completed by filling in between load-bearing walls with non-load-bearing metal stud and sheet rock partitions. The junction between these partitions and the load-bearing brickwork presented innumerable problems, particularly to achieve adequate fire protection, sound insulation, and cohesion between wet plaster applied to the brickwork and the drywall sheetrock of the infill party wall. Problems intensified as buildings settled and materials dried.

In the same project, mechanical services prefabricated to include all pipework also proved complex in terms of site operations. The supplier had tested each preassembled section (running from floor to ceiling) and was able to guarantee good workmanship. The subcontractor fixing the units similarly had to guarantee joints between stacked units for the full height of each block. The heating contractor, who made connections to hot and cold water tanks in the roof space, had similar responsibilities for that part of the work, and the gas company, insisting on control of final installation, was in and out to fix the supply at the base of the duct and final distribution to meters and stoves. Original intentions to employ an assembled kit to simplify site operations and thereby minimize conventional delays resulting from the usual trade waiting on trades was not borne out.

Loading prefabricated ducts, Adelaide Road, London.

The third category of capacity resides in excess material and additional components. How much extra do we provide to widen the range of initial choices and to facilitate changes of function or interpretation in the future? How much additional wiring and plumbing and how many water tanks, electric meters, and the like do we need in order to cater to last-minute decisions and future changes? How much thicker should floor slabs be to take unanticipated load? How many additional joists, heating radiators, or windows should be included? How much flexibility is appropriate, and how is this decided? Have we done our research and projections well enough to be confident in delimiting choices within boundaries set by our expectations?

Those who could afford to—and few of us could—initially advocated maximum flexibility, with interstitial floors grided out with wiring and junction boxes to service any conceivable configuration of dwelling plan. Facades became continuous planes of glazing, and sill heights were established in an atmosphere of "anything goes." Designers were unprepared or unwilling to commit their architecture to thematic constraints of site or to well-understood conventions of culture. Architecture was reduced to diagram, to an abstraction of technical building systems, to a universal shell. The more shell, the less structure; the more systems, the fewer constraints; the more ambiguity, the more freedom to plan as you will, do as you want.

And with more technology, the fourth category of capacity, so there would be even more flexibility. We got bathroom-kitchen cores that rotated at the push of a button and clip-on wall systems that allowed houses to be easily extended and elaborate systems of partitioning with inflatable or other easy fixing for quick demounting. Such technology and technial gadgetry dates back in modern history at least to the Weissenhofsiedlung exhibition in Stuttgart, Germany, in 1927. There are numerous examples. Jean Prouvé's houses at Meudon, France (1938), were designed on 1 m modules with all panels being interchangeable and the whole easily transferable from place to place. His *constructions modulaires,* in 1972, represented a fully industrialized system capable of being put together to make all sorts of building forms.

In Britain there was the Smithsons' Appliance House of 1958, based on cubicles with connection for food preparation, sanitation, communication, storage, and maintenance appliances. Even the Ministry of Housing and Local Government, in response to the call for more adaptability by Parker Morris in 1961, was experimenting with a 5 m flexible house in 1964. Spender and Rogers produced zip-up enclosures in about 1970, epitomizing "the 'popular mechanics' approach to flexibility. They are seen as prototypes for volume production aimed at unspecified markets" (Rabeneck, Sheppard and Town 1973, 724). In furniture and equipment manufacturing there were numerous parallels, such as Eric Mendelsoln's folding tubular bed and Heal's bookshelves that could become a bed.[7]

As building blocks in the construction of one idea, these projects made significant historical contributions. The trouble began, however, when they became perceived as solutions to problems of housing and production. Frequently they were little more than mechanical toys inspired by the lure of an ever-expanding technology. Designers found it hard to escape from the nineteenth-century concept of the celebrity architect, from the "dream of the factory-made house" pioneered by Gropius and Wachsmann and those "recurring bouts of the Henry Ford Syndrome" (Herbert 1984, 1), to produce houses like cars, to produce idealized systems—perfect, complete, controlled and mass produceable.

For these early architects of flexibility and for many who followed, believers in the technical fix and salvation to social ills, "the reward was in the creative and intellectual challenge inherent in the

---

7. See Housing flexibility? *Architectural Design* 43 (1973):698–727.

design itself, rather than with its ultimate realization" (Herbert 1984, 6). Many architects openly admitted that there was "greater satisfaction at the drawing board than in the market place." They tended therefore to paint an idealized picture of the problem and its solutions, "an exercise highly satisfying to the creative spirit, but not always productive of concrete results" (Herbert 1984, 6). No one believed that the rate at which change occurs in the conservative and romantic context of European domesticity warranted the high investment demanded by such technology, especially in view of the time needed to test prototype systems.

Some economists were pointing out that if the money invested in techniques and technologies to make buildings flexible were invested instead in a bank, it would earn enough interest to finance conventional conversions so long as the cycle of change was relatively long. The question then became whether the relatively long cycle of change in housing warranted investment in the kind of flexibility best suited to buildings with much shorter cycles of change. As Heath (1984, 160) concluded,

Flexibility then is easy to provide where the quality of the environment required is not too rigorously specified, where the level of servicing is low, where, it follows from this, changes in the nature of the use of space are not very great. If these conditions are met, and frequent changes are expected, flexibility is the obvious design approach. As we move away from these conditions, the premium paid for flexibility increases; and if we find that we are in fact building an additional floor of the building for each floor of usable space provided, as in the "interstitial floor" concept then it may be more rational to look at other solutions.

DESIGN PRINCIPLES

A number of important principles emerged from the early thinking and practice of flexibility. They offer some of the early building blocks of the support paradigm insofar as design practice is concerned, and they continue to influence design thinking.

First, flexibility embodied a formal recognition that change is an integral part of the performance of building and the design agenda. It is a way of making building functionally and symbolically permanent in the context of rapid changes in aspiration, life-style, family composition, work habits, and so on. Flexibility gives recognition to the concept of a better fit among people, territory, finishes, and costs—not as tailor-made responses to normative projected needs but as variable interpretive opportunities to package programs and interpret standards so finishes, space, and/or cost are variable. It falls short of expanding that variability to patterns of ownership, management, financing, or technology.

Flexibility recognized and then built on the differences or particularities of people rather than their similarities. These differences we could recognize as variety in patterns of informal development, which was difficult to model statistically or statically. Improvisation, extension, and addition are the three generalizable and dynamic ways in which change, fit, and personalization happen. Flexibility formalized these processes as themes in design, as responses, even requisites to change, fit, and variety. The question was, How much does one provide, and what does a designer do, if anything, to facilitate these things?

In this respect, flexibility induced the concept of capacity as a way of measuring the value of indeterminacy as a design strategy. These capacities are first created and subsequently analyzed in one or a combination of ways—in dimensions, in design reserve, in additional materials or components, and in technology.

But if the setting these buildings provided was to be an invitation to users to participate in creating an architecture of cooperation—a concept only primitively explored in the days of flexible buildings—then the size, position, and organization of space and materials would also have to perform in more than technically rational ways. They had to reference the choices available, promoting spontaneity and discovery, albeit within the constraints of the materials and systems employed and the legal and regulatory structure. The architecture of possibilities, in other words, would need to be legible and opportunistic and yet remain technically rational.

Finally, design participation, which was sometimes explicit and sometimes implicit as an intention of flexibility, was largely a misnomer. It was mostly restricted to arranging materials within a given space envelope, much as one does when arranging furniture or decorating. This kind of participation had little to do with shifting patterns of control and responsibility and even less to do with user satisfaction. It had little to do with people deciding the content and context of their housing—the character of neighborhoods, the politics of community, the management of resources—or with setting the terms of reference for design, building, and management. Flexibility, despite its importance as a theory of design practice, ultimately was commended more for enabling good and economical management by public authorities, builders, and manufacturers than for its social or political impact. And because the ideas were tied largely to large building projects and sophisticated building systems, they never got beyond a few demonstration cases, primarily in wealthy first world cities.

If flexibility failed to set the right conditions for participation, what then should these conditions be, and how can they be set up? What objections are conventionally raised against participation and what in favor? What is flexibility in the context of design that promotes participation?

REFERENCES

Fishman, Robert. 1982. *Urban Utopias in the Twentieth Century: Ebenezer Howard, Frank Lloyd Wright, Le Corbusier.* Cambridge, Mass.: MIT Press.

Heath, Thomas. 1984. *Method in Architecture.* London: John Wiley & Sons.

Herbert, Gilbert. 1984. *The Dream of the Factory-Made House—Walter Gropius and Konrad Wachsmann.* Cambridge, Mass.: MIT Press.

Ministry of Housing and Local Government. *Housing Standards, Costs and Subsidies.* Circular no. 36, 1967. London: HMSO.

Morris, Sir Parker. 1961. *Homes for Today and Tomorrow.* London: HMSO.

Pommer, R. 1978. The architecture of urban housing in the United States during the early 1930s. *Journal of the Society of Architectural Historians* (December): 37.

Rabeneck, Andrew; Sheppard, David; and Town, Peter. 1973. Housing flexibility? *Architectural Design 43* (November 1973): 698–727. Special issue.

Rowe, Peter G. 1987. *Design Thinking.* Cambridge, Mass.: MIT Press.

Sprague, Chester, and Testa, Peter. 1983. Public housing: Versatile building stock for changing clientele: Some thoughts prompted by change in design of four public housing projects: Fidelisway, Franklin Field, Jefferson Park and West Broadway. Cambridge, Massachusetts. Unpublished paper, Department of Architecture, MIT.

Taylor, Maureen. 1973. Towards a redefinition of user needs. *DMG–DRS Journal: Design Research and Methods* 7(2) (April–June).

Teicher, Jonathan L. 1989. Enabling housing. Master's thesis, MIT.

Ward, Colin. 1983. *Housing, An Anarchist Approach.* London: Freedom Press, p. 104.

Worthington, John. 1971. Housing—The economics of choice. *Official Architecture and Planning* (July): 518–20.

CHAPTER 5

Participation and Community

I know of no safe depository of the ultimate powers of society, but the people themselves; and if we think them not enlightened enough to exercise their control with a wholesome discretion, the remedy is not to take it from them, but to inform their discretion.

Thomas Jefferson
Letter to William Charles Jarvis
(September 28, 1820)

Participation: the slogan of community architects in Britain, of political radicals and community activists everywhere, something seemingly more connected with social sciences, politics, and management than with architecture, design, getting jobs as architects, and earning money. It started for architects as something trendy and then became necessary, but it is still viewed by the mainstream as benevolent, the domain of do-gooders, a bit further to the left than is usually comfortable, an ideology born of the 1960s and not easily taught or accepted in schools of architecture—something that, all said and done, gets in the way of professional freedoms, of building houses and making architecture.

Community participation as incorporated into the official jargon of planning and design is an ambiguous and powerful idea. It usually refers to the process by which professionals, families, community groups, government officials, and others get together to work something out, preferably in a formal or informal partnership.

The best processes of community participation ensure that everyone involved has a stake in the outcome and that therefore they have some measure of control over it. The best processes ensure that all concerned will share the responsibilities, profits, and risks of what they will decide to do. Their partnership is by necessity rather than luxury. The worst processes are tokenism. These are plans devised by a dominant group legislated to seek the opinion of others, who consult these others on issues that are preselected and may have little or no relevance to those invited to comment. In between, where most projects fall, are various shades of community participation, aptly represented by Sherry Arnstein's "ladder of citizen participation" (1969): co-optation, manipulation, therapy, informing, consulting, and placation.

People taking action on their own behalf—to build houses, protest housing conditions and poverty, protest environmental inequalities, improve neighborhoods—is a resonant part of the history of humanity's housing itself all over the world. These concerns captured the attention of moralists, architects, and reformers writing during the Victorian times in books like *Self-help* by Samuel Smiles and *Mutual Aid* by Peter Kropotkin. The first "exhorted its readers to apply thrift and self-improvement to their lives so that they could progress from rags to riches." The second "was a celebration of the ability to cooperate, whether amongst insects, animals or humans, intended as a rebuttal of the misinterpretations by Huxley and Wallace, of the implications of Darwin's theory of natural selection" (Ward 1981, 2).

Like most other reforms in housing, community participation was institutionalized out of necessity rather than benevolence and in response to growing public militancy as well as the demand for environmental justice. It was, unlike today, as Randolph Hester (1987) points out, a means to that end and not an end in its own right.

Participation was institutionalized in England first, and primitively, in 1956 and then with the Housing Act and the Skeffington Report of 1969. In the United States, participation in planning and design was incorporated into federal law in the 1970s and "used by local governments to set goals, to design housing and parks, and to recruit volunteers to reduce public spending. The latter alone accounts for a $30 billion annual contribution to the U.S. economy" (Hester 1987, 291).

In the developing countries, *community participation* became a buzzword in international urban development policy when the World Bank accepted sites and services as legitimate programs in housing in the mid–1970s. It received the backing of national governments and international agencies when it was discovered that formal construction amounted to excesses of three to four times what was built informally and that most formal construction was accessible to only 10–20 percent of people in upper- and middle-class households.

THE BEGINNINGS IN BRITAIN

The early days after World War II in Britain saw legislative attempts to involve people in the decisions of planners by offering the right of objection or appeal to development plans in case of new construction and of compulsory purchase of slum clearance. In 1959 developments that might affect environmental quality by increasing levels of noise, cars, and people had to be advertised on site. But as Ravetz (1968, 87) points out,

To "participate" in planning on the terms laid down was quite daunting, if not impossible, for the ordinary person. The gathering of information required facilities and skills that were normally available only to the middle class and the educated: use of telephones, typewriters, determination not to be "put off" by experts, and above all, free time in working hours. Public hearings took a quasi-judicial form, where the inspector presided like a judge and the planning authority had legal counsel and expert opinion on its side, so that objectors felt as though it was they who were on trial. All this, together with the fact that the most they could be guaranteed was for their representations to be "taken into account" required a special kind of intellectual tenacity and emotional stamina.

Real change in Britain, however, came with the Housing Act of 1969 (and later 1974), which, apart from all its other provisions, demanded that people be consulted before rather than after final plans. It came as a result of two major shifts in public policy, both inspired by public protest and by the "sheer burden of casework involved in planning appeals" (Ravetz 1986, 88). The first shift came as a result of the appalling destruction of hundreds of thousands of homes nationwide, implemented and executed by various plans devised by planners and traffic engineers to make way for new roads. And if all these roads could be carefully located to go through the slums of cities, so then you could relieve congestion of traffic and people, all at once, leading to much healthier, much tidier, and more manageable cities. The second shift, engineered partly in response to the first but partly also to the more general trend in policy away from wholesale redevelopment, with its socially destructive high-rise estates and failing industrialized building systems, and toward rehabilitation, came in 1966. Attention was brought to the vast but aging housing stock by various communities and their reports, including *Our Older Homes: A Call for Action* and later *Old Houses into New Homes*. In 1974, the government designated various general improvement areas and allocated significant funds for improvement programs. It was difficult, given the presence of existing communities, to ignore local people in the improvement plans of local authorities, all of which served to secure a much greater role for residents in planning decisions.

The results were numerous projects in which architects and planners worked with people in design and planning proposals. Some were of the consulting kind in which people were invited to confirm the conviction of their designers; others engineered partnerships with local community groups, integrating people into the design and planning process itself. Examples of both kinds and lots in between are numerous. Pioneering improvement programs included Project Assist (1972) in Glasgow,[1] Covent Garden in London, and the Black Road general improvement area No. 1 in Macclesfield, which began in 1968 and was completed in 1975.[2] Black Road was the first finished self-help rehabilitation project in Britain in which local residents, inspired by a resident architect, Rod Hackney (who later was to champion the cause of community architecture and

became president of the Royal Institute of British Architects), challenged the local authority's redevelopment plans with plans of their own for rehabilitation. It was an exercise in mobilizing community action, in proving local design, technical, and managerial competence to an authority to the extent of changing the local authorities' policies, and not just their plans. In the end, it was an experiment in partnerships and collaboration between professionals and the public—between the public and the local authority and between the public and contractors.

The 1970s also witnessed a growth in official public participation in the design of new projects, the mood for which was set in the planning fields. In 1970, there was Ralph Erskine's Byker project and Walter Segal's timber frame houses, which became acceptable enough to the Lewisham Council to experiment with a number of self-build houses. There were the PSSHAK projects in 1972 in Stamford Hill and at Adelaide Road in 1978. Bromley Council in 1978 allocated tenants their own architects to design houses, as well as numerous experiments in cooperatives, pioneered by Harold Campbell and intended to change the role and responsibilities of tenants, in some cases to offer them a stake in ownership of public housing.

THE BEGINNINGS IN THE UNITED STATES

Events in the United States were similar in many ways. The country has a long history of advocacy planning, which although rooted in the civil rights movement was not its major preoccupation (Hester 1987). But many urban removal programs did have the added agenda to those in Britain of removing the ghettos, which were substantially black:

At one point, urban renewal earned the nickname "Negro removal." Such projects were the spatial and natural resources elements of racism and exploitation of the

---

1. For a full description of Project Assist, see *Architects Journal: Assist*, part 1, November 10, 1976, pp. 901–9; Assist, part 2, December 8, 1976, 1089–1100; Assist, part 3, February 9, 1977, pp. 269–73.
2. See R. Hackney, Community architecture: An alternative self-help approach to housing improvement, in *Participation in Housing,* ed. N. Hamdi and R. Greenstreet, Working Paper No. 59 (Oxford: Oxford Department of Town Planning, 1982), pp. 38–71.

poor. . . . Participation meant black power. Getting people to participate by protesting urban renewal was the environmental policy strategy. Marching with thousands of clenched fists thrust into the air saying "I am somebody" defeated urban renewal in many cities and guaranteed environmental rights. Involving the impacted poor in developing alternative plans seemed a logical extension of the strategy, and was consistent with the tradition of architectural utopianism. (Hester 1987, 289–90)

Urban renewal in the United States got fully underway in the 1960s. "By 1963, the urban renewal agency had spent three billion federal dollars. It had demolished the housing of 243,000 households including 177,000 families, mostly poor and black, and mostly tenants, so they got little or none of the compensation. Besides new office and commercial property, the clearances had allowed for the construction of 20,000 public housing units," with hopelessly inadequate provisions for all the others who were displaced (Stretton 1978, 153).

There was, however, a substantial amount of community organizing, some involving architects, before official federal aid for urban renewal began in 1969. Both New York City and Boston, for example, fielded significant initiatives to get the poor directly involved in the struggle for better neighborhoods and improved housing conditions. In 1931–1932 "a group of unemployed architects and engineers formed the Emergency Planning and Research Bureau of Greater Boston" (Trolander 1975, 130) to find out the improvements that people living in the South End wanted for homes, businesses, and social improvement programs. They helped establish the South End Joint Planning Committee, which succeeded in establishing parks, playgrounds, and a housing consultation bureau to advise local residents on how to improve their houses. With the New Deal, however, local initiatives in planning received a setback in view of its thrust toward more centralized government, and it was not until the model cities program of 1967–1973 that citizens were given the right to negotiate and help direct government efforts to participate actively in policy

making. This was an experiment "to see if numerous federal programs which nobody had ever been able to coordinate very well 'from above' could instead be coordinated 'from below' where they converged at the neighborhood coal-face" (Stretton 1978, 154). This, then, was implicit recognition of the partisan rather than managerial style of urban governance and yet one that many officials still see today as undermining their abilities to govern effectively.

There are today hundreds and thousands of public employees, politicians, planners and theorists who have deeply vested interests in maintaining the strength of "national organization" against what they allege is the chaos of community control. The prospect for neighborhood government must be made to seem less threatening to those many who are dependent on centralization. Their legitimate interests must be accommodated if neighborhood government is to mature from a protest movement to a funding metaphor of public policy. (Berger and Neuhaus 1977)

THE BEGINNINGS IN THE DEVELOPING COUNTRIES

Reconciling this failure from above, with seeming loss of power and control for government officials that goes with innovating from below, has troubled planners and architects as well throughout the development of participatory planning and design, and no less in the developing countries. The same issues prompted the international community to reconsider its initiatives in and for the developing countries. The 1970s in general and the 1976 U.N. Vancouver conference in particular saw significant shifts in policy. Not surprisingly (since most policies continued to be engineered by Western-dominated interests and agencies and critiqued by Western academics) and in line with experience and developments in Europe and the United States, redevelopment gave way to upgrading; the poor were seen as a resource and not as a burden to the economy; the informal sector was productive and not consumptive in economic terms; housing agencies became supporters, facilitators, and enablers rather than providers; public expenditure or improvement programs were viewed as investment rather than charity; and so on. With these policies and the programs that emerged came community participation in planning, building, and management.

A number of projects are now well known for their ambitions, successes, and failures in this and other respects as milestones in the development toward support policies and as case studies for evaluation and critique. These can be grouped into three categories: as afterthought, where people wound up building their own houses and sometimes to preselected plans; explicitly stated as a function of the project program and broadened to include developmental considerations like employment and training; and as experiments in self-government.

The Dandora Community Development sites and services project in Nairobi (Chana 1984) is typical of sites-and-services projects and represents the conventional user participation stance—something that is more an afterthought than an integral part of the program. Started in 1975 and targeted at low-income households, it included some 6000 plots, some with, but most without, core houses and took a staggering six years for the project formulation and preparation stage alone. Significantly, however, like most other sites-and-services projects, people were less involved in managing the social, physical, and financial institutions of the development and its overall planning but more involved in building their own houses. Those who, for whatever reason, were unable to build or subcontract building on their own behalf were assisted by the Community Development Division to form cooperative building groups made up of about seven to sixteen members each to build for its members. Materials and loans were available to all households, as were some technical assistance and ready-made plans.

A second category of projects involving community participation in a much broader sense included a combination of upgrading existing slums and squatters and new sites with services. Forbes Davidson's project in Ismaili, Egypt, is one example, as is the program in Lusaka, Zambia.

The Lusaka project (Jere 1984), initiated in 1972 and stretching into 1975, was part of the government's second National Development Plan and substantially funded by the World Bank. Its objectives were to upgrade 17,000 existing slum dwellings, to provide 7600 serviced plots in overspill areas for resettling displaced families, and to provide 4400 fully serviced lots in six sites-and-services projects. But it was also an exercise in physical and social development and one that differed significantly in its stated intentions from conventional projects:

Local authorities could support and reinforce the residents' own efforts to improve their environment, rather than take over from them. It had to act as a stimulus to the investment of popular savings, skills and initiative, and was therefore to be seen as a phased program of development in which authority and the community determined at each stage the type of input that would help residents achieve their aims. (Jere 1984, 59)

There were a number of additional programmatic components and considerations. Community development workers, whose task it would be to inform residents of what was going on and to motivate them, were trained by the American Friends Service Committee, which with UNICEF was investing about 4.5 percent in the program. Collective, mutual self-help committees and organizations were formed to dig trenches; they earned enough money to invest in the construction of a new clinic in one case and a day care center in another.

Twenty-two percent of the total budget was allocated to materials loans, leadership seminars were held to strengthen skills and build confidence, and standards of layout and construction were treated flexibly. And yet most initiatives were not only conceived but also detailed and packaged from outside, ensuring that the participatory process had little or no influence over strategy. "Local participation was not brought into action at an early stage of planning, and when it was, all the financial details and expected objectives had been worked out in the board rooms of Lusaka and Washington" (Jere 1984, 64).

In contrast, the third breed of projects sometimes inspired by community activism are experiments in self-government. These projects use shelter as a vehicle for social and economic development; they see it as part of a larger system of initiatives designed to improve the conditions of poor or disenfranchised people. Unlike the first two projects, these have their roots firmly in the aspirations and politics of grass-roots organizations and in response to a common cause. Perhaps the most renowned and successful example in developing countries is the El Salvadoran nonprofit, nongovernment organization FUNDASAL.

FUNDASAL (Bamberger and Deneke 1984) is one of the largest nongovernment organizations in the developing world and probably the only one receiving direct funds from the World Bank to run sites and services and upgrading projects. FUNDASAL puts heavy emphasis on community participation and is quite blunt about what this entails. No project is allocated much without a commitment to be involved in one of the mutual aid construction teams. Its goal is to eliminate restrictive down payments and also to train people in building and management skills. In the long run, households participate in the maintenance of their settlement, in collecting payments on utilities and loans, and in lobbying for the installation of various services.

FUNDASAL's objectives, like those of most other NGOs, go beyond building shelter to building communities. The result is that yet more programmatic components are added to the project brief, in this case including employment opportunities, ensuring that projects are self-financing, and to build community organizations capable of sustaining development both socially and physically. In addition, international development aid agencies that operate through these organizations support their efforts in staff salaries, training, matching funds, working capital, expert help, and so on.

WHY WE NEED PARTICIPATION

What does history and the experience from cities as divergent in character and politics as London, New York, Lusaka, El Salvador, and Nairobi teach us about participatory planning and design? What does it tell us about building programs and making plans at the project level? What does experience so far suggest about why we need it? Under what conditions might it work best? Why, despite significant successes, are objections still dominant in official professional and governmental circles?

Much caution must be exercised in emulating programs that may have worked in one place for another. Land sharing in Thailand works because the Thais have conflict resolution built into their culture and because there is much political goodwill directed toward popular participation in planning. FUNDASAL was successful despite party politics because the El Salvadorans, mostly rural in character, have a long tradition of cooperation, which is built into their rural workplace. A few selective generalizations, however, may be helpful.

First, participatory programs are effective ways of building coalitions and fostering cooperation between government and nongovernment groups, between often competing government departments, between expatriate or outside experts and their local professional counterparts, and between community groups with sometimes differing vested interests, particularly early in program preparation. Partnerships do not happen, however, just because they are a good idea. Nor is it useful to talk in abstract ways about partnerships between sectors, such as private and public or formal and informal. Usually participatory programs happen if and when people and organizations are convinced that their interests will be better served with partnerships rather than without them. Many people, for example, accustomed to an informal way of life, may decide that cooperation with governments in formal planning will threaten their liberties and diminish their ability to act in the intuitive and spontaneous way they usually do.

Effective and operative partnerships begin with a discovery of common interests and subsequently with inducing a convergence of interests as a prelude to planning. Informally, these are processes that occur every day: "Individuals seeking information and action on their own problems, converge with other individuals with similar needs for research and action. . . . The convergence of interests . . . establishes a special phase of participant commitment and involvement which is continuously drawn upon and further developed as the process proceeds" (McGill and Horton 1973, 22).

Building partnerships is also a first step to strengthening institutional capabilities to initiate and then ensure continuity of work once experts pull out—another useful function of participatory programs and one already well argued by Silverman (1984). Institutional development is an idea very much in currency among supporters and funding agencies. Most discussions, however, focus on rationalizing, streamlining, or building capabilities within government organizations and existing institutions of government to increase their proficiency in receiving revenues, managing land, and controlling development. Although there are good reasons to strengthen the capabilities of institutions that must deliver land, materials, and basic services, there are equally good reasons to examine and strengthen local institutions, some of them informal—thrift societies, church organizations, and local law enforcement agencies, for example—which is the primary purpose of community participation.

The objective is to identify alternative institutional arrangements cutting across disciplines and sectoral lines and that establish direct relationships among the state, the market, and community organizations. Participatory programs therefore can help to emphasize the integrated nature of most urban development programs, as we saw with FUNDA-SAL and in Lusaka, building connections between health and housing, housing and employment, housing and infrastructure—connections that can be made explicit with the advantage that programs can reflect a more comprehensive and socially biased approach. While NGOs clearly play a vital role in this respect in mediating between government and community, one can foresee the possibility of direct partnerships between local government and communities (note I do not imply that they should be lumped together), as in some community-based projects in the United States and England, particularly when workshops bring representatives from each party face to face in negotiations.

"Some cases, such as those of Geneshnagar [Pune, India], El Augustino and Villa el Salvador [Lima, Peru]," suggests Turner (1987, 5), "show that local communities' own organizations can sometimes successfully negotiate with local and central government for the rights, goods, or services they need in order to implement their own programs. In most cases, the necessary supports for local initiatives are either provided through NGOs, either directly or through mediation between local communities and central authorities." Clearly this requires substantial goodwill and commitment by all parties.

Participatory programs can also provide a better way to collect, analyze, and interpret information. Development needs can be expressed by those who experience them and where they experience them before development begins.

If they are site based—in local schools or community centers, for example—they can mobilize the interest of the wider community and attract others who may not have had their interests directly represented but who can offer an additional point of view. In one case in Sri Lanka, local government officers argued they needed a playground as part of their village upgrading program, which would require converting some privately owned land to public use. While community representatives had no objection to a playground, they were unprepared to embark on lengthy negotiations with neighbors to release land for this purpose, which was, in any case, a low priority. School children who were not initially part of the workshop but were observing the proceedings with curiosity were able to be precise about their needs. They suggested that what they needed was equipment—goal posts for soccer and a net for basketball, to be more precise—which could be assembled anywhere and dismantled when play was over. The only space they required was for storage, which could be made available within the local school.

Broad policy objectives for improving health, education, and housing, for example, or even discrete proposals for building schools, health centers, or houses can be confronted and potentially modified by the values and perceptions of others who may have a better knowledge of conditions and a better understanding of what is likely to work. Representatives from the various interest groups involved have the opportunity to review the interests of other groups who may have very different interpretations of the symptoms and causes of problems, not only to see what they see but also to understand why they see what they do. The objective is to reach consensus on the best interpretation of position issues and problems in ways that will lead to more effective actions (Argyris, Putnam, and Smith 1985).

As Peattie (1983) suggests, "Information about processes and about invisible structures is not readily derived from counting things." Instead information and consensus on quality of information is sought first by observation, analysis, and explanation of what is seen and told. Observation provides a check on explanation and, vice versa, one interpretation may be refined by another until some consensus is reached over the issues or problems in question.

In story gathering or qualitative research, people are treated as informants and not as subjects or respondents. They are encouraged to "tell what has happened or is happening to them as a way of explaining how things work" (Peattie 1983) and not just what things are. The researcher uses these stories to find themes, priorities, and needs, uncovering what Turner calls hidden structures or networks, which can lead to a better understanding of appropriate action.

In some settlements, for example, residents take basic water taps and melt them down to sell for their metal value and turn into jewelry. Observation will tell that there is a problem and possibly who is responsible, but it does not tell what to do. Those who believe it does will replace the parts and tackle the symptoms but not the cause of the problem. Their response will be simplistic, incomplete, and short term in effect. If, for example, residents are unaware of the implications on health and sanitation created by the lack of water supply from removing the taps, the remedy will differ from that where taps are taken with full knowledge of implications. In the first case, education is called for and in the second, some mode of close supervision. What may emerge is a package of responses that will include replacement, education, and supervision. These examples illustrate that "open discussion among members of a community of practice can lead to agreement that one interpretation is more adequate than another, even in the opinion of those who originally held the less adequate interpretation" (Argyris, Putnam, and Smith 1985, 28).

Building local capabilities through action research can involve field training, another significant advantage of participatory programs. The kind of training to which I am referring runs in parallel with project work where projects are used as vehicles for teaching and where local participatory workshops can work well for this purpose. Running training in parallel to development work saves time and avoids more training later to enable participants to connect what they have learned with what they will have to do. Trainers must keep their explanations and ideas simple; communities will not let them get away with abstract ideas they do not understand.

The community design workshop is not a substitute for clinical teaching; it is an extension of it. For local professional staff, it exerts pressure of time, people, and place that would not otherwise be available. Under the urgency to act, decisions will have to be reached quickly, sometimes with few data and much uncertainty about the quality of these data. This urgency teaches how to distinguish and prioritize key concerns that are immediate from those that can afford to be resolved over longer periods of time. The urgency to act, coupled with incomplete knowledge, will teach ways of starting projects that can be completed incrementally as knowledge and more money become available and when more accurate means of intervention can be established. They teach ways of planning that improvise on themes taken from the physical and social content and without comprehensive, coherent plans—and, conversely, ways of making plans without the usual preponderance of planning.

CONDITIONS AND OBJECTIONS

Despite the advantages, there are nevertheless significant limitations to participatory planning and design that need careful consideration and are often raised as objections to the efficiency of participatory planning. The likelihood of success of most programs depends on a number of conditions that need to be understood.

It may be relatively easy, for example, to mobilize interest, secure commitments, reach consensus, and involve people in developing programs in neighborhoods that are integrated or parochial. In these places, people already share a common view; there is social homogeneity; they speak a common language; they may be ethnically related; and so on. Interventions in these kinds of neighborhoods, with the potential to organize, will be in stark contrast to those that are diffuse, stepping-stones, transitory, or nonneighborhoods.[3]

Most new subdivisions, whether of the sites and services kind or public housing, are *diffuse* in the sense that they start with little or no community structure. Interventions are difficult here because initially it is not clear whose interests need to be served. In *stepping-stone communities,* architects and planners face a different set of issues. In these places, people are transient, have no long-term commitment locally, and will probably move if dissatisfied rather than get involved. *Transitory neighborhoods* may be going through class or ethnic turnover— from black to white or from middle income to upper income, for example. There will be old-timers and newcomers, and their differences will be acute. In this context, how can differences be reconciled? Who is it one plans for? The nonneighborhood is most difficult for participatory planning and yet often in most need of collaborative action. They are often highly deprived socially, physically, and economically, devastated by new highways or other development, with abandoned buildings and derelict sites, and where communication is weak and loyalty highly fragmented. Each of these differences in social and physical configurations demands methods and techniques tailored specifically to the circumstances.

Participatory programs advocate a democratic process for reaching decisions. If they are conducted in a nondemocratic political climate, they will be viewed with much suspicion by local participants, who will suspect them as being set up by governments to expose local activists. Where the politics of project development do not match the politics of the country, those who count will not turn up.

---

3. From notes based on a lecture delivered by Phillip Clay, Department of Urban Studies and Planning, MIT, Cambridge, Mass., fall 1981.

This lack of proper representation can be a serious limitation to any participatory process.

Whatever the conditions and circumstances, sometimes community participation can inadvertently raise expectations. Local participants may come up with "wish lists" that local government officials might want to see implemented to appease their public and so will make promises that are ill considered technically, financially, and administratively and that later they cannot meet. Most who come to these sessions have a large measure of skepticism about official intentions given their past experience with government. Probably most of their contacts in the past with public authorities have been confrontational, and so many people may be bewildered by the new gestures. They will come to the workshops, if they come at all, ready to get what they can out of government. Under these circumstances, the question "What do you need?" can often draw the response, "What can we have?" Robbins (1988) describes this as the manipulative posture in participatory planning. "I was surprised by the friendly paternalism of the gentleman representing the GLC," wrote one local authority tenant. "I have never experienced such an interest in my housing problem by this hitherto rather faceless body, and I must admit to being suspicious."[4]

Sometimes the presence of high-ranking officials inhibits the participation of members who see themselves as subordinates and may therefore offer what Robbins (1988, 171) calls "the subordinate view." In this instance, people "will try to frame answers in ways which they feel will give [officials] what they want or that will carry favor or approval." They will be reluctant to voice opinions that may be seen to be in stark conflict with official policy.

In London, for example, the GLC held one of a series of workshops to determine the needs and priorities of families prior to completing detail plans. At first most tenants, confronted with the officials of the GLC, were cautious in expressing too strong a point of view for fear of prejudicing their chances of receiving a house. One tenant later wrote, "Perhaps I should have been more realistic and measured out room areas as compared with my present place, but I was so happy to move that I did not want to raise any 'lesser' matters that might impede a speedy getaway. I must honestly confess that any omission lay in my own reluctance to say too much."[5] On a separate page marked "do not publish," he proceeded to make suggestions for improvement to his dwelling and to the structure of the overall arrangement of space within the block.

At other times and for similar reasons, minority ethnic groups will be reluctant to express their concerns for fear of reprisals or harassment and fall in line with the majority point of view. It may be necessary to undertake separate workshops with the ultimate burden on local professionals to develop an equitable program.

Some say that participatory processes take too long, that people do not know what they really want even if asked, and even when they do know, they are not properly equipped to get it. Others say that given the chance, people will do silly things, and if they do not, they have neither the time, the commitment, nor the capability to be involved in decisions that can be very costly if they are wrong ones. Yet others hold that these participatory processes increase the burden of management on already overburdened administrators. They are often an excuse for professional incompetence. Participatory planning and design, they charge, is a measure imposed by poverty; most people do not want to get involved unless they have to.

There are, of course, truisms in all these criticisms. Do people want to get involved? Not always. If you are a tenant of a housing authority in England "who have produced generations of tenants

---

4. From a letter written by a tenant of the Greater London Council, London, in response to the PSSHAK participatory process at Adelaide Road. From personal files.

5. Tenant letter from personal files.

who become accustomed to the idea of the council as the automatic provider of housing services, then the idea of self-determination and participation is unlikely to hold much attraction. I for one," wrote Tony Judge (1981, 58), chairman of the GLC's Housing Management Committee between 1974 and 1977, "suspect that it is not the political and economic climate which stands in the way of more rapid development of tenant takeover. It is the tenants themselves."

Do these programs always serve the interest of poor or minority people, even when they are targeted to them? Not always. In cities worldwide, public participation has served in many instances to empower local communities to resist developments that may be of direct benefit to the poor. In Boston, the development of low- and moderate-income housing that the Public Facilities Department has pioneered on 747 vacant sites has been resisted by local residents because they know it will attract the poor, and usually blacks, which in time, they say, will increase crime and depress property values.

Finally, will community participation invariably lead to better maintenance, easier recovery of costs, and greater satisfaction? Not always. This is especially so for that preponderance of participation in house design that was the preoccupation of many during the 1960s and early 1970s.

Tom Woolley (1985) throws some considerable doubt on notions that quality and satisfaction follow easily from user participation in design. From three projects he evaluated in Britain, he drew a number of conclusions. Most design work emerges from the process and is not a direct result of clear participant choices. His projects were viewed as similar to good-quality housing that had not involved future occupants in design. He also found that the level of satisfaction achieved is closely related to expectations and that there was no real difference in price or standards between projects designed with users and those without.

The notion that user participation in design

would enable people to make special houses unique from others and so themselves special was also wrong. We have since learned that most poor people spend most of their lives being special in slums, shanties, or public housing projects; what they really want is to be ordinary. They see the services of architects and other professionals reserved for those who can afford to pay for them; far from despising these services, they see them as status, if nothing else. People want their own architects and planners, and they want assistance in having their wishes translated into physical buildable plans or, at least, in finding the means to do so.

I remember talking to one family on the waiting list of a local authority about the design of their new homes—about details of layout, kitchen arrangement, storage, lights, sockets, and the like. Throughout our discussions, they seemed quite disinterested, which I found puzzling given all our efforts to involve them in design decision making. I found out later that all six family members lived in one small room, shared a bathroom with four other families, and had only a hot plate for cooking. Their primary concern was to move into what was for them a more spacious and well-serviced new development, well located, and at the right rent.

I am inclined to agree with those who argue that design participation is the privilege and indulgence of the better off; only when a society is relatively well housed do their concerns turn to details of design.

PARTICIPATION: THE MEANS OR THE ENDS?

Community participation has been appropriated by planners for reasons of efficiency more than equity and in recognition of its important political and methodological advantages in shaping planning decisions. In planning, it has been equally effective in helping to ensure continuity in management, maintenance, and public administration—building on local people and institutions who can carry on when "outsiders" have left. In planning, it emerged in history because of demand from grassroots and neighborhood organizations, and not as something passed down from above.

In housing design, on the other hand, community participation emerged out of the conscience of liberal architects and concerned administrators. Few poor communities had ever been threatened by the standard dwelling types of Victorian pattern books and model plans, nor by Queen Anne revivalists, neo-Gothicists, nor even modernists. Few communities had ever demanded a say in design decision making, in the same way they had asserted their demand in planning. Designing was never integral to the body politic of housing and neighborhood development. Furthermore, design participation has been largely ineffective in ensuring greater community or user satisfaction with details of house plans or with built form. And in house production, at least in the industrialized nations of the West, there is little evidence to support its claims to reductions in cost—neither in product, nor in process—without significant measures of self-build and self-management, which is what people were doing all along before planners and architects started fussing about it.

Whatever the arguments, and whether in design or in planning, community participation is no substitute for professional or governmental interventions or for formal planning or design, but an intrinsic part of both processes. And just as when governmental and professional interventions of the wrong kind can distort programs in favor of the needs of those who dominate, so too can community participation. How much community participation, and in this respect, how much professional and governmental interventions—who participates with whom, who relinquishes control to whom and how much, and in what specific field of decision making—is something that can only be decided case by case and as an essential prelude to planning and designing. It cannot, it view of the complex net-

work of clients and client demands, be something that is planned as a palliative and then applied normatively.

Finally, a more coherent understanding of design and participation *is* emerging—one which recognizes design as the *subject* rather than *object* of community participation, not the result of the process, but the means to it.

In this sense, design can be an effective means of community enablement—a process that will improve the efficiency of design practice, will assert design as a part of the body politic of housing, and at the same time will promote an architecture of cooperation.

REFERENCES

Argyris, C.; Putnam, R.; and Smith, McCain D. 1985. *Action Science—Concepts, Methods, and Skills for Research and Intervention.* London, San Francisco: Josey-Bass.

Bamberger, Michael, and Deneke, Albert Harth. 1984. Can shelter programmes meet low-income needs? The experience of El Salvador. In *Low-Income Housing in the Developing World*, pp. 37–54. Edited by Geoffrey Payne. New York: John Wiley and Sons.

Berger, Peter, and Neuhaus, Richard. 1971. *To Empower People: The Role of Mediating Structures in Public Policy.* Washington, D.C.: American Enterprise Institute for Public Policy.

Chana, T. S. 1984. Nairobi: Dandora and other projects. In *Low-Income Housing in the Developing World*, pp. 17–36. Edited by Geoffrey Payne. New York: John Wiley and Sons.

Hester, Randolph T. 1987. Participatory design and environmental justice: Pas de deux or time to change partners. *Journal of Architectural and Planning Research* 4(4):289–300.

Jere, Harrington. 1984. Lusaka: Local participation in planning and decision making. In *Low-Income Housing in the Developing World*, pp. 55–68. Edited by Geoffrey Payne. New York: John Wiley and Sons.

Judge, Tony. 1981. The political and administrative setting. In *Participation in Housing*, pp. 41–58. Edited by Nabeel Hamdi and Robert Greenstreet, Working Paper 57. Oxford: Oxford Polytechnic Department of Town Planning.

McGill, M. E., and Horton, M. E. 1973. *Action Research*

Designs—For Training and Development. Washington, D.C.: National Training and Development Press.

Peattie, Lisa. 1983. Realistic planning and qualitative research. *Habitat International* 7(5&6):227–234.

Ravetz, Alison. 1986. *The Government of Space: Town Planning in Modern Society*. Boston: Faber and Faber.

Robbins, E. 1988. Doing socio-cultural analysis: Implications for practice in the field. In *Refugee Camps—A Primer for Rapid Site Plans—Land, Shelter, Infrastructure, Services*. R. Goethert and N. Hamdi, draft manual prepared for the United Nations High Commissioner for Refugees, Geneva.

Silverman, Jerry M. 1984. *Technical Assistance and Aid Agency Staff—Alternative Techniques for Greater Effectiveness*. Technical Paper 28. Washington, D.C.: World Bank.

Stretton, Hugh. 1978. *Urban Planning in Rich and Poor Countries*. Oxford: Oxford University Press.

Trolander, Judith Ann. 1975. *Settlement Houses and the Great Depression*. Detroit: Wayne State University Press.

Turner, John F. C., 1987. The Roles of Non-Governmental and Community-Based Organizations in the Improvement of Human Settlements. Paper prepared for Second Congress of Local Authorities, July 1987 at Nagoya, Japan.

Ward, Colin. 1981. Self-help and mutual aid in housing: the development of an ideal. In *Participation in Housing*, pp. 1–15. Edited by Nabeel Hamdi and Robert Greenstreet. Working Paper 57. Oxford: Oxford Polytechnic Department of Town Planning.

Woolley, Thomas Adrian. May 1985. Community Architecture: An Evaluation of the Case for User Participation in Architectural Design. Oxford: Unpublished doctoral thesis, Department of Architecture, Oxford Polytechnic.

CHAPTER 6

Enablement and Design

Enable: to give power to (a person); to strengthen, make adequate or proficient . . . to make competent or capable . . . to supply with the requisite means or opportunities to an end or for an object.

Oxford English Dictionary

Inasmuch as participation in housing is about shifting patterns of control—about communities and local organizations getting more of it—so enablement is the process by which people are empowered to exercise that control. In this sense, whether in program making, design, or development and significantly for professionals, enablement is centrally concerned with the practice of intervention—the why, when, how, and with what to intervene to get things going and then to keep them going. In this sense, it is the operational side of the support paradigm. And if flexibility demands capacities that widen the range of choices available, so enablement is the process by which that capacity is properly referenced—easy to take advantage of in programs, on sites, in buildings, in systems of management, and in financing.

Participation without enablement is like trying to drive a car without fuel. And both, without flexibility, are likely trying to drive the same car if it is programmed to move in only one direction and always predictably from A to B. The concept of steering becomes a pretense to freedom and the steering wheel no more than a symbol of control.

Enablement is far from being an abstraction of social science, public management, political radicalism, benevolence, or philanthropy. It can be an exciting initiative in building programs and in design.

In its evaluation criteria for the International Union of Architects (UIA) competition for students in 1983 entitled "The Architect as Enabler," the jury cited the criteria by which they would judge submissions: the degree of participation by users in the design process; the elaboration of mental and social tools for designing; the technical means of building as appropriate and sympathetic to the users; and the adaptability and responsiveness of the planning system, among others.[1] They did

---

1. See The Architect as Enabler of User House Planning and Design, special issue of *Architecture and Competition* (1985). The issue documents competition entries and reviews the concept of enablement.

not go as far as to suggest that the plan itself should be resourceful of ideas that are structured but indeterminate and easily readable.

Most significant, "the competition started with an unusual requirement. What was asked, was a method. Not one for designing a building or a housing scheme, but a method for organizing a participatory design process that would enable laymen to take active part in the planning and construction of their houses and neighborhoods" (Lambert 1985, 8).

What the jury got for the most part, and despite the talent, were various kits of standardized parts that could be arranged in all sorts of clever ways and various procedures instructing people on the planning process, construction methods, materials, how to use architects, and how to use the system provided. These "systems" came coupled with attitudes reflecting "a still current tendency among those seeking solutions to housing problems: the search for 'recipes' in the form of standardized and replicable programs" (Jury Report 1985).

Has enablement, and all the undercurrents of change inspired by advocates of design participation, appropriate technologies, flexibility, freedom to build, support, and housing by people, made any difference to the thinking, practice, and education of architects? By and large, the overwhelming evidence leads to a rather discouraging prognosis despite significant but rather isolated successes: by and large, most architects believe these issues are the domain of others.

What, then, is enablement in the context of design practice, and what professional commitments does it entail? What difference does it make to architects? How can it be useful in deciding interventions when setting objectives, preparing a program, and developing design? How can design, if conceived as a process of enablement—a process that builds capacities through the physical organization of sites and buildings—be descriptive rather than prescriptive of opportunities for habitation, community, privacy, security, ritual, comfort, health, and doing business and building wealth? An example will illustrate.

MAKING PLANS WITH MINIMAL PLANNING: AN EXAMPLE

The setting is an urban site typical of any in the developing countries today and any in the developed countries yesterday. It has been targeted to settle landless poor families, some already on the site or on the periphery, who have been there for some twenty years, and others who will settle from neighboring areas. It is an infill site, part of a larger program for area upgrading.

The site is unusually large for an urban infill with ill-defined boundaries, in public ownership with few utilities or services. There is very little money for its development. A road, consolidated but unpaved, runs perpendicular into the site, providing access to the few shacks already constructed as houses by families whose tenure rights to the land are unclear. The road peters out beyond the last of these houses into a marshy bog a few hundred yards into the site. A Lion's Club building sits in the middle of the site. A little farther to the west is a large lagoon, which always floods in the rainy season. Some of the existing lots are large, and some families are earning money by subletting parts to others.

The site plan indicates the extension of the existing road, intersected along its length by another unpaved road, which will form a spine along the length of the site and which in turn is connected back to the main road running along the boundary of the site. One function of this spine road is quite technical: to move people and vehicles along the length of the site and to locate mainline utilities so that they can be effectively distributed to the remainder of the site as it consolidates. Another function is opportunistic: to take opportunity from the site characteristics and existing activity patterns so that they can profit existing settlers and traders and as many of those who will come next. Yet another function is referential: to give reference to some of the different ways in which a strong community focus might be formed.

The spine road is positioned more or less to divide the site into two equal parts. Its position already gives reference to differential land values. We can expect that the value of properties that adjoin the road will be higher than those that do not because of their potential for commerce and because they will have easier access to utilities. The road deviates occasionally from its technically rational path to link the Lion's Club building with the lagoon, to avoid dislocating existing families, and to connect back to the main road at the point where some small shops and restaurants have been well established for some time. At its junction, the spine is widened a little. It makes a small piazza or stopping place for people and vehicles. We can guess that local traders will profit from the additional pedestrian and vehicular traffic routed to their front door.

Property values adjoining the piazza will likely be higher than along the spine road. Thus a hierarchy of land values is established. The public authority takes advantage of this likely potential and decides to develop properties adjoining the piazza for middle-income families and sell these at market rates. This, they believe, will attract enough capital to offset at least some of the infrastructure costs and to cross-subsidize some minimal construction of starter homes for the poorest. In addition, this initiative will please the donor agency, which is looking for evidence of self-financed projects as a condition to future loans.

A school and vocational center (a neighborhood rather than site facility) is located away from the main road but abuts the piazza, offering more potential profit for informal traders and more connections between the site and the larger neighborhood communities. We guess that this corner of the site might become a center to the neighborhood and differentiated from any center we might cultivate within the site itself. A hierarchy of open space is identified, each used and potentially controlled by varying clusters of people.

The location of public facilities, and even their design and construction, is used to give identity and status to this settlement. It can also satisfy the demands of local politicians who will want to make an event of opening the project by cutting the ribbon. They will demand something more than just roads, trees, utilities, and unfinished houses—houses that can be visited, that can be counted, and published, that look good enough to photograph.

The spine road is made a little wider along its length than standards would have it, reserving a minimum width for access for carts and vehicles and setting an outward limit for other functions—commerce, building extensions, spontaneous markets—that are less easily predictable. This margin of tolerance between public and private domain, and between what we know about and what we do not, will enable people to create their own specific demarcations and represent a generalization based on observations or even on an analysis of probability. The margin represents negotiable space between potentially conflicting functional and social demands rather than lines of confrontation. It is purposely ambiguous and functionally circumstantial. Some guidelines about the limits of what can and cannot be done may be set, although one has to be cautious about setting rules that cannot be monitored or enforced.

Where the existing site road and the proposed spine road intersect, both roads are widened a little more on the assumption that there can be another focal point, this time for the site. This is already in evidence because it is where the only existing standpipe is located; around it all kinds of social activities are already in evidence, activities that commonly cluster around the business of collecting water and washing clothes. Children play and women gather and socialize while they wait to fill their buckets. Close by is the only small store, selling candy, soap, spices, and vegetables. Nobody planned for a store; it is there because that is where people are, and it sells what it does because that is what is needed. Some additional physical elements are introduced to service the site and positioned to give the overall organization of the layout more formal expression. Street lights are provided along both roads and positioned to the inner limits of its width. Their spacing

Generating the site plan on the basis of a spatial model, including lots and circulation.

The model is easily adapted to suit existing patterns of settlement. *(From a studio project by John Englund, Sara Siff, and Andrew Slettebak, MIT, 1986)*

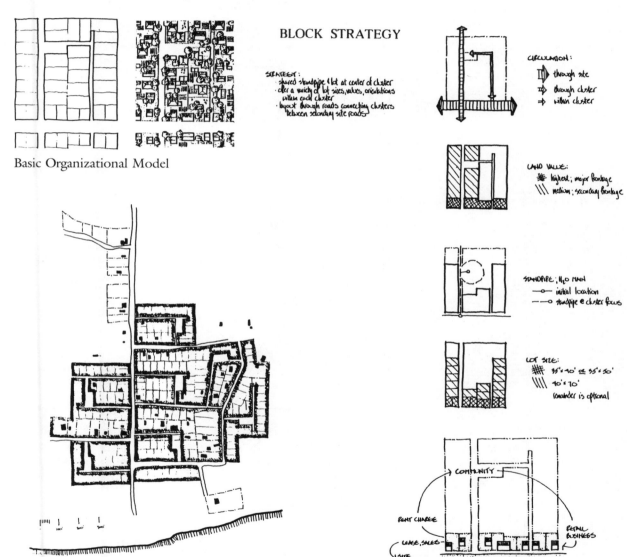

Basic Organizational Model

BLOCK STRATEGY

Transformations of Basic Model

Generating the site plan on the basis of a management model.

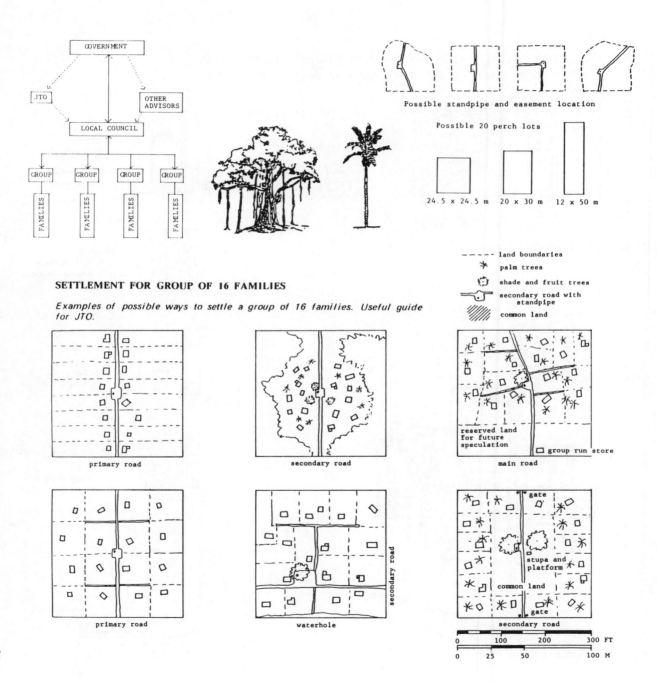

Possible standpipe and easement location

Possible 20 perch lots

24.5 x 24.5 m   20 x 30 m   12 x 50 m

- - - - - land boundaries
* palm trees
shade and fruit trees
secondary road with standpipe
common land

SETTLEMENT FOR GROUP OF 16 FAMILIES

Examples of possible ways to settle a group of 16 families. Useful guide for JTO.

primary road

secondary road

main road

reserved land for future speculation

group run store

primary road

waterhole

secondary road

gate

stupa and platform

common land

gate

secondary road

| 0 | 100 | 200 | 300 FT |
| 0 | 25 | 50 | 100 M |

PROJECTION TWO   PROJECTION THREE

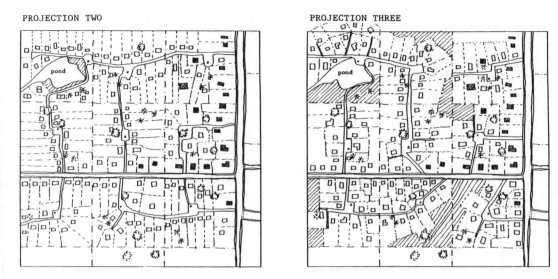

(From a studio project by Barbara Ruys, MIT, 1986)

may break with standards at the intersection, where more will be provided.

The bus line is brought into the site with a bus stop located at the intersection. A few trees are planted to give shade and visibility and physical definition to this public domain—to make things look good.

The remainder of the site—its circulation, subdivision, and utilities—is ordered by the combination of large parcels, each diagramatically modeled and each sized to accommodate a maximum number of lots. These parcels establish the thematic principles of the layout—an organizational typology based on size, proportion, position, and profile of lots, streets, utility points, walls, trees, and houses, and on relationships of fronts and backs, public to private, and so on. They are deployed like patchwork over the site, each its own entity and yet together giving structure and discipline to the site. Each par-

cel can be layered with as much physical and organizational structure as necessary, decided largely on the self-organizing or self-build capabilities of those who will inhabit them—their needs, incomes, aspirations—and so telling something about how much house, utilities, and landscape will be needed and how much outside organizational help will be needed to get things going and keep them going.

The capacity for change, transformation, and flexibility of use will be designed into each parcel based on consideration for dimensions, design reserve, the kind of materials and elements used, and the kind of technologies that can be easily appropriated. Each parcel as it is deployed will undergo a series of transformations to cater to site conditions and to existing families and clusters of families, to disrupt them as little as possible, and to cater to

(Text continues on page 96.)

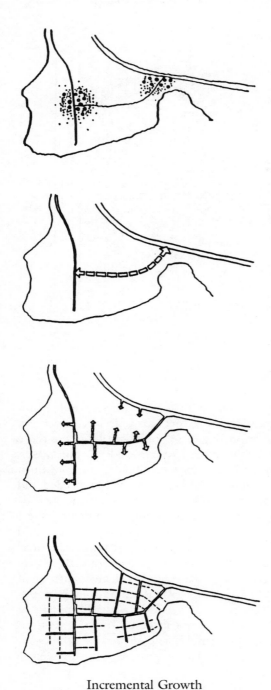

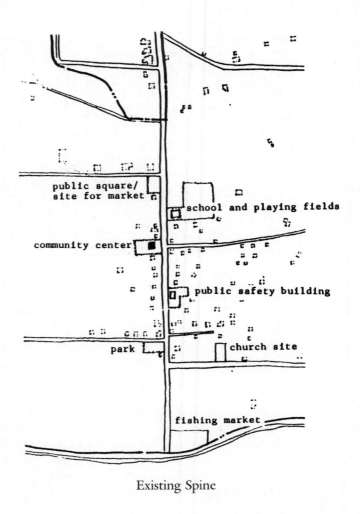

Existing Spine

94   Incremental Growth

Site consolidates based on incremental and phased development. Services, utilities, and land titles follow rather than precede development. *(From a studio project by John Englund, Sara Siff, and Andrew Slettebak, MIT, 1986)*

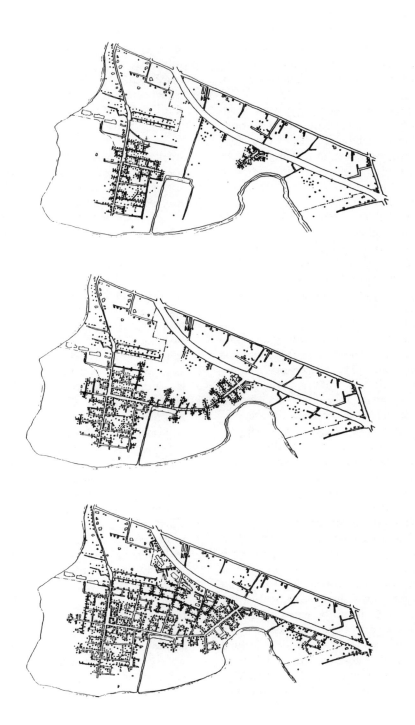

future adaptations. In some cases, these transformations may demand that the very principles that have ordered the model may need to be changed or even invalidated.

The theme may be interrupted with non-thematic models to cater to specific site conditions or to large buildings, such as schools or churches. Each parcel is carefully designated for effective land utilization and to encourage easy administration and maintenance. Responsibilities will be unambiguously designated either at the beginning or early on during habitation. Some useful comparative land use percentages and other design indexes can be looked up in the *Urbanization Primer* (Caminos and Goethert 1978) telling that there is a relationship between site area and desired lot area, expressed in relative percentages of private, semiprivate, public, and semipublic land.

Lots are sized to satisfy the demands of individual families, to meet broader community and government objectives, and to support the economic activities of households. Their size and arrangement, like all other elements of the plan, will be based as much on criteria that are technically rational (anticipated densities, anticipated use, expected dwelling type) as on those that are opportunistic and referential (location in the block, orientation, and frontage to allow subletting or easy access to backs in case of future additions).

Two types of circulation discipline its arrangement: through circulation, which links parcels (public), and circulation within parcels to gain access to individual lots (semiprivate), which for all intents and purposes is provided on a parcel-by-parcel basis. Access and circulation within each parcel is arranged in dog-leg fashion. The parcel can become a cluster with through access either visually or physically blocked, or it can be weaved into the fabric of the whole, a part of the larger network of streets and pathways. None of this will be decided until the site is settled. These parcels are relatively standard in size and geometry to facilitate surveying, pegging out, and the laying of utility lines but

later will not be uniform in terms of function or subdivision. Later they will be interconnected and combined as needs demand, as pathways are established and others blocked, as people inhabit the site.

Each parcel can be combined with others to make larger parcels, or subdivided further to make smaller ones with lots for rent or sale. Diversity of lot sizes and transformation of use emerge as a result of the actions of people and groups of people, because of personal ambition, aspiration, or wealth, or when social coalitions form and not because of ad hoc planning or architectural cliches or simply on the basis of pricing and affordability. The site will become denser as it consolidates in time, as people speculate with land, as they are joined by family members, as families expand, and as they turn land into capital. "In countries in which all forms of monetary savings are subject to the ravages of inflation, land may be the soundest form of investment (a principle likely to be as well-known to the poor as to the rich). For many families, therefore, the lot is not only the site of shelter, but it is primary insurance against any economic disasters the future might bring" (Peattie 1982, 131).

Usually governments go to great length and great expense to prevent subletting, doing business from home, or speculating with land with short lease holds, zoning laws, and even with identity cards that are periodically checked to ensure the original family remains in residence. The turnover of houses and land to the better off is quite common and, more, a measure of the success of projects.

In deciding both size and arrangement of parcels, we want to avoid discussions about optimums based on statistical averages of family size, social groupings, needs, habits, and incomes, which in this context will be difficult to establish and certainly difficult to control. Instead each parcel can be studied in terms of its capacity to accommodate a wide variety of lot sizes, the relative differentials in land values implied by size and location, the overall size densities that can be achieved, the way it might be serviced with utilities so that later individual connections can be made more easily, and the different ways one can circulate through and within it. Others can study its size and arrangement vis-à-vis tenure—as cooperative land trusts, land banks, or condominiums—and explore ways in which the community can build equity or income. Some of these options can be studied in terms of their trade-offs—the risks, commitments, and investments entailed, their advantages and disadvantages—so that we can distinguish what matters and what does not and where governmental help is most needed.

Will it matter, for example, if circulation is blocked, isolating one parcel from another as a cluster? Will it matter if some lots are combined and given over to cooperative ownership as common land? Will it matter if people rent, sell out, or build with temporary materials or extend into public land or if initial densities are exceeded? If it does, and we might want to know why and to whom it matters, it will need to be controlled formally, administratively, and legally. If it does not (and usually it does not), then it can be left to the free play of social and cultural conventions or even to market forces once the site is settled, self-determined by individual families, groups of families, or self-builders, and special interest groups. In this case, we may want to redesign or even dismantle legal frameworks that stand in the way.

If houses do need to be provided, and some will for the elderly and handicapped, then starter homes can be built with the same level of consideration for indeterminate usages, governed by choice of materials and by careful location on the lot to enable simple and easy extension and additions. Its location might leave enough space to the front, back, or side for an additional room. Its roof can be pitched to give more than minimum headroom at the front and back so that additions can be made with limited disturbance to the roof structure. Similarly, its sectional properties can enable a small loft to be added internally and even the rafters at the ridge to be extended to provide more space and light to a second

floor room. Structural columns or walls, dormers, windows, and front and back entrances can be positioned or indicated to allow multiple opportunities for internal division and subdivision according to intended uses and changing needs.

As people settle and houses are built, all of these simple, inexpensive gestures invite the participation of the community, who through a series of improvised and incremental transformations will give shape and meaning to what is otherwise an abstraction of place. For example, at the place of intersection between the existing road and spine road, the intensity of light will attract children to play and do their homework together in the evenings. It is unlikely that they will have electricity in their houses, at least to start with. Where children gather, so will informal vendors, who will wheel their candy and soda carts to sell their wares. Where buses stop, people will gather, sometimes for substantial periods of time, and so small shops and coffee houses will open up to serve them. Those same people will carry their goods to the city markets and will spread a sheet on the ground during their wait to sell to passersby. A marketplace emerges cheaply, spontaneously, incrementally, and in response to demand. No one "designed" the marketplace; no one contrived a "center." Instead the conditions for trading were informally structured so that if it wanted to happen, it could, and if it did not, no one would suffer.

As the site consolidates, various manufacturing industries will emerge for making cement and metal window grills, water storage tanks, and furniture. These manufacturers will not only get their raw materials (cement, plastic pipes, faucets) from formal markets but will also supply them (nails, water tanks, windows, doors). Linkages are therefore established between formal and informal systems of production, and systems of production, purchasing, and supply emerge that link local markets with urban ones. The multiplicity of large outlets, small manufacturers, and even pavement sellers offers variety in quality and price and therefore much

POSITION OF STRUCTURE AND SERVICES
PRINCIPLE FEATURES

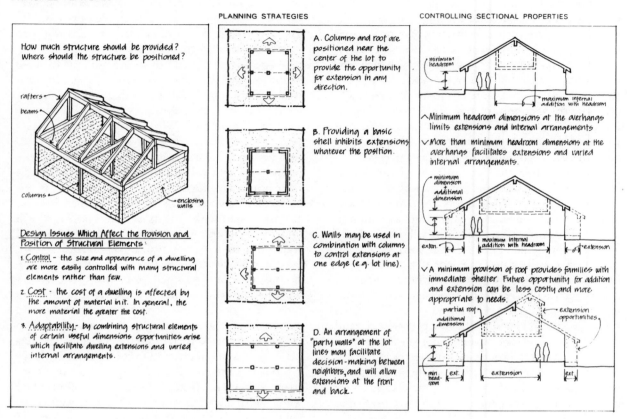

Design criteria that enable simple adaptive usages.
(Drawings by Brad Edgerly)

needed flexibility to local builders and families. Others will emerge who will recycle materials scavenged from building sites to use as temporary building materials. No one need decide whether standards of materials should be lower or higher or permanent or temporary.

All of these activities "stimulate productivity and employment in exactly the sector where these are most needed," and often they challenge conventional wisdom. Buying in bulk, for example, a legitimate form of government intervention to hold down prices of essential building materials, can disrupt local markets and wind up raising rather than reducing costs to families and small builders. "Larger producers of, say, construction materials, often use imported technologies and make products

UNIT LOCATION ON LOT
PRINCIPLE FEATURES

The position of the dwelling on the lot may either encourage or inhibit dwelling options. Assuming a dwelling lot is developed incrementally, the open space which exists initially will become partially or totally built. Care should be taken to locate the dwelling in such a way so as to create useful dimensions for the dwellings growth. The location of open space in relation to the initial dwelling and adjoining lots and roads is also a critical consideration in determining the type of building expansion that may develope.

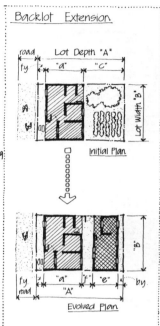

Backlot Extension

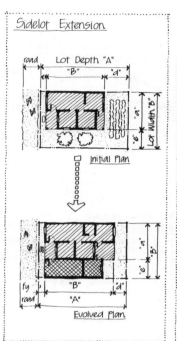

Sidelot Extension

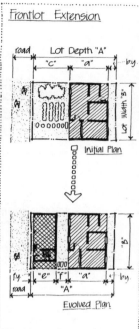

Frontlot Extension

adapted to modern sector construction, whereas cheaper grades might be perfectly suitable for low-rise residential purposes. Moreover, their more centralized locations may lead to transportation costs which offset production efficiencies. Local groups, operating through their own contacts, and with high incentives to economize, can frequently make better deals—for the exact materials they want—than public bulk buying" (Peattie 1982, 138).

Later various community organizations and groups of households emerge to buy into utilities—connections to sewers, mainline water, and electricity lines—and to appropriate services for street paving, garbage collection, and firefighting, for example. These opportunities will be facilitated by governments through programs of variable servicing packages, small loans and other assistance programs, and deregulation of standards.

Much of the construction activity itself will stimulate productivity and employment locally among groups of construction workers who will shelter under tents and move to where the work is. While this is a reality for the developing countries, it is also a metaphor for reality in all major cities of the United States and Europe.

Most sites and most dwellings constructed on them will be mixed use in function for commerce, manufacture, rental accommodations as small nursery schools, and dwelling and will serve more as productive infrastructure than as consumptive shel-

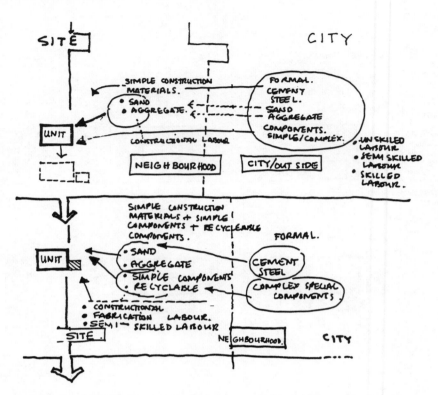

Building materials for construction are acquired from both formal and informal market sectors. *(Source: Soloman J. Benjamin)*

ter. Some people who will want to take advantage of existing walls or manholes for connections will negotiate usage fees with neighbors, as will temporary traders who may connect their canopies to private structures along the spine road.

Central government support will be crucial if these processes are to be considered mainstream rather than peripheral and an integral part of the project. Their interventions might typically include supplementary programs to generate employment and income, which for households help create opportunities for entrepreneurship. For the larger site

community, they might help create partnerships for cooperation and build skills and opportunities for production, services, and marketing. In all these respects, one might want to know who is already doing what, how existing small businesses got started, what is stopping people from getting started, and what skills might be underutilized (Rolfe, Rolfe, and Harper 1987).

It would be useful to know what natural resources are at hand, what is not being done that could be profitable, and what is that is not. What can the market in a broader urban context tolerate?

(Drawings by Orland Mingo)

Wanatahmulla in Colombo, Sri Lanka.

(Photo by Reinhard Goethert)

Construction is usually by families, small builders, or co-operatives, channeling funds back into the economy of low-income communities.

What equipment, working capital, or start-up cash is needed? What about staff and transportation? And before any formal intervention is actually embarked upon, one will need to understand the social and cultural practice regarding work in each of the different ethnic groups, how they organize, and their attitudes to cooperation.

What is getting in the way of people starting up businesses, building houses, finding jobs, getting their children to school, obtaining proper health care, and so on? Do local regulations impose restrictive taxes on employment conditions? Do building permits still take four months to approve? Are there restrictions on landownership, the use of common land, trading, renting, keeping animals, and so on?

On this basis, some initiatives may be contemplated that will have a direct bearing on the physical layout. Rather than direct financial or technical assistance to households, for example, cash may better be invested for broader developmental gains: proper drainage to encourage small gardens, retaining walls to prevent soil erosion, or a local plant for making bricks to discourage timber construction, which has been progressively deforesting fragile and sparsely forested hinterlands. In addition, a number of income-adding starters or small grants or loans to start projects like vegetable gardening or the manufacture of building components will influence the proper sizing of lots, the amount of communal land, the location of wells or standpipes, and the amount of electricity at least initially.

Finally, some of these activities will demand some measure of training to ensure the sustainability of the program. This may include vocational training in product manufacture, for example, or in bookkeeping or other services, such as drivers, teachers, or health workers. Some of these areas will have been sorted out during the program-building phase; most will be introduced progressively as the need arises. Careful monitoring will therefore feature in all project work. The conventional completion schedule of projects will be irrelevant, displaced by a program that will take years to consolidate.

DESIGN THINKING

What are the essential ingredients of this simple example? What implications does it hold for design in the context of enablement?

First, we see the importance of a plan that is at once technically competent and yet reliant as much on art and politics in conception and discipline. We see a very high level of indeterminacy in the plan, something conceived of as starting the process of habitation and not ending it. We can see the result of a process that avoids preemptive answers to commerce, housing, standards, and employment, none of which can be modeled in strict planning terms. Instead we seek to understand systems, networks, people, place, politics, and resources, which naturally produce the built environment and may need support.

We see a plan that in the end is based on inputs or interventions of physical and nonphysical components, and not outcomes or solutions. We see housing used for income-generating activities to the extent that sometimes there are more lots for commerce and manufacture than for dwelling. We see opportunities for a maximum range of house and lot sizes, all growing at different rates, and for the appropriation of materials, technologies, services, and utilities that match incomes, expectation, and priorities, all of them changing. We foresee the opportunity to turn land into capital, to speculate and build wealth, which more often for the poor is invested back into productive rather than consumptive sectors of the economy. We see housing as one link in a much larger neighborhood system of employment, income, health, manufacturing, training, child care and so on.

Later, we will see that the program has a pedagogic purpose as well: to teach others in principles of project and program design and development and expand the scale of local operations.

In all of these respects, the concept of enablement expands the definition of housing beyond the design and production of houses and places most professional activities, including design, in a technical, political, and social setting. And yet we see a tendency in favor of limited professional intervention because we have learned to reconcile what at first seemed to be conflicting and unreconcilable public demands for "more governmental services but less government," more professional support services but less professional dominance, more management services but less management of people, and more housing but less direct construction by public authorities.

Second, we see in the example illustrated, albeit implicitly, a way of working that does not rely for its efficiency on certainties or complete information. That means we cannot rely on the usual design program with its typically normative standards, styled most often for the expediency of management and production of large-scale systems, or on accurate surveys or site plans. Nor can we rely on the usual means by which these programs are devised—the kind of ethnographic and reductionist surveys that tell, for example, that people in India need 810 mm for polishing shoes, 1014 mm for dressing babies, or 1500 mm for telling stories, nor, in countries where most vehicles for transportation are made or adapted informally, can you guarantee that a horse and cart will always be 4500 mm wide.

The result resembles a planned land invasion with significant reversals in procedure to conventional practice. Cost recovery, community development, land registration, and even the bulk of infrastructure installation among many other usually preliminary planning steps are all done after rather than before settlement.

While we do need a good understanding of how and why things work, we want to avoid the rational, comprehensive world that demands "intellectual capacities and sources of information," as well as the kind of political goodwill, social stability, and skilled personnel that are rarely available in the field and consume months, and sometimes years, of planning. Our plan, and its underlying strategies, avoids rationalizing or aggregating the productively

disparate building process systematically into construction schedules, flowcharts, zoning diagrams, and critical paths that would demand the kind of expertise that in turn would displace marginal entrepreneurs in favor of project officials, businessmen, and contractors (drawn usually from the middle class and sometimes from foreign countries) (Peattie 1982).

Instead, as the example demonstrates, we see ample opportunity for each decision or action to tell us something about subsequent actions, which may induce a change of mind, a change in direction, or even a change in objectives. We want to set objectives and later decide interventions step by step with careful attention to existing physical, social, and economic patterns and conditions, building respect for and understanding of the fragility and resilience of place and for what people do and know how to do best.

Three ideas are crucial in this respect and for enablement planning in general help build on local capabilities and offer a way of tapping the ingenuity of ordinary people and community organizations: spontaneity, improvisation, and incrementalism. Spontaneity is vital because most problems and opportunities appear and change in fairly random fashion and need to be dealt with or taken advantage of accordingly. Sometimes problems appear all at once and not according to predictable patterns. One therefore has to be selective, knowing that once one problem has been dealt with another will appear equally randomly. When you have run out of resources but not out of problems, you improvise—inventing rules, tasks, and techniques as you proceed. Improvisations then become a means of devising solutions to solve problems, a process full of inventive surprises that characterize the informal way in which many poor people gain employment, make money, and build houses. The third idea is incrementalism. Most settlements grow, consolidate, change, and even disappear in a series of increments. Small businesses grow in a similar way, as do houses and communities. The question is to what extent these changes are inhibited or supported. And having answered that question, what kind of interventions are appropriate at the various developmental stages?

In the third place, there is the pedagogic agenda to use the occasion for training activities and to monitor the program as a resource for subsequent initiatives. The importance of this component of program development is currently reflected in international urban development policy. The World Bank's Economic Development Institute has recently increased its training activities and has embarked on a number of what it calls new initiatives: moving training courses out of Washington and into the countries, dealing with regional rather than national training centers, and focusing activities on training trainers.[2] All of these initiatives were due in part to the conclusion that "the establishment of a training institution in a specific country will be of greater importance than the provision of an additional 500 plots in that country" (Cohen 1983, 21).

One of the growing functions of the U.N. Habitat in Nairobi is to develop training materials and programs. In-country development banks and housing agencies (the Banco Ecuatoriania in Ecuador, for example, HUDCO in India, and BMICH in Sri Lanka) are also busy with new training curricula in various fields of shelter and urban management. The production of training materials has become big business in international development activities, as has the function of training in universities. In most European countries and in the United States and Canada, training programs in urban development are a growth industry. The resource pages of *Urban Edge,* for example, show the plethora of services and training programs offered by public agencies, private consultants, and universities.

---

2. See Huge training needs prompt strategic shift, *Urban Edge* 13(3) (April 1989).

This emphasis on training has unquestionably shifted the means of achieving ends but not so much the ends themselves. After all, we still need planning and design, management and coordination, information systems, and contract drawings, and we still need, in the end, houses, neighborhoods, and cities. What is different is the way we arrive at these ends—the people and organizations involved and the kind of social and political institutions set in place to deliver and manage housing, goods, services, and resources.

DESIGNING

Finally, what of the design process itself? Contrary to advocates of design participation, the plan is put together by architects, planners, and engineers and presented to the community for validation. These consultations might seem to feature rather low on Sherry Arnstein's ladder of citizen participation except that, in this case, what is presented are the ground rules or thematic principles developed locally and with all participants that later will be freely interpreted by the community. The plan is a technical representation of decisions made earlier through on-site program building workshops, which are an integral part of enablement planning and which most people were happy to leave to the experts.

No one, in any case, was interested in precisely where the spine road or bus stops were located, how the school or community center would be built, how the utility lines would run, or even in the design of houses. Instead they were keen to learn about and to control the implications of what was proposed on their individual and collective well-being: who would have to move, what they would have to do, how much they would have to pay, whether it would mean more jobs, and so forth. Will they be better or worse off after the fact? Involving people in decisions about matters they do not care much about, or do not want to know about is a waste of time and counterproductive.

Our first design responses will have been quite intuitive, diagrammatic, and inductive. They will have begun with a fairly theoretical stab at satisfying a whole set of objectives worked out with the various vested interest groups in a series of intensely participatory workshops. They will be laden with all the values and some of the prejudices of the design team, despite the community participation.

At first, we will have considered various ways in which community and government objectives could be met—the different ways of making a community center, meeting density requirements, planning the lots, or extending the school. These first considerations are based on how we think things fit; on experience of pushing these kinds of projects through the various approval processes; on how many people are likely to block it; on whether it feels right, seems reasonable, and looks convincing; on how likely we think we may succeed based on the implicit trade-offs that may be made of money, time, looks, or any other values we or other actors will hold or criteria that will come to mind.

Later, we will model our first intuitive responses with principles drawn from experience based on how we saw things worked elsewhere but which we know have to be reasoned with facts gathered locally that validate these principles. As much as we need intuition, in other words, we also need precision. Or as the artist Paul Klee once put it in describing his own work, we need "exactitude, winged by intuition."[3]

There will have been things we wanted to do *irrespective* of the site and shaped by our general knowledge of how we think things should work, by broader governmental and political agendas, and by the agendas of the funding clients. Then there will be other things we will need to do *because* of the site and community and shaped by an understanding of feasibility. One may therefore sketch about a

bit with the implicit desire to connect what one would like to do with what we need to do, and then both with what might actually be possible.

This is a cyclical process of inductive and deductive work that attempts to connect general principles, theories, and demands with the real world in which they will be practiced. It is by necessity inductive because we need to find good ideas or some vision of the future we intend to model, and it is necessarily deductive because we need to find good evidence that will help order ideas in ways that are locally specific and therefore practicable. As we have seen in history, people with lots of data but with few ideas wind up modeling the world according to some statistical average that is not accurate generally or locally and that is a poor reflection of urban and cultural systems. Conversely, those with lots of ideas but little data leave us with the kind of utopian visions that so far have been troublesome in practice. Ironically, both disconnect us from actuality because both are vague and incomplete. It is ironic that the field intellectually in this respect remains divided. In one camp are the empiricists with their view that "experience is the only source of knowledge," and in the other are the rationalists arguing that "reason alone rather than authority or spiritual revelation, or intuition, or sense data is the valid basis for knowledge, belief and action" (Petrossian 1985, 17).

In design, we need both experience and reason; local knowledge and general knowledge; intuition, art, and love; structure; empathy; and a lot of common sense. Like a collage, each step is pieced together in small increments; each move leads to subsequent moves guided politically and artistically but without any precise knowledge of where it might end. We do have objectives, but so far they have no form. As designing proceeds, it discovers its own ends, its own meaning, its own program of intentions, and its own order. Later we will reflect on what we have done to rationalize the intentions, images, and symbols embodied in the plan into something that makes sense to others and will even

---

3. Quoted from an introduction to the Paul Klee exhibition at the Museum of Modern Art, New York.

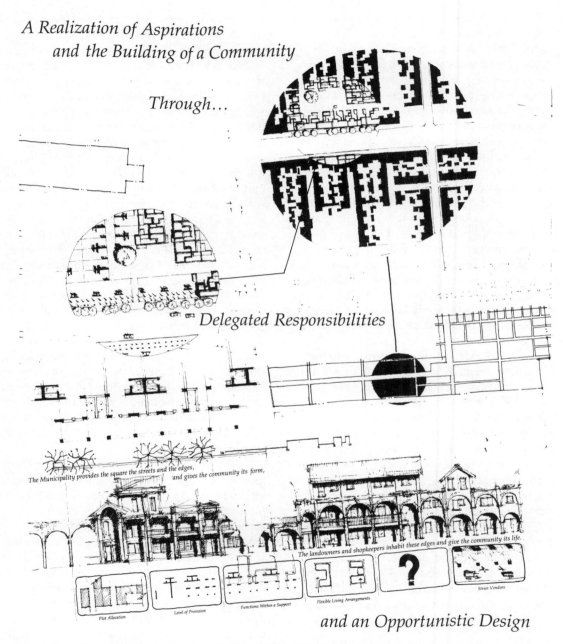

*A Realization of Aspirations
and the Building of a Community*

Through...

Delegated Responsibilities

The Municipality provides the square the streets and the edges,

and gives the community its form,

The landowners and shopkeepers inhabit these edges and give the community its life.

Plot Allocation

Level of Provision

Functions Within a Support

Flexible Living Arrangements

Street Vendors

and an Opportunistic Design

Design and enablement: how much structure, where does it go, and who decides? *(From a studio project by Paul R. Ries, MIT, 1986)* be useful and helpful. We may consider the conventions implicit in what has been done from what we have seen and heard from looking and listening as a part of the larger ordering framework—conventions that tell as much about community, privacy, and social and physical hierarchies as about fetching water, preparing food, and building houses. A number of themes emerge, which "once they are recognized can be used deliberately to foster teamwork and cooperation in the design process" (Habraken 1983, 6), to cultivate a participatory program.

This kind of design activity does not necessarily produce an architecture that makes its dominant impact through buildings. Nor does it produce the conventional master plan with its colorful designation of functions, circulation, and so on. "It will not seek to designate a desired 'end-state' for the simple reason that there is none, and it will not be based on zoning regulations and density standards, since the aim is to create conditions and not to impose restrictions" (Global Report 1987, 196). Rather it is an architecture of possibilities with very little that needs tight formal modeling. Most of the layout and its organization are loosely annotated with light, shade, trees, with walls, with some buildings, with geometry, with utilities, and with differential land values.

The plan is not a "sacred prototype" to be tested in its compliance with preordained rules. Nor is the design process concerned with problem solving, in the sense that a solution is expected to emerge at the end. Rather, the plan in its structure is an expression of creative opportunities, and more conventionally, a means of communication between designers, producers, policy makers, and communities.[4]

---

4. Alexander Tzonis in his book *Toward a Non-Oppressive Environment* (1972, Boston: i press incorporated, p. 101) suggests: "The making of a design product, for pre-rational man, had only two meanings: the exercise of creative potential through structuring (i.e., designing in its most fundamental sense), and the possibility this activity gave him of communicating with his fellow man."

The plan and the design process function to mediate between the demands of public authority and those of private informal organizations and individuals, between the demands of city systems and those of smaller settlements, between enough structure to provide effective overall physical organization and enough infill to make that structure habitable. The organization is constantly creating linkages between physical interventions and economic and social benefits.

As the U.N. Global Report on Human Settlements (1987, 196) put it, "Enabling settlement strategies must contain a response to two main challenges: how to deal with problems posed by very large numbers of poor people, and how to provide for effective autonomy of community-based groups. It will be impossible to find answers to the first challenge without the adoption of a settlement-wide approach, while the second challenge can only be met at the local level. Enabling settlement strategies must therefore fuse settlement-wide action with local initiative."

Our example, with its overall grid of roads, pathways, parcels and lots, disciplined thematically in position, size, proportion, and profiles of its physical and spatial parts, represents "a minimum of organization that would serve the benefits of planning, while leaving individuals the greatest possible control over their own lives." It is pluralist in nature; it aims "to sustain as many particularities (and interpretations) as possible, in the hope that most people will accept, discover, or devise one that fits" (Berger and Neuhaus 1977, 44). Far from being abstract design, the choice and organization of elements on the site go beyond the technically rational and take on characteristics that are in addition opportunistic and referential. They do not get in the way of ordinary people who are proficiently skilled at finding locally rational ways to inhabit the site and make it meaningful, comfortable, and profitable. The plan with its rules, opportunities, constraints, culture, and people serves legibly as a chessboard might to a chess player. As Habraken put it,

"The basic exercise gives us the ingredients of a design attitude. We see in the form at hand the moves available to us. We enter into a dialogue with the form. Our freedom is in choosing the next move, our skill is in choosing what leads us in the general direction we must take to satisfy a demand or a strategy; our knowledge and experience lie in being able to find many alternative moves. The result of such a humble beginning, if the process is continued, can be very complex and very rich" (Habraken 1983, 4).

REFERENCES

Berger, Peter L., and Neuhaus, Richard John. 1977. *To Empower People—The Role of Mediating Structures in Public Policy*. Washington, D.C.: American Enterprise Institute for Public Policy Research.

Caminos, Haracio, and Goethert, Reinhard. 1978. *Urbanization Primer*. Cambridge, Mass.: MIT Press.

Cohen, Michael A. 1983. The challenge of replicability—Towards a new paradigm for urban shelter in developing countries. *Open House International* 8(4):15–21.

Global Report on Human Settlements. 1987. Oxford: Oxford University Press for the United Nations Centre for Human Settlements (HABITAT)

Habraken, John N. 1983. The control of complexity. *Places* 4(2):3–18.

July report. 1985. *Architecture and Competition*. Special issue.

Lambert, Irina. 1985. Methods for the Turning Point. *Architecture and Competitions*. Special issue.

Peattie, Lisa R. 1982. Some second thoughts on sites and services. *Habitat International*. 6(1–2):131–39.

Petrossian, Robert Boghos Pour. 1985. Intelligent Computer Aided Teaching Systems for Structural Engineering. Master's thesis, MIT.

Rolfe, Chris; Rolfe, Clare; and Harper, Malcolm. 1987. *Refugee Enterprises: It Can Be Done*. London: Intermediate Technology Publications.

CHAPTER 7

Looking, Listening, and Measuring

I see what I see very clearly, but I don't know what I'm looking at.

V. S. Naipaul, *The Enigma of Arrival*

How was the plan described in the previous chapter put together? The process is best illustrated by an example that is set in a developing country, although it holds many lessons for the developed world.

The first objective is to be well enough informed about people, politics, and place to get started, keeping in mind that information is scarce and ambiguous. Our task is to establish a frame of reference for design work based on principles that are practicable locally and recognizing that most information has costs, so the more that is spent on knowing, the less there may be to spend on doing. Each vignette in this chapter contains information about the site and illustrates important principles of design and planning as processes of enablement.

The context is Sri Lanka, a small, poor country that nevertheless has a high literacy rate, a low mortality rate, and a zero rate of urbanization. It has a well-established and well-developed welfare system that reaches out into the smallest villages. Sweeping land reforms initiated between 1972 and 1976 enabled nearly 1 million acres to be placed in public ownership, which later enabled the National Housing Development Authority (NHDA) substantial flexibility and control of development. In addition, the ceiling on the housing property law of 1973 transferred some 12,347 properties, or 71.6 percent of all tenements to state ownership.[1]

Immediately prior to 1982, Sri Lanka was very much a provider. Its 100,000 Housing Program (to deliver 100,000 houses to the villages) launched in

---

1. Most of my data are drawn from Housing mainstreams—A case study in learning, unpublished paper prepared by Susil Sirivardana for the National Housing Development Authority of Sri Lanka (n.d.). For further reading, see Disa Weerapana, The evolution of a support policy for shelter—The experience of Sri Lanka, *HABITAT International* 10(3) (1986) (a clear and succinct presentation of how the MHP policy was developed.) Also see Susil Sirivardana, Reflections on the implementation of the MHP, *HABITAT International* 10(3) (1986) (an overview of implementation written in September 1985 that documents the pilot phase during 1983–1984).

1978, and which was to consume some 12 percent of total public sector investment from 1979 to 1983, did include a substantial amount of direct construction (36,000 units), albeit with a large share of aided self-help (50,000 units). Its NHDA was set up in 1979 to deliver lots of subsidized houses and to coordinate the national effort. Policies shifted considerably with the election in 1982, however, partly due to the pressure of party politics (the pledge of 1 million houses that the new government had made with only 3–4 percent to be allocated out of gross public expenditures would be difficult to achieve without a new paradigm) and partly due to the influence of international trends (notably influential funders and prestigious universities) but mostly due to a number of influential Sri Lankans who saw it both correct and expedient to shift substantially to support policies. These same people saw an opportunity to gain international visibility from their program and to endorse their national status in a wider intellectual and political community—all legitimate aims. A small country willing to experiment needs the cushion of international respect, and it needs to have its successes and mistakes, if and when they occur, legitimized in the interests of learning.

Sri Lanka did not invent the support paradigm. The country is significant in this context, however, because its objectives more or less follow those of supporters as I have defined them and because of its effort to translate a number of theoretical and somewhat abstract ideas into support policies.

Urban and rural development programs, for example, have shifted away from renewal and redevelopment and toward upgrading in both rural and urban areas. A housing options and loan package provides rural loans for a variety of construction investments—utilities, repair, extensions, and new core houses at interest rates of around 6 percent. Substantial decentralization to local district and village councils has occurred. A nationwide training program was launched to strengthen local traditional institutions and to organize, build, manage, and finance the various programs. These included thrift societies, village organizations, and community development councils.

Various tools have been developed to assist local organizations in planning, design, bookkeeping, and maintenance. These include the home owner file, which helped families control the construction and financing of improvements, as well as numerous guidebooks on how to build, organize, and manage.

The Sri Lankan program has avoided simplistic problem-solving techniques, recognizing the complexity of shelter as a system involving people, actions, intentions, and events. Sri Lankans recognized that their program, if it was to work as a support paradigm, had to strike a careful balance (always shifting from place to place and from time to time) between community needs and governmental objectives; between adequate off-site preparation and on-site development and implementation; between the need to know, to inform action, and the desire to act, to build knowledge, and experience. Most important, it is a housing authority staffed with people who are enthusiastic, if sometimes uncertain, about what they are doing.

KNOWING THE ACTORS

Let us assume an urban site in Sri Lanka, typical of any other in developing countries. The design process starts with a series of community design workshops located on site, first to elicit the interests, concerns, problems, and priorities of the various groups who have a vested interest in the site and subsequently to figure out how these interests will feature in the plan. We will want to know each of these actors insofar as the attitude they will hold toward any proposed project or program: will it be hostility, indifference, tolerance, sponsorship, or active promotion (Salas 1988). The success of the projects will depend significantly on how differences can be resolved and how much cooperation can be engineered among participants as a prelude to design. The principal actors typically are housers, municipal engineers, community builders, politicians, international funders, and dwellers.[2] While most are openly sympathetic with the government's new policies, most are skeptical and some suspicious. They are present to argue for maintaining the status quo.

The housers are the architects and housing authority technical and management staff, mainly interested in self-help housing, sites and services projects, urban upgrading, land management, and the improvement of services and utilities. They see these programs as a means to attract badly needed international funds, to increase land tenure security, and to direct more of people's savings toward building and improving their own houses.

The municipal engineers are primarily interested in public health. They see most infrastructure and upgrading programs as a means of removing serious health hazards through the provision of clean water, the collection of refuse and sewage, and increased public safety.

The community builders are mainly concerned with community organization and development. They see physical improvements as generating issues of common interest around which slum dwellers can organize effectively.

The politicians are mainly concerned with extending and consolidating their ability to govern and see housing and urban improvement programs, particularly of the support kind, as an effective way to assist the poor visibly without incurring vast public expenditures and without unnecessarily alienating the support of the middle class or the landowning groups on whose votes they count.

The international funders are primarily concerned with disbursing capital for development projects. They see housing and improvement pro-

grams as a means of providing international assistance that can reach the poor. For them, these programs are appealing because per capita expenditures are low, because they do not distract attention from rural development efforts, and because they can be justified economically as increasing property values in improved areas over and beyond the initial capital investment in infrastructure, which should, in their view, be recovered from the dwellers themselves.

Finally, the slum dwellers are primarily interested in not getting hurt by heavy-handed government intervention. They see whatever programs are offered as an effective means of getting something from the government, which is clearly better than nothing but which they know falls short of what they feel they deserve and know they should get.

GETTING ORGANIZED

The design workshop begins with some visits to neighboring settlements with as many of the principal actors as possible. Walking through the most recent squatter area, the most recent public housing project, and others that have been there for the last twenty years or so will tell much about how and why things work well and what things do not. It is an exercise in listening and understanding. It is therefore about learning, drawing on local references and precedents that may be useful in design. As Stretton (1978, 116) puts it:

For a quick test of a developing country's urban performance, do not ride from the airport by the motorway to the Central Planning Office to inspect the Regional Structure plan or the metropolitan strategy plan. Instead, find the newest shanty town outside the capital and see what, if anything, is keeping the sewage away from the drinking water. See if the layout of the shanty town would allow power and deep drainage, bus routes, local schools and services and solid housing and small workshops to be developed without bulldozing anyone. Then start walking towards whichever government office in the city centre should know whether sites and services and housing construction are getting two percent of the nation's recorded

2. I have paraphrased these accounts from S. Angel, Upgrading slum infrastructure, *Third World Planning Review* 5(1) (February 1983).

⑥ 2 SCHOOLS CLOSE BY - ¼ Mile (PRIMARY)
½ " (SECOND)
1 " (2 EVENTS. SECOND)

- SHOPPING AVAILABLE LOCALLY BUT
PREFERENCE TO GO TO GRANDPASS

- ENTERTAINMENT - SOME LOCALLY AVAILABLE
OTHERWISE G.P.

⑦ - LIKE SENSE OF COMMUNITY - WELL
ESTABLISHED TIES.
- LACK OF LIGHTS AT TOILETS
- LONG LINES AT PUBLIC FACILITIES/TAPS.
- NO PROPER GARBAGE COLLECTION/
DISPOSAL.
- PROBLEM OF DRAINAGE - PARTICULARLY WITH
ELEVATION OF NEW ROAD

Story gathering as a basis for understanding hidden structures.

(Photos by Reinhard Goethert)

economic activity, or ten, or what figure in between. By the time you get there you should know the answer well enough from what you have seen along the way.

Before going out, we prepare some simple guidelines. We ask: What are we looking for? What general categories will direct our inquiry? What issues, objectives, theories, and policies we may already hold, either implicitly or explicitly, do we want to inform or are we looking to validate? We sketch out a framework for our investigations on a large piece of paper and make checklists in our notebooks. We avoid questionnaires or the kind of systems analysis that we have learned usually fails to consider "much free or variable or unpredictable behavior, or once only historical events or willful changes of mind or anything that cannot be reliably measured or modelled" (Stretton 1978, 64).

But we do need some convenient way of making an inventory, some convenient categories. We could, for example, organize our inquiry under three categories: frame, fabric, and function. We could organize the documentation for each under two more general categories: features that are thematic and those that are not.

Throughout any town or settlement there will be themes that are observable and even measurable; they provide structure and continuity based on conventions, materials, technologies, and social habitat. The pattern of front streets, back streets and squares, for example, or the rhythm of doors, windows, stoops along a facade. There will be systems of rules that may be implicit and will find expression in the different ways people organize and use buildings, streets, squares, and parks. There will be differences in value attached to notions of public and private. There will be a nonthematic building or open space demanding its own system of rules—the church, the town hall, the marketplace, the school. It breaks with thematic rules, demanding its own presence and providing surprise, interest, and punctuation to the city's fabric. These traits are present equally in the informal settlements of developing countries as in the most historic cities of Europe.

Under *frame* we will ask what elements, built and unbuilt, social and economic, characterize people and place. We need to know which are the most recurrent and give the city its basic organizational discipline socially and physically: roads, pathways, houses, churches, public squares, front streets, back streets, in-between streets. How many children, old people, single-headed households, and unemployed are there? How much do people earn, and how do they earn it?

For *fabric*, we may consider how these pieces fit and work together. What linkages are strong and can be built on? What are weak and need to be strengthened? We look at linkages between houses and streets, streets and squares, public and private, backs and fronts, this neighborhood and others. Other linkages are those between quality of utilities and health, between how much they earn and how they build, what they produce and where they sell it.

For *function*, we want to know how these physical pieces are used, how people and cars move about, how trading takes place and where, who uses what, where people sit and work, where buses stop, where children play and go to school.

We might want to consider frame, fabric, and function at the settlement scale, at the scale of a typical block or cluster, and also the scale of the lot or house. The group of observers could be divided up in various ways to cover most ground: according to categories, according to scales, or according to those who will look, those who will talk, and those who will read. This last group will spend some time in city offices asking questions. What is the record on cost recovery? How much are people willing to spend on their housing or for utilities? What proportion of gross national product is invested in housing and infrastructure? Are there any figures demonstrating that self-help construction is cheaper than direct construction? Where are the nearest schools, clinics, and so on?

Some of this information will come from plans and some from public records. Most we can get from walking about—listening to stories people tell, reading newspaper articles and ads, and talking to public officials, bus drivers, nurses, children, people in ethnic minorities, the elderly, and others. We can count the number of people waiting at standpipes and spot the kerosene van or horse-drawn water tanker delivering fuel and water, the lines of illegal wires tapped to main supplies, and the donkey and cart carrying garbage to learn much about how utilities are delivered, how they work, and who, if anyone, is profiting. We can count the number of people urinating in back alleys as clues to how public latrines are working or count the number of people waiting at street corners to get a rough measure of the number of unemployed.

At first, these walkabouts are viewed with skepticism by the assembled group. "We've seen it all before," someone said. A one-day workshop can make the point, sensitize participants to the issue, and win confidence. It is a training session that the consultants feel is necessary before starting actual project work.

A small settlement was randomly selected for the exercises. During the first phase, participants, who were divided into two groups, attempted to identify problem areas, which would subsequently enable local technical officers to decide what to do. The first group was asked to represent the various professional and technical officers usually involved with upgrading and the second to represent the residents. Both groups were to undertake a preliminary survey of the settlement. The exercise was entitled "deciding what to look for." The professional group was instructed simply to observe, talking to no one and listing the issues and technical details that, according to their professional judgment, would merit funding or other forms of public intervention. The second group was instructed to talk to local villagers and observe the physical environment through the eyes of resident families.

Both groups then returned to report their findings. Predictably the professional group was primarily concerned with improving conditions to meet prescribed standards: improved accessibility to pedestrian paths; providing cement rendering to plinths to prevent erosion and reduce maintenance; adding windows to poorly lit and "inadequately ventilated" rooms, to name but a few. The resident group reported the infinitely less tidy (and therefore professionally unsettling) day-to-day and largely invisible issues that affect the quality of life, including broader community concerns: small decorative improvement in lieu of pending social events; easier access to health facilities; more employment opportunities; improved water supply for both irrigation and drinking. Both groups then proceeded to price their respective needs. Not surprisingly, the technical specifications of the professional group were significantly more costly than those of the residents. dents.

This vignette highlights a number of common and therefore generalizable issues. First, neither professional judgment nor resident opinions on their own provides an accurate or complete understanding of place. Second, the group did not find out things they either had not known or could have known without looking, talking, and being in the field. Third, people in impoverished areas rarely demand the unreasonable. To the contrary, it is the government and government officials who want more for their people than people want for themselves. Fourth, reaching consensus over problems and issues is not only socially expedient but can lead to less costly solutions. Finally, people may be more willing to pay for improvements that they have helped to identify as necessary rather than those gifted by governments.

LOOKING AND LISTENING

In the field we see along one alleyway flowers planted outside every house and carefully tended, and the street is kept immaculately clean. The street comes to a dead end. What we are looking at is a semi-private street shared by a community of about thirty small houses, with its own informally estab-

Water lines, Sudan.

Observation as a basis for under-standing systems.

Garbage collection, Egypt.

Garbage collection, Sri Lanka.

Dental services, Chile.

Kerosene fuel delivery, Egypt.

lished organization for cleaning and maintenance made easier by restricted public access. Around the corner is another cul-de-sac, but this time it is significantly wider—some 40 ft or so. We see lines of laundered clothes draped over makeshift fences or laid out to dry on the ground, women working over kerosene stoves, and small children playing. Outside one home, two men make furniture. We are looking at a cluster whose semi-private courtyard has been appropriated and used as an extension of house, like a large, multifamily compound. Rather than build their houses to the front limit of their lots, which could have offered small, individual restrictive back yards with the usual narrow alley at the front, families agreed to begin building at the back of their lots, each offering their fronts as part of the collective whole. Later they might extend to the limits of their lot boundary, but at present, their arrangement serves their individual and collective purpose well.

Walking back along the main street, we come across a dumpster piled high with garbage that clearly has not been emptied for some weeks. Some-one mutters the usual abuse at the city authorities for failing to provide regular pickups. Later we learn that what we were looking at was an assignment of dumpsters provided as a gift by a donor nation that was incompatible technically with the pickup trucks given by another nation. Children were largely responsible for carrying garbage to these collective dumps, and they were usually unable to lift their loads high enough above their shoulders and over the sides of the dumpster. In addition, we heard tales of an administration too poor to extend services to the informal and squatter settlements regularly and too poor to maintain their trucks, which were often immobilized for lack of spare parts. Administrators complained that numerous foreign consultants had visited and had concluded after extensive surveys that garbage collection and disposal was a serious issue, but no one had proposed any workable plan for dealing with it. In one case, plastic bags had been distributed to neighborhoods on a monthly basis, but people could see no logic in putting out such a valuable material with garbage. They preferred to use the bags instead as a

Land clearly designated in terms of responsibility.

Controllable semipublic land.

Uncontrolled public land. *(Photo by Reinhard Goethert)*

Simple structures can create a focal point.

roof material or floor covering or to store grain and animal foodstuffs. In some instances they cut holes for head and arms and used the bags as rainwear.

In another settlement, a small community center had been built with money from a local nongovernmental organization (NGO). It was the first step in a more comprehensive program for upgrading—a quick, cheap, and visible intervention while more complicated details of land regularization, street paving, and utilities were being worked out. It served as a meeting center for the community. A small nursery school had been started, as well as various skills training programs, including bricklaying and carpentry. It had served to create a focal point to an otherwise physically dispersed community. Most important, it provided legitimacy to a settlement that during its five years of existence had been considered illegitimate.

One activity seemed to dominate: a small soap-making industry set up by an international organization as part of its income-generating activities, this time directed at unemployed single mothers. Although a worthy cause in its own right, this industry was being heavily subsidized with foreign money and imported materials. What we were looking at was an industry whose products were distorting local prices for soap in the informal market and creating substantial resentment among local retailers, who were unable to compete in price and quality. In addition, it was doubtful that such an activity would be sustainable in the long term given its dependence on imported materials. Nevertheless, it was a visible project for the agency in charge—more visible than delivering small loans, tools, materials, and even technical assistance to the hundreds of small enterprises already in existence—people repairing bicycles, making aluminum sheets from soda cans, or shoe soles from old rubber tires, working as scribes, or operating coffee houses. Many of these people need credit and a market for those goods and services. But the agency, bent on soap making, could lay claim to starting something new and could

Infill shop, Scotland.

Shop stall in a public housing project, Egypt.

Shop stall on public land, Sri Lanka.

Shop stall selling pickles, Philippines.

Front rooms converted to workshops, Philippines.

Major streets and walkways afford commercial potential, often reflected in the value and size of adjacent properties.

locate this small industry centrally to impress international visitors or spend its budget in one easily manageable sum.

In the same settlement along one of the more densely used streets, we observe the usual plethora of small shops and trading establishments, cafes, and even video parlors. We were looking at people who were profiting from their convenient location, trading habitable space within their dwellings for commercial space. Some people talked of selling out when streets were paved and electricity had been supplied, to open up small businesses in more central areas of town. Others, in view of the likely restrictions that government was intending on the resale of land, would consolidate their houses and rent to newcomers, while they would join relatives in the adjoining squatter settlement.

This same street had been laid out by engineering standards and according to some master plan to a width suitable for vehicular traffic (some 2 percent of residents actually owned vehicles). Its width was provided with a generous setback, allowing, we were told, for the usual contingency of street widening in case of increased traffic. In addition, these setbacks also appeared to guarantee adequate levels of privacy between dwellings. And should buildings go up to three stories or more (few had done so even in the most consolidated settlements), the additional width would guarantee abundant light, sun, and air.

We paced the street and found it to be about 60 ft wide—precisely the same width used by many local authorities in England to safeguard privacy and light. Could a single number be suitable for cultures as diverse as England and Sri Lanka? These findings confirmed the suspicions of the antirationalists in the group—some housers, some community builders—who, as always and rightly were weary of the candid and colonizing way in which occidental standards, theories, technologies, and even morals are transferred across cultural boundaries with little or no thought to cultural differences.

Ironically residents were happy with the extra space provided by the setback standards. For them this was extra space in an already cramped settlement, and it functioned in all sorts of useful ways. Some houses had extended out to the boundary of this setback line. Others, at corners, had built adjacent structures and were renting them as shops or small dwellings. The additional width enabled temporary structures to be built—small kiosks for selling goods and services, small shelters for mechanics and bicycle repair workshops. Every Saturday an informal market appeared, occupied the entire street, and then disappeared. Some homeless families had built makeshift shelters and were squatting. Most of these activities were officially illegal, but so long as there were no local objections, the authority had decided not to interfere.

Later we went to the city's Town Planning Department to look for an explanation of standards—how and why they were set up and who they served. We dug up a memorandum dated July 1940, prepared by a British consultant hired to advise the government. In it he recommended housing standards for improving the slums that reflected attitudes held by the Victorian evangelists of England rather than the realities of Sri Lanka: the separation of sexes over ten years old, ventilated cupboards for storing food, piped water supply, and a lavatory for each house. He wrote that each house should be "kept in a proper sanitary condition and in a good state of repair and decorative condition." In the same memo, he offered recommendations to build satellite towns to provide new housing (still being built in many developing countries) modeled on his success in such towns as Aberdeen, Scotland. "The building of a satellite town has obvious advantages over piecemeal rebuilding," he suggested. "Following the example of Aberdeen, other cities, particularly Manchester and Liverpool had already begun similar schemes just before the war. I would urge the Colombo Council to consider the possibility of building such a satellite in the Colombo region" (Holliday 1940, 19–20).

In the same settlement, we come across a row of

houses that are not very well built but are painted all sorts of bright colors. The architects in the group become curiously animated and busy themselves taking pictures of what they believe are useful ethnographic references with which to color code their new project with claims, no doubt, of symbolic counterstructures. Actually a consignment of paint had fallen off a truck, and in the usual entrepreneurial way in which things happen, the paint had been acquired by one resident and sold cheaply to neighbors.

Around the corner, a long, monotonous street of largely single-story dwellings with flat facades is interrupted by one building set back about 5 ft behind the others, with a canopy projecting to the street. Someone in the group remarked how well this provides relief to what is otherwise a monotonous street facade. In fact, no one we talked to had ever thought the street facades were monotonous, and certainly the setback and canopy had little to do with relieving monotony. In fact, it provided valuable information about social habit, climate, and the function of the space covered. The building was a small clinic/dispensary. When we asked why the canopy was there, our informant told us that people who visit the dispensary bring their families, who wait outside while their kin are treated. They need shade and a place to sit while they wait. Unless this amenity was provided, people would go elsewhere, and the dispensary would lose money.

Brief discussions with one of the clinic nurses underscored the importance of an integrated approach to problem solving. Most of the complaints were associated with water-borne disease. Although standpipes had been provided by the municipality, people continued to collect water from a nearby canal of largely stagnant water, where there was also space for washing clothes, for bathing, and for children to play. The standpipes had been positioned along main roads, where none of these opportunities were available, and were in any case crowded by lines of people waiting to fill their buckets. At home, the water would become polluted from

standing in open containers and would be decanted for cooking and drinking with soiled containers. The residents could not afford the additional fuel to boil water before drinking, which would also entail the sort of household management and discipline that was unfamiliar. The nurse said that if the problem was to be solved, people needed to be informed about the hazard to health of unclean water and would need adequate space for storing water at home. What we were hearing was that water provision, storage, and training were mutually dependent parts of an effective clean water delivery program. Technical, social, and spatial considerations were necessarily part of the package.

A little farther along, two houses distinguish themselves from the others in contrasting ways. The first is falling down and seems to be poorly maintained. Our guide from the housing authority is critical of the occupants; he charged that they had not taken advantage of the government's cheap loans to upgrade their dwellings. In reality, what we were looking at had little or nothing to do with family's ignoring the program, about which, in any case, the family knew or cared little. They were recent arrivals and were renting from an absentee landlord. The other house had elaborate additions—balconies, carved balustrades, glass in windows, and a clay tiled roof. This family was pointed out as a good example of how effective the government program had been through its program of loans, craft training, and other incentives. In reality, the family had two daughters working in the Middle East as housemaids and sending money back to the family, who had become quite well off and could afford to pay a local builder for the renovations.

In one of the many coffee shops, one man told of the difficulties the settlement had been through to convince the authorities to extend postal deliveries to them. They wanted a postal service to reach into their shanties not because writing letters was common but because it was the best way of getting their food stamps and welfare vouchers. This in-

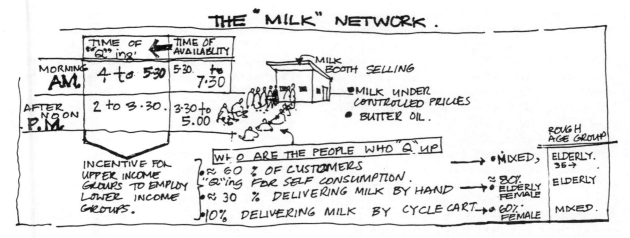

Stories tell how and why things work and who benefits.

(Source: Soloman J. Benjamin)

volved the postal service, an urban-scale organization with its own hierarchy of decision makers and its own standards. For letters to be delivered to each household, houses needed to be numbered, but numbering could be done only with legal title to each property or at least some other form of legitimacy for those who have settled the land. This involved a national organization, the National Housing Authority, which designates titles. But the authority needs to refer the matter higher up to the Ministry of Housing and Construction, to the body

politic itself. The ministry would need to decide whether giving title to squatters or shanty dwellers is politically expedient. Even if it is, titles cannot be given until the land is regularized and until property boundaries are made precise. That brought into play two additional parties: the local authority, whose task is to do such work, and the families, who may dispute boundary lines with their neighbors and therefore will demand some voice in how boundaries are set and how much land they have a stake to.

In his example, our informant illustrated how the simple business of delivering mail became an unwieldy entanglement of people and organizations from all levels of decision making, each of whom waited on the other before it could act, which took years to sort out. The technical issues could not have been simpler. We were learning that, any proposal would have a greater chance of success if the decision involved in its implementation could be contained within the same level of organization—in other words, the fewer decision makers, the quicker and easier it would be to move. In the end, our informant told us that a community-based postal drop was finally established—an obvious solution in hindsight that gives legitimacy to the existence of the shanty but avoids doing so, for the time being at least, to individual families, avoids regularizing land, and avoids numbering houses.

Later another man joined us, introducing himself as one of the community representatives appointed by the local authority to watch over a nearby upgrading project sponsored by an international agency. It took little prompting to get him to talk. He told of the agency's plans to establish a cooperative in his settlement to self-manage, build, and organize his community in ways that would enable them to participate in decision making. He recalled the man in charge, a foreigner, arguing his case in all sorts of ways: cooperatives create integrated communities, he said, not only for housing but for education and other facilities; they provide internal control to prevent speculation and illegal transfer of land and make collective financing and repayment simpler; they are a good way of mobilizing savings, providing collective maintenance, and accumulating experience that can be institutionalized locally and therefore more easily passed on to others. Our informant recalled being puzzled by the enthusiasms of the foreigner, who was arguing advantages of little interest to him or to his community. In the end the program failed because these forms of formal social organization were viewed by the residents as inspired by government and presumably therefore representing government interests, and so were not to be trusted. They were viewed as attempts to get people to participate in government initiatives from which, given past experience, few people saw much to be gained.

The main hub of the settlement in which we were sitting was a wide strip of public land that was once a canal, now filled, for which the city planners had all kinds of intentions. It was a place where buses and trucks stopped, where market stalls were set up, and where all kinds of small commercial and light industrial activities were going on—mechanics, metal workers, appliance repair shops, and the like. Set apart to one side was a curious, tired-looking concrete post and beam structure built some five years previously and looking like stables for horses. In fact, it was the beginning of a broader civic plan, a marketplace for rent as individual stalls. It had never been used because no one could see any purpose to paying rent, which would have to be reflected in the price of goods. And because it was removed from the major center of activity, people feared they would lose trade. In any case, the midday temperature within these stalls reached over 100°F and was far less comfortable than squatting out on the street.

Later, back at the city offices, the full plan was revealed. A colorful map of circles and arrows with patterns of green, grey, and red (all fading a bit) painted a world that was utterly in contrast to what we had observed. It was described according to some plan that views the world as discreet functional bits separated into tidy, manageable zones, to a backdrop of posters and photos of Chandigar, Brasilia, and Milton Keynes that draped the wall of the planning office. The terms used were abstractions of reality, picked up no doubt in planning school: "magnets" to attract circulation, "communication nodes" instead of "bus stops," "lines of pedestrian communication" instead of "walkways."

MEASURING

After a few days or so of looking, listening, and talking, we start measuring, turning our attention to lessons more detailed and more technical in nature. Our purpose is to draw up some general guidelines indicating alternative ways of overcoming the most common hurdles encountered before, during, and after project implementation and developing some indexes for infrastructure design and for land development as a basis for evaluating our proposals later. We do this first by locating on site within a project completed some five years previously and second by asking each group of participants to bring along their favorite project for evaluation and comparison. None of the assembled junior architects and technical officers had ever made an evaluation; this was usually left to foreign consultants and international agencies, serving to emphasize the divisions between doing and learning. None had read the boring project evaluation reports prepared by respective agencies, directed more often than not to the central office rather than to fieldworkers.

On site, a conventional sites-and-services project, we identify specific problems encountered, the symptoms that helped identify the problems, as well as possible causes (Table 2). Is the problem real, or is it only perceived as a problem by those who might not be knowledgeable about how and why things work the way they do? Once the causes are known, consideration can be given to alternative actions to take and to the implication of these actions before deciding the most suitable alternative.

During the two-day workshop, community members, NGOs, housing managers, and technical staff involved with the project report on successes and failures. The process of allocating lots—who should get the large ones, the front ones, the back ones—for example, had created tension among settlers, especially between those who were allotted the larger, and considerably more attractive, road-front lots and those on smaller back lots. The initial size differentials, of course, had been based largely on anticipated differential land values and on ensuring that the front lots would have the spatial capacity to house small workshops and other commercial activities. A more flexible arrangement with differentiation based on need and affordability rather than anticipated pricing would have worked better.

The requirement to complete construction within a three-month period—a demand placed by the authority as a condition of securing tenure and issuing loans—had strained some families. They were using hard-earned savings on materials and construction, which they did not want to do in view of other priorities for food, education, and business. They had been prevented from bringing with them their scrap materials and were required to build from permanent materials.

Some informal small builders had overpriced their work, others were building to unnecessarily high standards for foundations and superstructure, and others who had demanded payment up front had disappeared. The result was that money had run out, and some building had come to a standstill. The housing managers expressed the clear view that more supervision was needed; because residents were required to build in unfamiliar ways and to manage contractors, many would have preferred the authorities to build the houses.

The phasing of site construction was poorly planned; work completed out of sequence was being damaged by subsequent work. Drains, for example, were damaged by contractors' trucks, and already consolidated tertiary roads and pathways were dug up, the clay and gravel used for fill for individual houses. Communal garbage dumps were located alongside communal washing facilities, without any easy access to collection vehicles. Loans were too small to complete work but too large to pay back.

The arrangement of clusters had seemed to differentiate one class from another, one income grouping from another, one ethnic group from

Table 2
Coping with an Inadequate Water Supply

Possible Causes	Alternative Actions	Implications
Inadequate pressure Inadequate main supply or failure or lack of capacity of pumps. Sometimes informal connection to mains reduce pressure.	Reduce number of standpipe services	More crowding of remaining taps
	Increase pumping capacity	Longer walking distance
	Increase number of sources, or the storage capacity	Higher running costs, more maintenance
	Schedule water supply on a rotational basis, so not all standpipes are not serviced at once	Extra costs if extra storage needed
		Requires extra management
	Consider supplementary supply with carried water	May not prevent people from walking to quality checks, more difficult to control
	Increase capacity to store water on lots	Potential employment generation if people can carry out operation; may require increase in size of lot
		May lead to increased pollution of water in storage containers
		Requires extra storage containers
Poor maintenance Lack of staff or unclear designation of responsibilities; perhaps too public	Designate 1–2 persons in community to maintain standpipes	Raise issues of pay; perhaps offer land near standpipe as incentive
	Technical specifications may be difficult to maintain	Charge service fee for water to cover maintenance
		Expensive structural changes may be necessary
Theft of parts (faucets most commonly stolen)	Greater control, preferably locally	Locate standpipes in clear view of community
	Install improved standpipe that is more tamper proof	
Unanticipated density	Increase number of standpipes	Supply may not be sufficient to allow increase
	Increase capacity to store water on site or lot	May need to find additional source

Table 2 (*Continued*)

Possible Causes	Alternative Actions	Implications
	Encourage water to be carried in by residents	May find suitable location
		Increased cost, which can be high
		Increased difficulty in maintaining nonpolluted supply
		Can be used as employment generation

Source: R. Goethert and N. Hamdi. 1988. *Refugee Camps: A Primer for Rapid Site Planning,* pp. 158–159. Draft manual prepared for the United Nations High Commissioner for Refugees, Geneva.

Note: The symptoms were long lines at water points, use of polluted sources, and a high incidence of disease.

another. The arrangement had reinforced differences and had created unnecessary competition. It had served to inhibit free movement and had created a new hierarchical social order within the site.

The second set of exercises is quantitative. Some indexes drawn from a broad range of case studies are useful here, offering technical rationality and reflecting the performance of previous projects (Table 3). For each of the projects brought as cases, we measure land utilization percentages, circulation length area ratios, and density. We count the number of manholes and service connections, establish where the highest land values might be, and then look at where the greatest commercial activity has occurred. We attempt to correlate the relative percentages of public-private land to the burden on maintenance and administration.

These measurements are used to point out the importance of differentiating hierarchically between major lines of access and secondary lines of communication so that responsibilities for maintenance can be distinguished and standards for construction differentiated. It may be worth pointing out that

roads and pathways should be considered not only for their primary function of movement but also for recreation, commercial activity, and firebreaks. One might indicate that details of dimension and location will need to be considered: how large elements should be, how much or how many of each, where they should go, and who will maintain and control them. In all of these cases, benchmarks drawn from case studies may indicate desirable circulation length-area ratios of, say, between 150m/ha and 285, and land utilization percentages of between 20 and 25 of total site area.

Through these evaluations, one can point out, for example, that the percentage of land allocated to plots and that allocated to facilities and services is a vital indication of the future health of a development. Too much land for services increases maintenance costs and unduly limits the amount of land and the number of people to accommodate. To determine the percentages, we divide the total development into land that is used for circulation (streets, walkways) and open spaces (playgrounds, parks, and any leftover areas of unclear definition) and land that is allocated for the plots. (Experience

Table 3
Considerations in the Design and Evaluation of Projects

Main Features of Site	Land Utilization	Circulation Network	Blocks, Lots, Clusters	Lots	Utility Infrastructure	Community Facilities	Community Focus
Location context	Public land	Function	Size	Expected dwelling type	Communal versus individual	Schools	Coherence between elements
Approaches	Semipublic land	Width	Number of families	Expected uses	Individual	Community center	Reinforcement between elements
Topology	Semiprivate land	Surface	Dimensions	Position in site	What is provided	Health clinics	
Boundaries		Location	Legal covenants	Position in block	Location	Parks	Physical and legal tools
Hazards		Spacing		Area, width, length, proportion	Distance to use	Administration	
Legal restrictions		Hierarchy			Technical standards		
Easements, existing structures							

suggests that less than 50 percent of land for lots is a warning to reevaluate the layout).

Similarly, we point out that the layout pattern effectively fixes the cost of infrastructure and affects maintenance costs. To determine the ratio, we divide the total length of streets and walkways (in linear meters) by the total site area (in hectares). A ratio greater than 286 linear m/ha is a warning to reevaluate the layout. Density is useful in determining the amount of facilities and service required for a given population. Very high density can rapidly overload facilities and increase social pressures; very low densities imply a high per capita cost of land and services and are not cost effective. Precise values are difficult to determine and depend on the social and cultural situation. Approximately, we suggest that a gross density of 350 people per ha (600 p/ha net density) is an average value for a community, dependent on lot size and size of project, but values of 1000 people per ha (gross density = total people divided by total area) and above are not uncommon for some squatter settlements, or older residential city centers.

EXAMINING THE INFORMATION

By the time we get back to the drawing office, we will have a reasonable understanding of how and why things work the way they do and will have enough clues and hard data to prepare a plan. We will have at least a frame of reference on the basis of which to decide intervention to compare what we want to do with what is actually possible. We will have found out, for example, that low-income groups do pay for land and services—anything between 10 and 30 percent of their income—especially when they have had a voice in decisions affecting the design of services, costs, repayments, and tenure status. We will have come to understand that housing programs have to be designed according to effective user demand and not according to preconceived notions of adequate housing; that most self-built housing costs some 30 percent less than that built by private developers and some 60 percent lower than that built by the government; that the rate of cost recovery has been on the order of 58 percent over those projects with no community in-

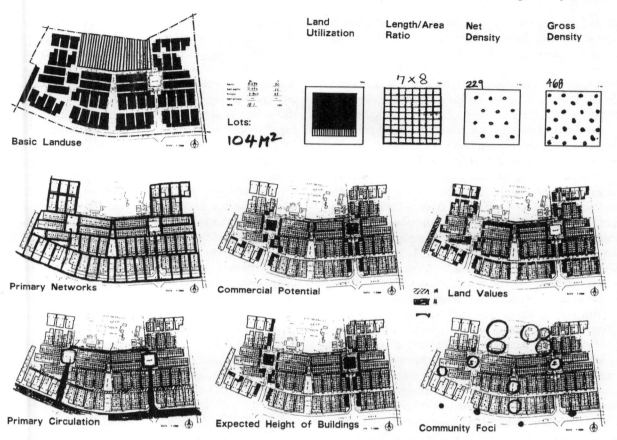

Land Utilization Length/Area Ratio Net Density Gross Density

7 × 8   229   468

Basic Landuse

Lots:

104 M²

Primary Networks

Commercial Potential

Land Values

Primary Circulation

Expected Height of Buildings

Community Foci

Learning from projects: Measuring plans and developing design indexes.

volvement and up to 95 percent where there was and where affordability and willingness to pay have featured prominently in government calculations; that the government spends somewhere between 2 and 7 percent of its budget on housing and urban services, well below what would be required to build completed houses or to provide infrastructure according to standards usually demanded by the engineering department in other parts of the city.

We will have noticed that a preponderance of land in public ownership—anything, say, over 30 percent of the total site—is difficult and expensive to maintain and usually, if designated as open space, winds up as a depository for garbage. It undermines the tax base of a neighborhood and ends up burdening everyone.

We will have seen a significant relationship between the location of residential lots and their potential for commercial use, sometimes reflected in the size of the lot itself and sometimes in the far quicker time it takes for these lots to be built up.

We will have confirmed John Turner's principle that what housing does is as important, if not more so, as what housing is, recognizing that houses improve health, generate money for their occupants, place them close to their source of employment, and can help develop building skills, which people can then market both formally and informally.

We will have come to understand that standards must be flexibly applied, that plans must be resilient to "free or variable or unpredictable behavior," that both physical and nonphysical components of design are intrinsically related, that people build at different rates, and that settlements take years to consolidate. We will have learned something of the resourcefulness of these settlements and will use these as starting points for design.

But we will know that all this knowledge and all these data and most of what we have observed will give us only a partial understanding of questions that will need answers, problems that will need definition, and conflict that will need to be resolved in answer to questions once design begins. How will land be allocated among families? What level of utilities will be provided? How many houses should be built? What categories of circulation will be provided, and where will they run? For all of these questions, we can foresee conflicts of interest, conflict of priority and taste, and conflicts among technical alternatives. "Inventive design can reconcile some of the conflicts, but never all of them. Good neighborhood plans have elements of exact surveying, engineering, forecasting, and cost, but they are also works of art, and politics—or at their best, perhaps, works of love and justice" (Stretton 1978, 81).

How can some of these conflicts be managed? How can interests be converged? How can problems be properly positioned so that a viable set of options for design, planning, and construction can be identified? How in all these respects and given the frame of reference we have gleaned from looking and listening do architects and planners decide on interventions in building their programs and making plans?

REFERENCES

Holliday, Clifford. 1940. City of Colombo memorandum on town planning. Colombo: Department of Town and Country Planning, July.

Salas, Julian. 1988. An analysis of Latin American autoconstruction: A plural and mass phenomenon. *Open House International* 13(4):2–11.

Stretton, Hugh. 1978. *Urban Planning in Rich and Poor Countries.* Oxford: Oxford University Press.

CHAPTER 8

Building a Program

The life of a modern nation or city is very complicated. The citizens have intricate patterns of common and conflicting interests and tastes and beliefs, and individually and collectively they have very unequal capacities to get what they want for themselves or for one another. From that tangle of powers and purposes comes a social life so complicated and partly unpredictable that any understanding of it has to be incomplete.
Investigators therefore have to put up with knowing less than everything. They have to choose what questions to ask and what general types of answers to accept. They have to select and simplify.

Hugh Stretton, *Urban Planning in Rich and Poor Countries*

The place is a local community center, familiar to everyone and within walking distance from the site—the one, for example, described in Chapter 7. The center has enough room for everyone and enough space for hanging paper. Chairs and tables are borrowed from a nearby school. Large sheets of recycled paper, tape, pins, colored markers, and a site plan, if it exists, are at hand.

The objective is to build a program that will entail sorting out objectives; devising various ways in which they can be achieved; getting some sense of their priority; considering the trade-offs among all the alternatives that seem reasonable; figuring out what we have versus what we need in money and resources to get the job done, and then where to get what we need; sorting out who does what, where, and how; and finally establishing conflicts and opportunities among all the things we want to do as a way of evaluating our proposal and taking most advantage of it. The objective in a more general sense is to expand the scale and speed of housing activities by training community people to become trainers and community developers and to do this without sacrifice to efficiency. This will entail accumulating knowledge of the kind that helps improve performance as we go along. The idea is to create knowledge that can be used to produce action. It must be channeled directly to those who must act.

Learning and therefore training become an integral part of the program and the approach we will adopt in ways that are dynamic, based on discovery rather than curricula. Three principles will be critical here: time, because we cannot afford to lock ourselves into months or years of costly study; relevance, because we want to judge what is transferable from site to site, place to place, and even culture to culture; and partnership, because not only do we seek to understand our actions through the eyes of other parties with whom we have been involved but also because we want to understand how and why they see what they see in the way they do.

The method is an intensely participatory design

Residents and Housing Authority staff at a community center in Colombo, Sri Lanka, the site of a planning workshop. *(Photo by Rita Sampat)*

workshop, held on or close to the site. The workshop staff have already been assembled and were part of looking, listening, and measuring. Those who will lead the workshop are consultant architects, paid in this case directly by the governmental agency. There will be someone who will deal with day-to-day logistics, the project officer who will be responsible for ensuring that what is decided is actually done, and a number of facilitators who will sit with the working groups to keep time, document decisions, and help overcome shyness. In addition, there will be the technical team—architects and engineers—and health and social development workers because money for the housing authorities program is coming largely from an international organization whose interests are primarily in this field and want these interests explicitly represented.

A number of meetings have already been held with the existing site community, arranged and conducted by a local nongovernmental organization (NGO) in this case, one established by the Catholic church. These preliminary meetings are useful to explain the purpose of the program and to answer some general questions of concern. Will we have to move? Will we be compensated for losing a day's work if we come to your workshop? Will we have title to the land? Will we have to pay for utilities and how much? A representive group is selected to participate in the workshop by calling for volunteers and through nominations. The community will ensure that those who count for them will be there. The NGO ensures that minorities are represented and that the final group of about twenty people is a reasonable cross-section in terms of age, sex, the employed, and the unemployed. The NGO also knows that there will be some groups who will not volunteer to participate and others who should but cannot because they will be new incoming families who will not yet have been identified. The NGO will therefore have the important task of mediating between these groups and those who will have representation and between the community and the authorities until there is a more formal local organization to take on this task, which it will help to build.

After the usual introductions—the top brass are all present to give the occasion credibility, including the mayor, the chairman of the housing authority and the district housing manager—the tables are arranged in three groupings—one for each of the communities, representatives from government and from the funding agency, and the health and social development personnel. The technical and professional staff are dispersed to each of the three groups to advocate their cause, help them with technical details, and advise about procedure. In this first session, each group will identify the issues, problems, needs, and desires that concern them most and that they want considered when preparing a proposal. Each group is asked to prepare a list of these based on what they have seen and heard and what they have learned and, in addition, to give some thought as to why a particular problem or issue is thought or known to be so identified and also to whom specifically it is of concern. This will help later because any proposal will have to deal with both cause and effect and because it will help identify whose interests will be served if money and labor are invested in any one project area as opposed to any other.

IDENTIFYING AND POSITIONING PROBLEMS

As objectives and problems are identified, they will be positioned and then prioritized. Strategies for dealing with each problem that arises during the discussions can be recorded. Later other strategies can

be considered and the initial ones reviewed, their relative trade-offs (technical, administrative, and financial) evaluated, and the list prioritized on the assumption that not all that is decided will be affordable and some of it be technically infeasible or politically inexpedient.

After an hour or so, the results are hung on the wall for discussion. The task at this stage is to review what has been decided so far with four objectives in mind: to avoid preconceptions about solutions; to flag potentially conflicting demands; to observe where there is already consensus about demands; and to read what seem to be differences but are in fact similarities expressed or interpreted in different ways. The coffee break is a useful time for workshop staff to review results.

After the break, discussion and debate get underway. The desire for a local school, for example, is expressed in different ways by the community and technical groups. One says "want better schools"; the technical team says "build a new school." The technical team argues its case in terms of persons per facility and catchment areas according to anticipated densities, age groupings, and national standards. The workshop leader asks the community group to explain its demand (under "why" they had curiously listed "better jobs"), hoping to articulate the issues more precisely and leave open the precise solution. The community representative explains that they need more skills or vocational training for their youth, expecting this to be more profitable later and pointing out that with all their schooling, 14 – 19-year-olds had difficulty finding jobs. Moreover, the local schools required uniforms, which many families could not afford, and schooling, much as it was desired, took youth away from activities that made money for their families. The demand "want better school" seemed better expressed as "want skills and vocational training." Similarly, the demand "build a school" became more precisely "establish a vocational facility with training and schooling activities." Both were grouped and listed on a

(Text continues on page 137.)

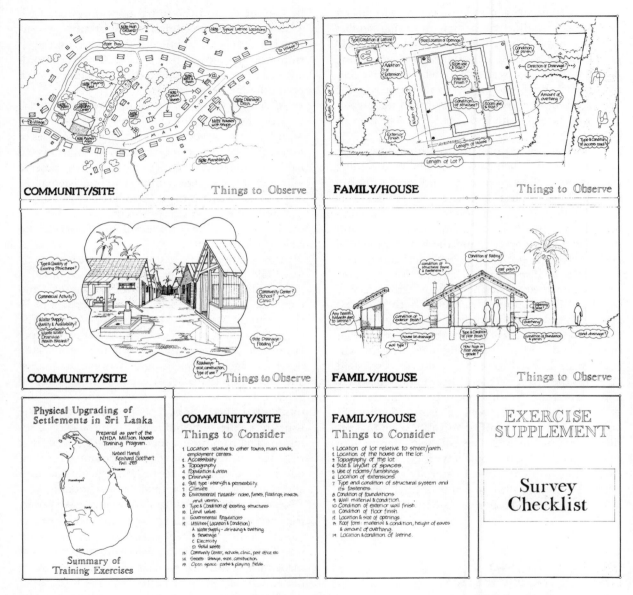

These exercise diagrams illustrate the planning methodology as organized and applied in Sri Lanka. In an extensive program of training of junior technical officers from the National Housing Development Authority, professionals role-played both family and community, helping to build their awareness of local concerns relative to housing, services, and utilities. (*Drawings by Brad Edgerly*)

1. Interview

2. Discussion

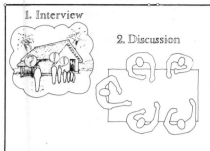

3. Findings

user bias
* Need New House
* Need New Roof Timbers
* Need Loans for Repairs
* Need Materials for Repairs
* Lavatory Inadequate
* Improve Drainage
* Repair Plinth

FAMILY/HOUSE PERSPECTIVE
USER BIAS

1. Survey

2. Discussion

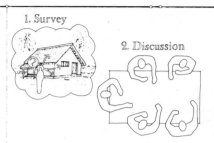

3. Findings

professional bias
* Repair Wattle & Daub Walls
* Replace Roof Timbers
* Replace Cadjan
* Replaster Plinth
* Improve Ventilation
* Improve Drainage
* Need Seepage Pit
* Improve Latrine

FAMILY/HOUSE PERSPECTIVE
PROFESSIONAL BIAS

1. Interview

2. Discussion

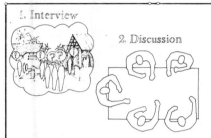

3. Findings

user bias
* Need Dispensary
* Better Drinking Water
* Need Post Office
* More Cultivated Land
* Community Center
* Better Internal Roads
* Electricity
* Better School Equipment
* More Small Industry

COMMUNITY/SITE PERSPECTIVE
USER BIAS

1. Survey

2. Discussion

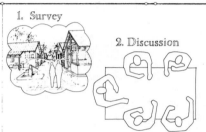

3. Findings

professional bias
* Repair Access Road
* Electricity
* Better Transportation
* Community Center
* Primary School
* Better Irrigation
* Need Small Industry
* Better Water Supply
* Post Office

COMMUNITY/SITE PERSPECTIVE
PROFESSIONAL BIAS

Materials & Equipment

1. Base plan
2. Checklists as aid to survey/interview
3. Notebooks & pencils
4. Blank chart to list problems
5. Polaroid Camera
6. Tape measure

Things to Consider

1. Local residents know more about their circumstances than trainees. They should be used as informants
2. Use checklists as a guide, not a questionaire. Let people tell their stories (encourage them!).
3. Practice interviewing techniques before visiting the site.
4. Do not edit information.
5. Use "official standards" to technically evaluate site.
6. Keep survey time short.
7. Sketch technical problems at site.
8. Highlight incompatibilities in the discussions between user group and professional group.
9. Use travel time to review procedures.
10. Trainer should give on-the-spot help during surveys, interview, and discussions to insure exercise is proceeding correctly

Physical Upgrading of Settlements in Sri Lanka

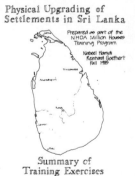

Prepared as part of the N.H.D.A. Million Houses Training Program

Nabeel Hamdi
Reinhard Goethert
Fall 1989

Summary of Training Exercises

EXERCISE ONE

Identifying Problems

Day :
Time :

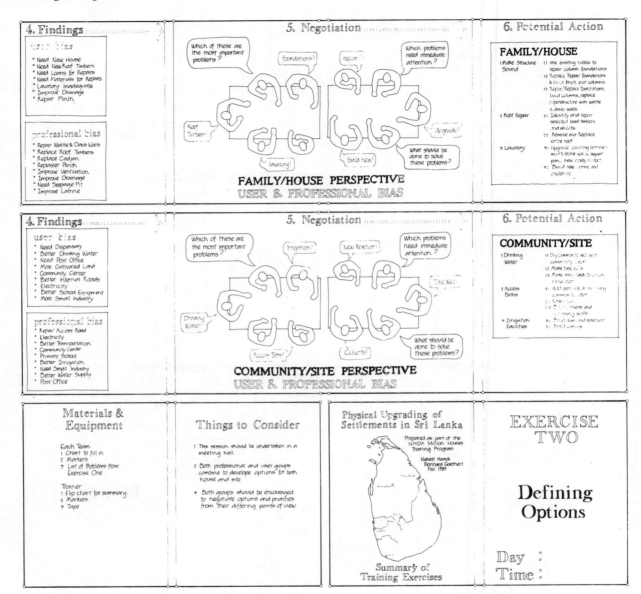

7. Potential Action

FAMILY/HOUSE

1. Make Structure Sound
   - 1.1 Use existing rubble to repair column foundations
   - 1.2 Replace/Repair foundations & build brick pier columns
   - 1.3 Repair/Replace foundations, build columns, replace superstructure with wattle & daub walls
2. Roof Repair
   - 2.1 Identify and repair selected roof timbers and sheets
   - 2.2 Reconstruct/Replace entire roof
3. Lavatory
   - 3.1 Upgrade existing latrine - mud & stone walls, squat pan, new cadjan roof
   - 3.2 Build new latrine and enclosure

8. Negotiation

FAMILY/HOUSE PERSPECTIVE
USER & PROFESSIONAL BIAS

9. Selected Action

FAMILY/HOUSE

Option	Repair/Replace Foundations		
	User Choice	Professional Choice	Other
Who?	Owner	Community Help	Contractor
How Long?	Two Weeks	Three Days	Five Days
How Much?	450 R/ft³ Hire Craftsman	600 R/ft³	1250 R/ft³
Other	Health Issue	Climatic Interruption	Climatic, Labor, Schedule

7. Potential Action

COMMUNITY/SITE

1. Drinking Water
   - 1.1 Dig community well with community labor
   - 1.2 Make tube wells
   - 1.3 Make mini-tank to catch rainwater
2. Access Paths
   - 2.1 Add open side drains using community labor
   - 2.2 Form steps
   - 2.3 Build culverts and retaining walls
3. Irrigation Facilities
   - 3.1 Build dam and reservoir
   - 3.2 Build canals

8. Negotiation

COMMUNITY/SITE PERSPECTIVE
USER & PROFESSIONAL BIAS

9. Selected Action

COMMUNITY/SITE

Option	Provide Tube Well (user choice)	Dig Well (professional choice)
Who?	Water Board	Community Labor, NHDA - materials & supervision
How Long?	Nine Months	Three Months
How Much?	75,000 R (by Government)	12,000 R (Community donates labor)
Other	Allow 2 weeks for mechanical failure	—

Materials & Equipment

Each Team:
1. Chart to fill in
2. Markers
3. Charts from Exercise One & Two

Trainer:
1. Flip chart for summary
2. Markers
3. Tape
4. Pointer

Things to Consider

1. The proposals are only general indications of what to do. Avoid too much detail.

2. Encourage negotiation during the selection of options. What may be feasible to one group may not be to another.

3. It may be necessary to do this exercise twice in order to assure that everyone understands what to do

Physical Upgrading of Settlements in Sri Lanka

Prepared as part of the NHDA Million Houses Training Program

Nabeel Hamdi
Reinhard Goethert
Fall 1988

Summary of Training Exercises

EXERCISE THREE

Selecting Actions

Day :
Time :

IDENTIFY AND CLARIFY CONCERNS

WHAT ARE THE CONCERNS	WHO IS AFFECTED & WHY	WHAT OTHER OPPORTUNITIES

- NEED HOUSING FOR LOW INCOME FAMILIES	- CHILDREN OF HOMEOWNERS
	  - MAY HAVE TO LEAVE N'HOOD
	- LOW INCOME RESIDENTS
	  - MAY HAVE NO OTHER PLACE TO LIVE
	  - PAYING TOO MUCH FOR RENT
	  - WANT TO STAY IN THE NEIGHBORHOOD
	- BUSINESSES - NEED PLACE FOR WORKERS
		-

- MUST PRESERVE NATURAL OPEN SPACE	- ALL RESIDENTS
	- ENVIRONMENTALISTS
	- CHILDREN
	  - RECREATION
	  - HEALTH
	  - RELIEVE CONGESTION
		- POSSIBILITY TO DEVELOP ONLY PART OF LAND - LEAVE OPEN SPACE

- RETURN VACANT PROPERTY TO USE	- CITY GOVT.
	  - HELP TAX BASE
	  - IMPROVE IMAGE OF TOWN
	- RESIDENT ABUTTERS
	  - REDUCE CHANCE OF CRIME
	  - IMPROVE NEIGHBORHOOD IMAGE
		- JOBS CREATED BY CONST. WILL ALSO HELP LOCAL ECONOMY.

Sample chart from the Planning Assistance Kit.

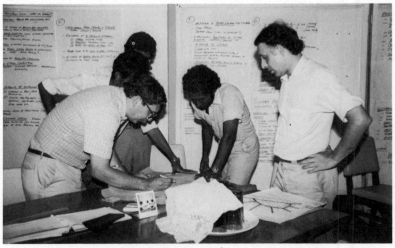

Local workshops in session: Group identifies issues and proposes strategies. *(Photo by Rita Sampat)*

master sheet summarizing all agreed-upon issues, problems, and demands, a sheet that would be added to as work proceeded.

One community member wanted to improve the health facilities in the area. The community asked for a new clinic to be built, expecting this to be the obvious route to improvement. After more analysis, local officials argued that a clinic existed within a short bus ride for most families and that investment in building was neither justified nor necessary. In theory, they were right; in practice, they were wrong. They were right because their investment in "building" could not be justified. Official standards suggested a perfectly adequate match between the existing facility and its catchment, its size, location, and the services if offered. They were wrong because the problem had been incorrectly diagnosed and the assumption "clinic" theoretically unfounded. At this point, the desire for better health facilities expressed by community members might have been ignored. More analysis, however, revealed that the real issue of concern was not the availability of a clinic but accessibility to it. People were intimidated by the formal procedures for making appointments (which in the absence of telephones usually required at least two trips), by the long wait once there (for which many would lose a full day's income), by the preference given to those of higher income or class, and by the expense of the bus ride. Thus, a very different set of issues was revealed.

In theory, then, even had it been acceptable to build a clinic, it would have been a wrong decision. In real terms, however, a problem did exist, and it was both legitimate and immediate. Some general approaches were prepared based on the support principles that had become part of the government's policy. Policy provided a general theoretical framework for making decisions: building self-reliance, local manageability, participation, and sustainability, for example, all framed within the general desire for governments to support rather than dominate local initiative and local enterprise and to leave the precise mechanics, standards, and form of the solutions to be decided locally.

The first options considered included a mobile service facility, converting an existing unused building into a medical center, and creating a special unit within the existing clinic to expedite diagnosis and treatment. In practice, however, the medical team argued that the most common cause of complaint was diarrhea (something they had learned on their tours) and its associated symptom of dehydration. If this was so, they argued, then local community-based paramedics might be trained to identify symptoms and to train families in the use of oral rehydrations, a simple self-administered procedure that would relieve the burden on central medical facilities, speed the process, cut costs, and save lives. They might need to train people in personal hygiene and food preparation, storage, and feeding and therefore correct the conditions that caused the problem. When symptoms are not diagnosable locally, families would continue to be referred to the existing nearby clinic, where paramedics might mediate between families and doctors and so facilitate access.

In this example, community member expressed a desire or objective for a particular facility. The professional team (teachers) then identified the legitimacy of their demand and the source or cause of their complaint. What might have been a simplistic, inaccurate, and wasteful response became a package of responses: training paramedics, training families, a well-tried process of self-help treatment, and locally staffed informal clinics serviced periodically by a mobile unit. A system emerged more suited to the complexity of conditions actually encountered and substantially cheaper than a fully staffed new building.

In a third example, the problem was to provide a constant supply of clean water. The professional team had suggested shallow wells as a temporary measure, knowing that the city's main supply was already overburdened, with low pressure in the pipes and a number of cut-offs scheduled during each day on a rotating basis and to the various low-income areas. The community, however, knowing that temporary measures have a habit of becoming permanent, preferred tube wells because shallow wells often ran dry and were often polluted. Management argued that tube wells would be too expensive. Community members proposed, however, that they might raise some of the money by organizing carnivals and fetes if this could be matched through government funds. It was inconceivable that this might have been proposed formally, but the managers rightly decided to profit from what was proposed, and a private-public partnership was forged.

One issue—the question of playgrounds for children—seemed unresolvable in discussion. Someone had suggested playgrounds as an essential component of any future plan in view of the lack of play facilities for children, particularly for the 8–12-year-olds. Yet other community members doubted its value and held it low on their list of priorities. Had anyone talked to children about play and about their needs for space, equipment, location, and the rest? They had not.

One group of workshop participants returned to the site to observe and talk to residents. They found that the desire for a playground was an expression not of play but of security. Families were concerned not about the needs and habits of children but about the fact that the existing road into the site where most children played was heavily traveled and therefore the cause of a number of accidents. The problem was not lack of play facilities but security. The result was a very different set of options to consider, including the provision of play elsewhere but also road signs to indicate children at play or even closing the road to traffic during certain periods.

Perhaps the strongest conflict of interest arose over the issue of density and therefore lot sizes. The technical team had listed densities per hectare that reflected the number of people they expected to settle on the site. Without question, this implied a reduction in lot size for most existing families, threatening their economic base. Most families remained dependent on animal husbandry, vegetable gardening, and other small-scale industries for which land was needed.

The managers were intent on regularizing land and meeting their density needs. Two issues were dominant. The first was equity; all families should have more or less the same size lot, though some will be larger than others to reflect pricing differentials. The second was the number of lots and the homeless they wanted to settle. The equity issue is misnamed. It comes from the managerial point of view that to make all people equal (a misnomer in its own right), you service them all the same. There is no single city, no single squatter or slum area, where this is true, and nowhere has this cured social unrest except where the divisions are extreme. The second issue is also misidentified. Most neighborhoods do become denser over relatively long periods of time. They do this in response to market pressures where families divide and subdivide selling pieces of land they own. Blocks are filled in, stories added, extensions built, rooms added and rented. It is a dynamic process that occurs where people are free to speculate, a privilege usually of the rich. The poor are usually prevented from turning their land into capital; theirs is the only sector of the population where the restrictions apply, at least in democratic societies. In any case, most families who were to be housed, we later found, were not the homeless but those being relocated because of slum clearance. Under these circumstances, it might be the role of public authorities to tackle the density issue by introducing market measures designed to encourage densification where both sides can profit—in other words, to cultivate the conditions for densification rather than provide lots.

This issue and others that remained unsolved were listed on a separate sheet identifying issues needing further discussion. Even when settlement starts, the plan will have holes in it that will be filled

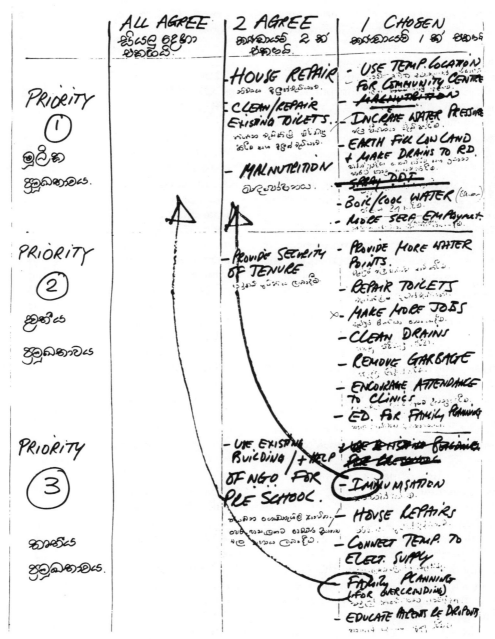

Prioritizing objectives and options based on consensus.

in response to informal negotiation among families and to market demands from which families can profit, socially and economically.

The following day the session begins late—there is a "work to rule" in all public offices in support of a claim for higher wages, and most public transportation is on strike. The previous day, we had noticed that attendance at open sessions was lower than we had expected. There is no sure way to guarantee that those who count will come, but after a bit, they usually do, if only out of curiosity. On the second day, we decide to so something small but visible to show good intent to those skeptical about the exercise.

One small part of the program entailed repaving a piece of roadway. All the workshop participants went to the site and began the construction. The local newspaper covered the event and published a photo the following day. The mayor made public the government's intentions. And on the next day, everyone turned up at the workshop.

During our deliberations, we have kept each group separate, setting out its priorities and developing wish lists. The technical advisers will be learning how to talk to ordinary people and other specialists not normally part of their team (funders, for example, or health workers). They have facilitated discussion and helped work out alternatives. Many of them probably have never left their drawing boards, except for the occasional site visit. Up on the wall are three lists of priorities—one each for community, government, and health and social workers.

We now begin to make a master list. Priorities common to all lists are automatically included on the master, as are those listed by two of the three groups. If only one group has raised the issue, we ask its members to explain their reasons to convince the others of their cause. Usually we ensure they win. The master list is therefore quite long at first. Then we make another list taking only the first three or four priorities from each of the separate

groups. These represent the least that needs to be done.

IDENTIFYING OPTIONS AND ESTABLISHING A PLAN OF ACTION

Now we rearrange the groups and intermix them. We make three working teams, each with funders (government staff), community members, and health workers. Each group has technical experts. None of these people will probably have sat at the same table before. It is a symbolic gesture of cooperation. Each group or team develops different ways in which the strategies already identified can be implemented. Where these have not been developed, some will not yet have emerged and they will need to be developed. We suggest that the process should indicate the easiest way to achieve our goals and then work toward more elaborate but still appropriate alternatives.

If, for example, one priority is for a community center, the simplest way of establishing one is to designate a place under a tree. The only equipment this may entail are some chairs and perhaps a sign. A more extreme but more conventional alternative is to get the government to build a center. If this is desired, then designating a place under a tree may be the first step. In other words, the alternatives may not be mutually exclusive. The community will need to understand, however, that money spent on a new building may leave little elsewhere. Perhaps community members may be prepared to contribute their labor to get the center built and to offset some of the costs.

Options are worked out with respect to how to pay for, build, and manage the school, the clinic, the road, and so on. The assumption that government will provide is dispelled; instead a sense of cooperation is cultivated. For each option we devise, we give some consideration to the risks involved,

PRIORITIZE OBJECTIVES

ELM ST. COOP
MAY 1, 1984

CRITERIA	Build on Vacant Land	Provide Play Area	Provide Low-Income Housing	Provide Elderly Housing	Build New Parking Spaces	Provide Security Lights	Require Local Contractors	Keep Some Open Land	Explore Coop Ownership	
TIME	1	2	1	1	3	4	2	3	2	1 = TAKES MOST TIME / 4 = LEAST
COST	2	3	1	1	3	3	4	3	3	1 = MOST EXPENS / 4 = LEAST
EFFORT	2	4	1	2	4	4	2	2	2	1 = HARDEST TO ACHIEVE / 4 = EASIEST
TOTAL	(5)	(9)	(3)	(4)	(10)	(11)	(8)	(8)	(7)	LOWEST = MOST DIFFICUL / HIGHEST = EASIEST
IMPORTANCE	3	1	2	1	2	2	3	3	2	1 = MOST IMPORT. / 4 = LEAST IMPORTAN

Prioritizing objectives and options based on trade-offs (sample chart from the Planning Assistance Kit).

the investment entailed, and the commitment demanded, based as much on intuition as on fact. How likely will we get what we want if we ask for a new school building? Should we modify this demand? How much money will it entail and what investment of time and energy? To what extent will it tie me down over the longer term in repayments, tasks, time, and so on?

We facilitate this process, make the point, and edit the alternatives further by attaching a budget number to the program—say 10 (1 is the least amount of money, 10 is the most). We attach a budget number to each alternative, and the total must not exceed 10. We price alternatives in two ways: by considering what the authority will build or do in their usually direct construction approach and by considering the community contribution and therefore stretching the money. The point of this procedure is to encourage the team to come up with alternatives that may not be immediately evident, to discover opportunities that we may have missed, and to build on local resources of labor and knowledge that experts and agencies may not possess.

By this time, various objectives will have become clear. We will have a good sense of the time, money, skills, expert help, materials, permits, and favors needed to get the job done. We will also have some sense of what will block our path—the sort of technical, political, legal, and local social institutional hurdles that still stand in our way.

Why, for example, in one previous project were

ASSESS WHAT YOU HAVE & WHAT YOU NEED

OPTIONS	HAVE		NEED	
	APPROVALS	RESOURCES	APPROVALS	RESOURCES
SHARP SUBSIDY	- NON-PROFIT STATUS - MUST BE NEW CONSTR.	- MIN. OF 25% LOW-INCOME	- UNITS TO BE APPROVED BY EOCD - MUST LOCATE IN "HOUSING DEVELOPMENT AREA"	- CONSTRUCTION MORTGAGE
MODULAR CONSTRUCTION		- DRAWINGS & SPECIFICATION - VACANT LAND	- BUILDING PERMIT - ZONING APPROVAL - APPROVED MODULAR CONSTRUCTOR	- CONSTRUCTION MORTGAGE

DECIDE WHERE TO GET WHAT YOU NEED & WHEN

(N) = NOW   (S) = SOON   (L) = LATER

	NEED	WHERE TO GET IT
APPROVALS	- UNITS MUST BE APPROVED BY EOCD (N) - MUST BE LOCATED IN HOUSING DEVELOPMENT AREA (N)	- EOCD, LOCAL HOUSING AUTH. - EOCD FOR CLASSIFICATIONS - LOCAL COMMUNITY DEVELOPMENT DEPARTMENT
RESOURCES	- CAPITAL TO INVEST AS EQUITY (N) - ABILITY TO ADMINISTER & HANDLE STATE PAPERWORK (L)	- FUNDRAISING FROM PRIVATE FOUNDATIONS - SYNDICATION - HIRE PROPERTY MANAGEMNT CONSULTANT

Samples from the Planning Assistance Kit.

142

An open meeting where ideas are presented and discussed with the larger community. *(Photo by Reinhard Goethert)*

households prevented from building houses with scrap material and instead committed to the expense of masonry, clay tiles, and timber frames? Why were some people prevented from subletting and others from keeping animals or building up to three-story heights? What prevents the community from borrowing money from the government's housing bank, forcing people to borrow from local informal money lenders charging interests at more than double the official rate—up to 20 percent a month? Why in one rural cottage did residents refuse to install trenches to irrigate their fields despite the government's investment in farmers? Was it complacency, mistrust, or ignorance? The answer was that the trench "has to pass over land owned by big landowners who extracted a tax for the use of the ditches—a tax the farmers could not possibly pay."

At this point, we figure out what we have versus what we need to get the job done. What kind of willingness in time and commitment and what kind of skills in carpentry, plumbing, and masonry do we have within the community? What kind of approvals or what kind of influence and political clout do we possess to push proposals through? Do we have the tools and the equipment? Who can make bricks, window frames, roof sheeting, and so on? Apart from all else, this kind of inventory will be helpful later in promoting various income-generating activities and building on what exists rather than inventing industry.

In other words, we assume at the beginning that substantial local resources can be tapped before going elsewhere for help. Later we establish what we need and where to get what we need, organized in some general order of priority relative to the sequence of work. We do this by arranging what we need relative to now, soon, and later.

An action plan emerges. Not everyone is satisfied, but we get to the point where we can be reasonably confident that no single party will block any other party's decision. Now we figure out who will do what, how, and when. Next there is a meeting open to everyone who wants to attend, and the proposals are presented by one of the community representatives. Volunteers are elicited to work on a management team and to monitor progress to ensure that momentum is not lost.

EVALUATING LINKAGES

Now we give more careful attention to ensuring effective linkages among the parts of the program. We want to judge how some of the objectives, strategies, and the solutions are interconnected—how dependent or independent they are of each other. "Within each functioning system, some parts are more crucial than others. Components that handle the planning or steering for the whole system are more critical than those that take care of some small aspect of a technical routine. One may ask: on what does everyone and everything depend? On what do many things depend? Relatively few things depend? Rather than a condition of equality or a classless state, we find arrangements of subordinate and superordinate units" (Winner 1977, 184–85).

We ask which components or clusters of components will have greatest bearing on the proper functioning of the whole. A hierarchical order will appear and will need to be understood to avoid delay in project development and later to prevent it from self-destructing. We may want to review each of the strategies devised in the early phases of programming in view of these linkages—not to change ideas or reshuffle priorities but perhaps to rearrange our approach, introduce components of design that may not have featured, or devise alternatives that are more likely to succeed. This is an evaluative and reformative phase of work that in addition suggests the proper phasing of work and the kind of additional interventions that may be demanded from government and professionals.

Linkage analysis ironically presents us with an ap-

parent conflict of objectives. On the one hand, those who advocate an integrated approach to planning seek tight, coordinated packages because they think that unless we do, the chance of the whole falling apart is high and the opportunity to control the whole efficiently is diminished. But the concepts of integrated planning, although they recognize the importance of linkages and are attractive in theory, have no basis in practice. Few of the projects have worked because they not only demand sophisticated administration but also need large sums of capital invested to get them started. They need a level of sophisticated management and institutional coordination that few countries have. The result is that you cannot start doing A unless you do B, and you cannot do B unless you do C, and so on. It is a recession to the old paradigm of doing projects rather than a new paradigm based on discrete incremental intervention, because we come to realize that you cannot do anything until you do everything; therefore nothing is complete unless everything is complete. This same holds true in the design of most systems or buildings. We want to avoid the absurd dependencies that inhibit change or modification because we find that "to change a window mullion is to change a corner, is to change the structural system, is to change the plan, is to change the concept" (Correa 1987, 12).

On the other hand and because of the unwieldy characteristics of integrated projects, we need to disentangle and reduce dependencies between the program components and between the various organizations involved in implementation and management. The fewer people involved and the fewer dependencies, the easier it is to get things done. The result has often been fragmentation, and many opportunities for building the strength of urban systems have been lost.

Two things to think about, taken together, may help to clarify the issues and give us a better basis for marrying the two seemingly conflicting objectives. The first has to do with the hierarchical order of importance of components and the second with a clear categorization of the different types of linkages.

The first is best illustrated by a simple example. It is common practice for public utility lines to be installed along public thoroughfares. The water line is installed in the road rather than through houses, with spurs feeding individual houses. It is done this way so that if there is a breakage in any one house, the entire system is not interrupted.

The laying of pipes assumes a hierarchical order. Even decisions on whether households should receive individual supplies or whether to charge for their utility does not delay the installation of mains. This hierarchy of pipes sets up hierarchies of organization. The main supply is managed and controlled by a collective body—a community group, a local authority, a cooperative. It need not interfere with details of house design and construction, which it would do if the pipes ran through houses. It can install its utility before, during, or after house construction. It is independent of house connection and even independent of deciding how many households there will be, precisely where they will go, and how tall buildings will be, except in the most general way. The household manages and controls its own installation. It can even choose to ignore the main supply if, for example, it does not want to pay for it, and continue to fetch water from the nearby standpipe or pay for it through local vendors. Simple as it is, the arrangement provides substantial flexibility, achieved largely through commonsense design.

The second thing to think about in linkage analysis is the nature of the linkages themselves. We go about this task by considering three categories, which I will call consequential, complementary, and conflict. In the first case, there will be things we need to do to ensure the success of what we want to do. We need to supply clean water to improve health; we need training if clean water is to remain clean until the time it is consumed. Providing more

ample and direct water supply to each household, with all good intentions to control the quality of water and prevent disease, could result in much poorer sanitation and an increase in health risks, unless better systems of wastewater removal are also installed. "There is no point in designing a scheme which is dependent on daily solid waste collection, or monthly emptying of septic tanks, if the only services available are weekly or annually" (Kirke 1984, 237). In the second case, there will be things that because we need them can be used to greater advantage when linked to things we want to do in the interests of broader community, urban, or national gain.

Let me first illustrate how consequential and complementary linkages can work. Let us assume that a water-borne sewage system is proposed as one component among others for improving conditions in a settlement. Two consequential links are immediately identified to ensure the success of this proposal and to validate the decision in the first place. The first is an adequate supply of water; the second is an effective system for controlling garbage disposal. In different ways, both ensure that the system will remain free of garbage, although each may be independent so far as installation and timing of installation are concerned. In this case, decision-making responsibilities are clearly defined and independent other than the usual task of coordinating the work of contractors, sewage, garbage, and water.

In the second case, links may need to be made so that initial interventions can contribute to broader developmental gains. In the previous example, we may want to link the control and disposal of garbage to an equivalent program on health education and connect garbage directly in people's minds to the health hazards facing every family. Garbage collection may also be linked with employment generation. Here it could be handled by local enterprises, releasing the burden on local administrations and generating income in the process. Depending on the scale and organization of this enterprise, garbage can be recycled, generating small-scale commerce and industry and so more money. Government may even contemplate two further interventions to support these activities. First, they could create a market for these goods. The Zebaleen in Cairo, for example, were less interested in the government's efforts to upgrade their area but more interested that they should guarantee the purchase of pigs who feed on the garbage collected. Second, they may issue small business loans and even tools to encourage the enterprises.

One further point is worth making here: most problems of high priority usually take the longest to implement, and their success and impact are usually measured and felt over relatively long periods of time (examples are employment generation, health improvement, and better education). Effective services, such as garbage collection, cannot be delivered without access to settlements. And access cannot be secured unless there is some measure of land regularization. Communities with garbage collection at the top of their priority list will need to know why work starts by regulating land. And having discovered this, community members may decide that regulating land will be too disruptive because people will have to move, houses will have to be removed, some will lose land for road widening, others will quibble over the precise boundary to their site, and people will appear on the tax register. For all these reasons, residents may seek alternative ways to dispose of garbage, not necessarily based on access for the municipality's trucks. An important distinction has to be made between priorities and starting points; the two are often muddled.

The third kind of linkage, which completes the analysis, is to expose connections that could lead to conflict. Even when all parties have agreed, for example, on solution A, conflicts may arise because in doing A we find we will also have to live with B. If B outweighs the advantages gained by A, then A clearly is the wrong course of action, whatever its merits. In this case, we may either change or modify

A or, more likely, work toward A over a longer time frame by first ameliorating B. The situation is made more complex if A is something demanded by one party and yet the impact B will largely be felt by another. In this case, the second party will have to convince the first that what is likely to be bad for them will also be bad for the public at large. In other words, their interests in dealing first with B will have to converge to avoid delay and prevent raising expectations.

We need to consider the trade-offs involved, which may be social, political, financial, technical, environmental, or administrative in nature. In measuring trade-offs and figuring out potential conflicts, some assessment of likely impacts of decisions and desires will need to be made. This need not entail lengthy study or analysis because not all impacts will be predictable. Instead, we might play the if-then game: if we do this, then these are the likely trade-offs. In this case, some information from other cases and other countries might be useful. When we did A in country X, this is what happened. Is it likely to happen here, and if it is, does it matter in the same way as it did there? This game entails some measure of logic, experience, technical competence, negotiating skills, and common sense.

As far as possible, we want to avoid introducing a strategy devised to deal with problem A, only to find that in solving A we have created problem B. We tackle B but create a further problem C. Examples are plenty. In a social context, there is Fathy's (1973) classic example in India, ''where certain villages were supplied with pure water on tap in houses [but where] the girls still preferred to go down to the river to bring back dirty water carried on their heads. This was because fetching water was their only excuse for going out, and thus their only chance to be seen by the young men of their village. A girl who stayed in the kitchen drawing water from the tap would never get married.'' Another example is cited by Amos Rappoport (pers. comm.) in recalling tribal habits in central Australia. There, conflicts between tribal groups are sorted out at night, in the absence of light, each group separately signaling its position and response to the other in purely auditory ways. They have learned to resolve problems and avoid conflict in this way. The introduction of electric lighting would inadvertently destroy these patterns of negotiation, with dire social consequences.

In one city in Egypt, the issue was how to relieve congested traffic in the central area and so improve its commercial and recreational facilities. The idea was to model the revitalization program on some European or U.S. notion, which included parkways and pedestrian shopping areas. This was a ludicrous strategy, with little or no consideration for how people shop, conduct commerce, or pursue leisure-time activities in Egyptian cities. Nevertheless, to start with, a road would be routed at the periphery of the city to carry through traffic. This bypass, a common strategy in many European and U.S. cities, created an unfortunate problem: being well serviced and easily accessible, it encouraged squatting and other informal building activities that were not in their own right undesirable but were in their encroachment on prime arable land. And since government policy was to control, if not prevent, such encroachment, regulations were subsequently introduced to limit the growth of the secondary cities. The problem this in turn created, good as these regulations might have been, was how to enforce them, something never achieved. The multiplier effect for the delta region as a whole has been catastrophic for a country that relies heavily on agriculture.

METHODS AND ASSUMPTIONS

The process I have described demonstrates one method for discovering locally rational ways of doing and planning while at the same time building the capacity of local institutions and communities to act. In the broadest sense, its objective is to increase the efficiency of production to match the

scale of supply with demand, with more people involved in production, more variety of responses tailored to fit, and more learning. We have called the operational side of these efforts *micro planning* because they are result oriented, locally enacted, and deal with community plans rather than urban districts or national strategies.[1] The term emphasizes that these efforts are on a small scale and depend on simple administration or sometimes informal organizations for management and on small entrepreneurs and builders.

This approach for building programs is based on a number of assumptions. First, neither lack of knowledge about place nor ability to tackle problems is usually at issue. Technical skills are usually available locally, albeit in rudimentary form but sufficient to deal with the problems at hand. At the community level, awareness of what works and what does not is rarely an issue because the problems are known and finite. What is lacking in most cases is a forum for articulating problems accurately, a community of inquiry, a framework that provides the structure for drawing out problems, modifying interpretations, defining solutions, and building consensus and partnerships. What is lacking is the use of a plain common language so that everyone can figure out what is going on.

Second, not enough mediation takes place between the demands of public authorities, and those of private or individual communities. There is a lack of consensus among those involved about problems, issues, objectives, priorities, and actions, a lack of "mediating structures" between the demands of public administration and private needs.[2]

---

1. Micro planning, including the field manual and case studies in Sri Lanka and Chile, is recorded in R. Goethert and N. Hamdi, *Making Micro Plans—A Community Based Process in Programming and Development* (London: Intermediate Technology Publications, 1988).
2. See P. L. Berger and R. J. Neuhaus, *To Empower People—The Role of Mediating Structures in Public Policy* (Washington, D.C.: American Enterprise Institute for Public Policy Research, August 1979).

We need a way of crafting workable links among various sets of demands, various groups of people, and various scales or organizations that so often compete for dominance and so exclude the benefits each has to bring to the design and planning processes. We must mediate between the need for some measure of strategic planning to safeguard health, ensure security, protect minorities, and sort out larger city systems like transportation, schools, and health, setting longer-term objectives, with their implicit desire to create reforms to improve conditions generally. At the same time, we must satisfy the demand in planning for spontaneous, more intuitive action so that problems can be solved immediately and profitably by those whom they effect and so that trading can take place, markets can appear or disappear, houses can be built, improved or extended and so on. We need a way of disentangling public agencies from private organizations and strategic planning (large, usually public organizations, national objectives, strategic plans) from problem solving (small, usually private organizations, local objectives, action plans). We need a process that is bottom up in terms of problem solving and top down in terms of coordination and management. But we need both with some measure of balance and each with a large measure of give and take.

Too much coordination or strategic planning will slow the process. It will inhibit the ability to act spontaneously, finding this usually threatening to its order and therefore to its objectives. It will tip the balance in favor of general needs or policy and will be too abstract to the people for whom they are intended; they will have to accept their objectives without really knowing why. Too much spontaneity, on the other hand, is threatening and abstract for the government. In this situation, the government will be unable to control the pace of development, allocation of land, standards of construction, and supply of money, materials, or infrastructure. They see the ad hoc interventions and the variety implied as an additional burden, particularly to their

management tasks. "Part of the problem is that the relationships between houses, jobs, services and transportation are crucial to the success of enabling settlement strategies, and efforts to consolidate and improve these relationships demand decisions that can only be taken at the [larger] level" (Global Report 1987, 196).

Where the demands of these two positions when taken together remain unresolved, as they so often are, governments usually adopt a position of appeasement. Projects are built that may be visible but are simplistic responses to complex issues and thus short term in benefit. Most governments (and their supporting agencies), after all, are committed to spending their budget in the time allocated and to meeting the political promises that put them in office, and so they will respond, for example, to the need for health improvement by building hospitals, which we later find that most who need them cannot get to; to housing by building houses, which we later find the poor cannot afford to pay for; to play, by building playgrounds that we later find no one uses; to commerce, by building marketplaces that often wind up in the wrong place, and so on. These projects serve little purpose other than for political expediency.

They fail to recognize natural scales and limits within which programs serve people, beyond which we get "the universal schoolhouse, hospital ward (housing project) or prison" (Illich 1973, xii). Appeasement projects wind up serving managers and systems of governance and displacing the very people for whom they were intended. One example is Le Corbusier's Chandigarh in India, graphically documented by Madhu Sarin (1982). Another comes from those who operate the buses in London Transport: "A local authority, told that its bus drivers were 'speeding past queues of people with a smile and a wave of the hand' replied that 'it's impossible for drivers to keep to their timetables if they have to stop for passengers'" (CBI 1983, 3).

The third assumption is that not enough people are encouraged locally in production. Systems of production cease to be self-regulating and become self-serving. This issue has been well illustrated in the analysis of large technology systems, where four conclusions have been reached (McDermott 1969). Such systems encourage (1) centralization of control, (2) development of a technical elite, (3) decision-making processes that consider the needs of the system rather than the needs of outsiders affected by the system (the public), and (4) the development of mechanisms to prevent external criticism or to discredit those who may make it.

Fourth, and because of the proved inadequacies over the longer term of prescriptive methods, we need to consider a methodology less directed at telling what to do and then how to go about doing it. No method is a substitute for professional competence and resourcefulness nor for common sense. Indeed, no methods for planning are good at solving problems. Problems cannot be solved in a general way. They can be solved only according to locally specific circumstances, with some general help. Our intention should not be to produce problem-solving methods. Instead, we need ones that indicate alternative paths that could be explored locally in search of solutions, indicating how to proceed, and what to expect as one proceeds.

We know that good methods do not necessarily produce good products or results. Good judgment, tempered with experience and intuition, does. Good processes facilitate good judgment, which is what methods set out to do. Their efficiency is measured in their capability to adapt and change and yet remain relevant, not in the ability to predict or the capacity to control.

Fifth, despite the importance placed on project monitoring and evaluation, not enough learning takes place. And even if it does, it usually winds up documented in extensive reports that no one knows quite how to use. While these reports represent a substantial accumulation of data and sometimes analysis, they remain nonoperational. If they were, we might avoid repeating the same mistakes in design and planning. There are, of course, all kinds of

people who make evaluations and numerous reasons why various methods are used. There will have been municipal authorities, political groups, international funding agencies, central government housing authorities, church groups, user groups, architects, planners, and engineers, all of whom will have had some voice (some more than others) in programming and implementation. Most likely each will have been looking to judge outcomes based on their own history of success or failure, to validate their approach, invalidate their competitors' approaches, safeguard the status quo, or get more work. Each party will be selective about what it measures and how it measures what it sees.

Unfortunately most monitoring ends up as little more than bookkeeping, and most evaluations are self-serving. Neither has much to do with learning. We need a more qualitative and participatory approach to evaluation, a sharing of knowledge about networks that make planning work and a much greater role for those who will be affected by what is found out.

We need to create conditions in which members of a community can engage in ''public reflection on substantive matters of concern to them, and also on the rules and norms of inquiry they customarily enact. . . . To be effective, fact finding [learning] has to be linked with the action organization itself; it has to be part of a feedback system which links a reconnaissance branch of the organization with the branches which do the action. The feedback has to be done so that a discrepancy between the desired and the actual direction leads automatically to a correction of actions or to a change of planning'' (Lewin 1947 in McGill and Horton 1973, 13–14).

This demand is in stark contrast to the conventional way of working in international development. Not only are professionals considered the prime source of knowledge, makers of projects, or builders of programs, but also most of the knowledge finds its way out of the countries and institutions it is supposed to serve and on to the shelves of the libraries of distinguished universities and agencies in foreign countries. These universities and agencies probably know more about the countries they serve than the countries themselves.

All of these claims and assumptions are easily stated. No doubt, they would elicit condescending nods of approval from any assembled group of academics, practitioners, international agencies, and even government officials. But what do they add up to methodologically for enablement planning, and how can they be made workable as theories of design practice? How can we best model the process of building programs so that we can identify where and how know-how and resources may be needed and where and how intervention can be decided?

REFERENCES

Confederation of British Industries. 1983. *Working for Customers*. London: Confederation of British Industries.

Correa, Charles. 1987. An essay for JAE. *Journal of Architecture Education* 40(2):12.

Fathy, Hassan, 1973. *Architecture for the Poor*. Chicago: University of Chicago Press.

Global Report on Human Settlements. 1987. Oxford: Oxford University Press for the United Nations Centre for Human Settlements (HABITAT).

Illich, Ivan. 1973. *Tools for Conviviality*. London: Calder and Boyers.

Kirke, John. 1984. The provision of infrastructure and utility services. In *Low-income Housing in the Developing World,* pp. 233–48. Edited by Geoffrey K. Payne. New York: John Wiley and Sons.

McDermott, John. 1969. Technology: The opiate of the intellectuals. *New York Review of Books,* July 1, pp. 25–35.

McGill, M. E., and Horton, M. E. 1973. *Action Research Designs—For Training and Development*. Washington, D.C.: National Training and Development Press.

Sarin, Madhu. 1982. *Urban Planning in the Third World—The Chandigarh Experience*. London: Mansell Publishing Ltd.

Winner, Langdon. 1977. *Autonomous Technology—Technics-Out-of-Control as a Theme in Political Thought*. Cambridge, Mass.: MIT Press.

CHAPTER 9

Deciding Interventions: Methods and Models

The idea that civilised life consists of a fully conscious, intelligent, self-determining populace making informed choices about ends and means and taking action on that basis is revealed as a pathetic fantasy.

Langdon Winner, *Autonomous Technology—Technics Out of Control as a Theme in Political Thought*

There is a pervasive dilemma which recurs in research, in planning, and in politics. How much can you afford to know before you act? How much time can you afford to spend making sure that you will all act together? How far can people share power without destroying the power they share?

Hugh Stretton, *Urban Planning in Rich and Poor Countries*

Developing programs cooperatively and deciding interventions involve three general clusters of activity: sorting out intentions and setting objectives; acquiring know-how, which sometimes demands acquiring expert help and sometimes training; and collecting resources—whether land, money, materials, skills, or influential people. These clusters are common irrespective of formal-informal development demarcations.

The first cluster requires coming to grips with the way we see what we see and therefore with building knowledge and interpreting values about the physical and social makeup of place. It entails understanding sometimes fragile networks of relationships between people and organizations, between dwelling and commerce, buildings and ritual, between the desire for modernity and respect of tradition, to name a few.

Setting objectives entails documentation and analysis. What have we got, and how do things work? What are the problems, why and for whom, and in what general order of priority? What opportunities are available to us? Setting objectives also entails people, local informants, a community of clients, all of whom will have their own social, political, technical, and economic agendas and most of whom will provide a substantial amount of knowledge about function, values and symbols, history, and the structure of its institutions. This "knowledge required to understand the actions of people is embedded in the ordinary language of social practices of the community in which this action occurs" (Argyris, Putnam, and Smith 1985, 26) and in the expression of that language in the way people build and organize their physical environment. Inasmuch as it is impossible to paint pictures of reality without the multiple interpretive expressions of those who are part of that reality, so it is risky, and even dangerous, to change that reality without the cooperation of those who know it best. If they are, artificial systems for regulating change, imposed from outside in the form of standards, laws and institutions will be introduced that usually are difficult to sustain. Most systems of this sort require persistent external vigilance to maintain them, which especially in poor countries, are difficult to get and keep going, for lack of money, administrative capabilities, skilled personnel, and political commitment. External systems of vigilance also induce apathy and dependence. Lacking the opportunity for self-determination, ownership, and control, people who need something done typically wait for someone to come and do it. And when no one comes (the typical case), apathy and resentment set in and environments deteriorate rapidly.

Setting objectives therefore entails collecting stories and identifying themes that bind people, are common, and are repetitive. It entails developing a mutual understanding of interests and later of interpretations of issues and problems so that they can be properly positioned and properly tackled.

The second cluster of activities is about collecting resources. Can we achieve what we have set out to do with the resources available? How do the resources we have—the land, the money, the skills, the materials, the influence—shape or reshape our means and ends? Given what we need to do, how can we get the resources and where? How to get the resources is not our primary concern here; finding out what we need and what we can do with the available resources is an intrinsic part of enablement planning.

The third cluster of activities is about building know-how—specifically know-how of the system and how to manipulate it. This cluster is about project work, which satisfies not only its primary purpose of building shelter, delivering services, and improving health but a number of other purposes as well. People will need to be aware of things to consider, things to watch out for or to worry about, problems and hurdles that may be encountered, the sorts of people and organizations that always seem to get in the way, the kinds of bottlenecks that always seem to appear despite planning and preparation. People need to know the options available, the risks and commitments that are entailed, the investment of time, energy, and money that will have to be made, the resources they will need, and so on. One may ask: What hurdles can be anticipated before, during, and after implementation?

Many of the risks, bottlenecks, and hurdles people will encounter will have to do with managing the system and trying to find their way through it or around it:

What [people] need is a guide through the thickets of legislation and regulations that stand in the way of anyone doing anything. How do we get our aims through the local authority planners? Through the building control department which administers regulations which are by now incomprehensible to the layman? How can we qualify for improvement grants? How can we win a loan from the Housing Corporation? How can we put together a package of mortgage loans from the various sources of housing finance, which might include that body and the local authority, and an insurance company or a building society? How do we qualify for any of that urban aid money that comes from central government under a bewildering and ever-changing series of initials and acronyms? Can we use any of that free, job-creating labour provided by the Manpower Services Commission to massage the unemployment statistics? (Ward 1987, 29)

MAKING STRATEGIC CHOICES

These three clusters of activity—setting objectives, collecting resources, and building know-how—demand significant changes in work habits for architects and planners and in method. They also demand better communication techniques and innovations.

We attempt to create a community of clients. The dynamics of such a group is very different from that of individual clients most architects are accustomed to dealing with. In previous examples and those to follow, I have used community-based workshops in a variety of forms geared to the different circumstances. Our techniques have varied according to purpose, the scale of the project, the amount of time available, and the prevailing political circumstances.

Most collaborative planning work includes usually one or a combination of role playing, games or gaming, and negotiation. Wall charts, models, and cognitive maps are typically used to structure the decision-making process, record information, and avoid personal confrontations. Most methods view planning "as a process of strategic choice . . . in which activities of making plans, decisions and policies can come together in quite subtle and dynamic ways" (Freind and Hickling 1987, 1, 5) and full of surprises rather than contrived by overly tight and preemptive schedules, agendas, and curricula.

Most processes of strategic choice entail games or gaming, played under structured circumstances to help develop alternatives and to compare choices. They enable each alternative to be properly understood in terms of its likely impacts.[1]

Those directed at communities and community planning typically assume that solutions are more likely to be appropriate and problems more likely tolerated when design and development decisions are made by those closest to the situation and most affected by those decisions. In addition, community-directed methods assume that nonexperts may lack knowledge of alternatives, the resources to achieve their goals, and information about or trade-offs among choices. They may also lack the skills needed for negotiation and to work out technical and financial details. Communities may also lack knowledge of hurdles they are likely to encounter during planning and sometimes organizational and leadership skills. Various games and other techniques will need to be designed to help build any one or a combination of these missing elements. Some games are designed to simulate potential outcomes (if you did this, then this is likely to happen).

---

1. See, for example, Clark Abt, *Serious Games* (New York: Viking Press, 1970). See also Henry Sanoff, *Designing with Community Participation* (New York: Hutchinson Ross, 1978).

Others are used to teach skills or build awareness. "Serious games combine the analytic and questioning concentration of the scientific viewpoint with the intuitive freedom and rewards of imaginative, artistic acts" (Abt 1970, 11–12).

GAMEPAK

Some games can be designed to inform and build awareness of planning procedures, potential hurdles, and alternatives for funding, tenure, and management. This was the intent of GamePAK (Hamdi, Goethert, and Mongold 1989), which was designed for the Massachusetts Housing Partnership as part of a larger Planning Assistance Kit (PAK) that contained gaming methods designed to assist communities in delivering and managing their own housing and improvement programs.

GamePAK is designed to instruct people about PAK and utilizes a series of metaphors to model the planning field. People play the game at the beginning of the planning process with three primary objectives in mind. First, it familiarizes people with the planning jargon. It informs them about the approvals they may have to be familiar with, programs for funding and ownership, potential risks, and commitments and investment. Second, it identifies typical hurdles, bottlenecks, basic choices, people, and organizations likely to be confronted and what they are likely to demand. Third, since it is played before work gets underway, it is designed to break down barriers between "them" and "us" and to build a sense of cooperation among participants.

GamePAK is significant as much for its structure as its content. It is designed so that the content can be filled in by participants as a prelude to playing the game itself. This enables the game to be played in a variety of contexts and also enables participants to brainstorm and talk about options, terminologies, resources, hurdles, and potential bottlenecks. In other words, the character and content of the game can be established by those who play it.

COGNITIVE MAPS

Yet another useful function of gaming has to do with documenting and interpreting information, ideas, and decisions. The issue here is to undertake these exercises openly so there is constant feedback among all participants and information can be modified and reinterpreted until themes are identified and used to build programs. One example was illustrated and successfully employed in 1979 in Topeka, Kansas.[2]

Unlike conventional examples, the documentation went further than developing lists and monitoring information to mapping events in people's past and present experience. Constructing stories in this way—using cognitive maps—revealed social and political relationships that might in the end influence proposals.

The area, known as Tennessee Town, was founded in 1879 by freed slaves; it is typical of many poor inner-city areas. The migration of more affluent families to the suburbs, lack of financial resources, and neglect of the environment combined to erode the physical and social characteristics of this once-cohesive and largely self-sustaining community. Decay was compounded by the displacement of locally owned businesses, the increasing number of absentee landlords, and the large elderly and transient population, with conflicting interests, needs, and aspirations.

The planning and design process started with a team of student architects who roamed around the six-block area, talking to families, the elderly, children, shopkeepers, and those who had come in for business and others who had business going on in backyards, in basements, and in front rooms. Large maps of the entire area were made on stiff cardboard and put up in an abandoned school within the

neighborhood. The school later became the center for planning activities and later still converted to a permanent neighborhood facility with day care, community legal services, and community gardens.

In the second phase, a community workshop was organized, the first of many, and located locally in the Buchanan School. The map filled one entire classroom. Piles of construction paper in all colors, scissors, pins, tape, colored markers, and pencils were at hand. Professionals, government personnel, and residents recorded their perceptions, feelings, sentiments, prejudices, nostalgia, opinions, wants, needs, and suggestions. Over the next three months, people would drift into the school, on their own or with friends, review how the maps were developing, and make additions or adjustments. Information was layered progressively on to the maps, and equally progressively, stories emerged that told as much about physical needs as about people with influence—who owned what, how various territorial claims worked among different age groups, different religious orders, and different minorities; who went where and when; who used what; who worked for whom; and so on.

The student architects checked information and sometimes made drawings to pinpoint areas of potential work to clarify ideas and to build an inventory of the kinds of things and ideas that could feature in a potential program.

In the third phase, areas selected for work were recorded on 8½ × 11 cards, each identifying a specific category of work. Among the projects that emerged were renovation of the Buchanan School to accommodate a number of community facilities and community gardens; new housing; winterization of some existing houses; the management of garbage; incentives for local businesses; and historic markers to highlight the importance of the neighborhood and its buildings, both locally and nationally (the Buchanan School was one of three cited in *Brown* v. *Board of Education of Topeka*). Each category was pinned to a wall, and residents and others brainstormed ideas for dealing with issues and re-

2. This year-long project was undertaken with students from Kansas State University and is reported in Tennessee Town Neighborhood, *Openhouse* 6(4)(198): 41–50.

Mapping:

Putting information on maps
of a Tennessee town.

(Photo by W. Mike Martin, Architecture Department, CAL POLY-SLO)

155

Discussing project areas and working out options.

solving problems. A newsletter was started to publicize events and record initiatives.

Finally, work teams were set up to work out in detail proposals that seemed feasible and to lobby community agencies for money.

This and other examples model their methods on the assumption that decisions about strategies will be made in a climate of uncertainty under conditions where information is incomplete, where demands are not consistent, and sometimes under pressure of conflict of interests, of urgency, to get on and do something, and of competition for limited resources. The best methods in dealing with this complexity are active rather than passive and use techniques that communicate openly rather than intimidate. They use simple language in words and in graphics that inform rather than bewilder.

PLANNING FOR REAL

One method that brings all these attributes successfully together is called Planning for Real.[3] It was devised and is widely used in Britain, primarily for neighborhood improvement. It all comes in a kit with cutout buildings and other neighborhood facilities (playgrounds, pools, laundries, etc.) and with information cards, wall charts, case histories, and hints on how to be effective. Its focus is on bridging the communication gap between professionals and between professionals and the public. Tony Gibson, its innovator, had come to the conclusion that ''an

---

3. See Tony Gibson, *People Power: Community and Work Groups in Action* (London: Penguin Books, 1979).

'alternative currency' to words was needed in order to sustain effective exchange between people with the gift of gab and the technical jargon, and others without the verbal means to convey their own knowledge and experience" (Gibson 1980). In Planning for Real, local people first build and then work around a model large enough to ensure that there will be no room for the conventional platform party and audience.

The kit contains over 150 suggestions marked on cutouts that people put on the model gradually, sorting and sifting them out until consensus begins to emerge on what most people want now, soon, or later. The model, which is made in sections, is carried around the area—to bingo halls, churches, schools, shopping centers, and even playgrounds—to attract attention.

Part 2 of the kit contains information about how to publicize the model and promote public meetings. Instructions advise on how to record ideas, update information, or express disagreement with someone else's suggestions. Anyone can walk up to the model and turn someone else's suggestion card over, which has "disagree" written on the back. Later all of the suggestions that have not been turned over presumably represent proposals about which there is consensus.

Gibson has everyone mill around the model, which, "instead of the eyeball-to-eyeball confrontation you get in traditional meetings with the fluent talkers having it all their own way, it's more likely that everyone's eyelines will be converging on the subject matter—the model and its possibilities" (Gibson n.d., 3). Personalities become less distracting, the suggestions on the model no longer have a particular person attached to them. Confronting subjects rather than people avoids intimidation.

In the third part of Planning for Real, people make concrete proposals—adjustments to buildings, gardens, adventure playgrounds—to improve the neighborhood. Very soon what matters to people appears evident: "in one case 16 adventure play-

grounds appeared on the same model in the first 20 minutes" (Gibson n.d., 4).

The final part of the kit has charts for ordering and positioning the suggestions according to what people feel is most important, other suggestions that need to be done soon, and those that can wait. Later, small groups are formed to work out details and to negotiate between still conflicting interests and priorities.

Gibson suggests that Planning for Real (and other processes like it) works because it begins to establish working relationships as some of the "us" and "them" prejudices disappear. "This is because," Gibson (n.d.,5) suggests, "everyone, professionals included, can start out non-committed, without making promises or proposals which have to be stuck to (for fear of losing face) even when a second or third thought looks better."

The model enables people to see the problems and the possibilities as a whole, and suggestions and priorities can be identified and written on a chart: "Seeing all this makes people more confident and adept at exploring the ways and means to overcome obstacles and get things done. And this goes for professionals too, as they begin to look across interdepartmental barriers and to see how to bring together scattered resources of official manpower, money, materials and equipment" (Gibson n.d., 5).

Whether with models, wall charts, gaming, or role playing, all of these processes help improve dialogue between public officials, professionals, and community people and empower local people to negotiate priorities.

In Planning for Real, as in microplanning, planners are not simply inviting opinions or seeking reactions to proposals, which is so often the window dressing conveniently labeled participatory design, or planning.

The materials used for the models and the charts are not sophisticated or slick. No one is intimidated by the packaging: It's all disposable and most can be picked up free wherever good paper, card, boxes

Planning for Real. *(Source: Tony Gibson)*

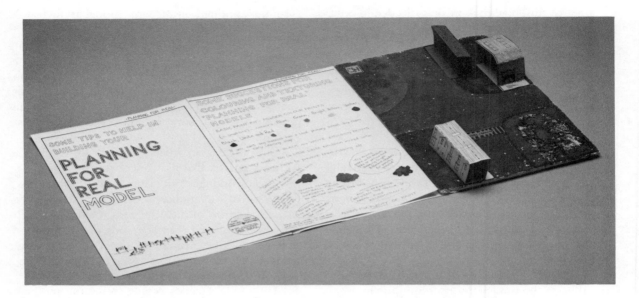

(Photos by Reinhard Goethert)

Working with Planning for Real with the Riverside Cambridgeport Community Corporation, MIT SIGUS Workshop, Cambridge, Massachusetts.

are being thrown out. An architect observing these processes in Liverpool said: ''The thing which impressed me was the speed with which they worked out and resolved the problem. . . . They arrived at decisions together very quickly without a great deal of conflict. One of the best things of watching people design without us making suggestions is to see what their priorities are'' (Gibson, 1980, 204). A community group in Nottingham observed:

We saw what we were doing. You could translate words into actions. . . . There was a definite affinity growing up, just as two people who live together can start off a sentence and you know the rest of it. . . . We got on to common ground quicker, because with words everybody's words are the same; but the imagination may be different. . . . In the mind everybody can be seeing a different thing and therefore not come to that consensus, stick out for their thing, because they could not see in

their mind what was making it impossible. . . . But where you have got the model . . . you looked at the thing and said, ''let's try this.'' (Gibson, 1980, 204)

A PRO FORMA ATTEMPT AT PUBLIC PARTICIPATION

Now consider, in contrast and more typically, attempts at public participation that are pro forma. These exercises conventionally wind up in public meetings, held in town halls, where people get talked at by officials and experts. At a platform an official of the housing authority explains his authority's intentions to build a large housing project. Other specialists sit with the speaker to answer specific questions if they arise. They are there because they are required by legislation. The speaker has a long pointer, which he uses to pick out features of his new project, presented in full color, which he flips through with the aid of his flip chart.

At the other end of the room sit about forty people; some are abutters to the proposed project and others hope they will receive one of the houses being built. Also in the audience are the activists and others who are there to champion the cause of "power to the people."

Few in the audience can see what the speaker is pointing at (he uses feasibility drawings done to 100th scale), and even those who can might not understand what he is really saying because his language is obscure. "Spatial configuration of the plan, derived on the basis of deductive reasoning," he says. "It is an optimally functional synthesis of user demands, based on months of surveys." He talks of internal streets and spines instead of corridors, and so on.

Most of the forty people present shuffle about impatiently; the meeting has been in session for over 2 hours. Some nod off to sleep, and others eye their watches nervously (it is getting late for the baby sitter, the stores will close in a half hour). Finally, the speaker summarizes the salient points and turns to his experts to ask if he has missed anything. Then he asks for comments or questions from the audience. This is usually followed by a silence; no one wants to expose themselves more than they have to. Then one of the activists complains about the poor quality of sound insulation between dwellings in his own project. His comment has little or nothing to do with the purpose of the meeting, about which by this time most people had in any case forgotten.

The speaker winds up the session by thanking everyone for coming, by assuring them of his best services, and by encouraging them to visit the town hall within the next week between the hours of 2 and 5 P.M. (when most will be at work) where the drawings will be pinned up in case anyone has any suggestions to modify the plans. Everyone gets up and leaves. The platform people congratulate themselves on how well it all went.

A METAPHORIC MODEL

In all of these examples (except the town hall meeting) and in many others, despite desirable and necessary variations in sequence, emphasis, technique, and the timing of work, a general pattern emerges that enables us to construct a model of the decision-making process in ways that facilitate professional and governmental interventions and can be a basis on which to design most program building workshops. It is a model that helps make more explicit where governments and professionals can step in and help, what they should leave alone, and how to get things going and keep them going. In all projects, decisions have to be made with an understanding of the options available, the resources at hand, and the hurdles that have to be faced.

Consider the following: a site ready for development, a settlement targeted for upgrading, or a building earmarked for renovation. Now consider a set of objectives reflecting the aspirations, needs and vested interests of a composite client body made up of users, funders, politicians, activists, abutters, special interest groups, ethnic minorities, and the rest: a community center, some houses revamped for the elderly, some lots for self-build, some small loans as business starters, extending the bus line and adding a convenient bus stop, extending a small school.

Initially, a number of ways in which each of the objectives can be met come to mind—the different ways of making a community center, planning the lots, or extending the school. Our first response is probably quite intuitive, based on our values, our knowledge, and our experience. Then a number of questions will have to be asked: What are the different ways we can fund our project? What are the different ways of building, owning, and running it? What should go where? There will be other questions more specific to content or of special interest to particular clients. How do we guarantee security? How do we keep cars away or reduce noise or other environmental impacts? How do we control speculation?

Each question identifies a potential field of exploration, each with a variety of options, each placing demands on the resources of people and local organizations, and each demanding certain approvals. Each option will involve risks, investments, and commitments, with differences in cost, in the time needed to get them done, in their sequence relative to all the other components of the program, and in their degree of indispensability.

One way to model this complex process more simply and to expedite passage and decide interventions is to use a number of metaphors.[4] Consider, for example, that each option is like a gate, access through which will depend on a number of conditions. In any field, there are at least three kinds of gates. First are those that are known and readily accessible, provided the means and the authority to gain access are available. Known and accessible gates usually have legal legitimacy; access through them can be officially offered and has been preapproved. The question, of course, is to whom they are accessible and for whom they were put there in the first place. Known gates come and go depending on party politics and, in international development, the policy of development agencies. Each field can be cultivated and controlled by the number and types of gates available within it, which can sometimes frustrate rather than support local freedoms of choice. In the field of tenure, for example, gates might include freehold ownership, cooperative ownership, land trusts, or condominium. In finance, there are gates through both public and pri-

vate channels or in partnership between public and private.

The second kind of gate is hidden and needs to be "discovered." These gates are hidden either because the problem or issue is poorly defined or positioned, because we do not know about them, or because they are purposely or inadvertently concealed. In this last case, government, agencies, and professionals may be bent on pushing a particular option and may therefore try to conceal others. Involving people in selecting from an already preselected set of options is manipulative and perfunctory, as Sherry Arnstein (1969) has shown. She pointed out that in the United States "survey after survey has documented that poor housewives most want tot-lots in their neighborhood where young children can play safely. But most women answered the questionnaire without knowing what their options were. They assumed that if they asked for something small, they might just get something useful in their neighborhoods. Had the mothers known that a free pre-paid health insurance plan was a possible option, they might not have put tot-lots so high on their lists."

The importance of the concept of hidden gates is to legitimize discovery as part of planning—the idea that you can stumble on good options, that you have the freedom to devise one that fits, that you can legitimately search for alternatives in the face of adversity. This applies to government as well as to communities. In Jakarta, for example, where public land is in short supply, guided land development schemes were invented as a kind of land sharing between government and private landowners. Government would improve roads and rights of way on private land to gain access and settle people. Landowners would benefit from higher land values, as would the government by levying a tax that would cover long-term payments for the improvements. Other good examples of hidden gates that have been recently discovered with government support include land sharing in Bangkok—a partnership between owners and renters to appropriate and

---

4. The choice of metaphors and the basic concept for the model is derived from John Turner's barriers and options ideas. See John Turner, Barriers, channels and community control, in *The Living City*, edited by David Cadman and Geoffrey Payne (New York: Routledge, 1989), pp. 179–89.

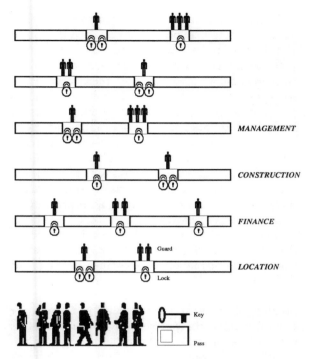

MANAGEMENT

CONSTRUCTION

FINANCE

LOCATION

Guard

Lock

Key

Pass

Fields, gates, locks, guards, keys, and passes. *(Drawing by Sevag Pogharian)*

develop land for low-income housing. In Sri Lanka thrifts have been formalized as effective local institutions for savings and small loans. In the Philippines, in response to difficulties in acquiring public land for housing projects, loans are offered to private developers, who then establish joint ventures with landowners.

Once hidden gates are discovered, they may nevertheless remain inaccessible. They may be blocked by governments or well-organized neighborhood groups, or they may be too expensive. The public may reject them if they do not meet expectations. In Africa, for example, innovations in mud technology were rejected in favor of concrete blocks because many Africans view concrete as the first rung of the ladder to modernity.

The third kind of gate is the *emergency* gate. It usually represents last-ditch options that one might adopt if all else fails. Some of these may be known but are considered illegitimate—for example, tenant takeover, tent cities, illegally tapping utilities. Others may be hidden and discovered in response to specific conditions—the city of the dead in Cairo, for example, where local cemeteries are inhabited by the poor. Governments may even informally legitimize emergency gates if there are no alternatives or if they fear political reprisal. In other cases, governments may informally co-opt the services of influential private individuals. In Pakistan's Katchi Abadis, for example, as in many other countries, peripheral land is often developed and sold by independent private persons who do not have legal title to the land but are informally legitimized because of acute land shortages. The illegal developers will ensure connections to basic services and guarantee some security from eviction.

Sometimes what starts as an emergency gate may well end up with the official backing of international agencies; it may become a known and legitimate gate, such as the case of squatting in most third world cities. Policies to upgrade squatter settlements legitimize de facto squatting as an inevitable way in which cities consolidate and grow.

In the informal settlements in developing countries, emergency gates are often a good way for the poor to make money. In Quito, Ecuador, the space under the public stairs in the old tenements is rented to some who otherwise would live on the street.

Finally, emergency gates conceptually differ from gates placed in any field because there is an emergency. Examples include bed and breakfast accommodations for the homeless or special shelters for the elderly or homeless.

All gates are locked and guarded, some more than others. Those who wish to gain access need both the means and the authority. To continue our metaphor, locks represent a measure of the private resources that any specific gate demands of anyone

Institute for Community Economics Revolving Loan Fund

Development Loan Fund

Low interest loans made available to CDCs and other community based developers who are involved in low income housing and land trusts. Loans may be used for acquisition and construction or rehab and other development expenses. ICE loans frequently are made available to land trusts and limited equity cooperatives that have found it impossible to get financing elsewhere.

How To Get More Information:
Call or write: The Institute for Community Economics 151 Montague City Road, Greenfield MA 01301, (413) 774-7956

Approvals Needed:
-Must be a project that involves keeping land and housing off the speculative market.
-Must be unable to arrange sufficient financing through other channels.
-Must have preliminary analysis of feasibility of project (flexible).
-_____
-_____
-_____
-_____
-_____
-_____

Resources Needed:
-Must have technical development capacity or appropriate technical assistance available.
-_____
-_____
-_____
-_____
-_____
-_____

Each option demands approvals (passes) and resources (keys) (sample from the Planning Assistance Kit's InfoPAK).

seeking access. And gatekeepers safeguard the public realm. They may prevent access even if an individual or group has the resources to open a gate.

There are at least two kinds of locks: resource and procedural. More simply, there will be resources you need to have—a certain income, a down payment, a particular skill, a certain amount of know-how, an influential contact—and there will be procedures you will need to follow—file certain applications, undertake preliminary surveys, acquire references, or register an organization. Who decides these demands? Who places locks on gates? Are the procedures for gaining approvals appropriate? Can they be changed? How?

Some resource and procedural conditions are endemic to the option, and usually these are technical. These conditions are placed there in good judgment and in the knowledge that if they are ignored, the option selected will not be effective. It is no use installing flush latrines in the slums of Caracas, for example, unless the water supply is adequate. It is difficult to drill a tube well without the right equipment and the money or influence to get it. A brick wall demands a foundation. Equally, there are procedures endemic to certain options. Whether you are laying foundations, building pit latrines, or constructing a timber roof—in all cases there is good and well-tried practice that is known to work and needs a building permit and the approval of building inspectors. The trouble is that even good practice can demand standards (guards) that put them out of reach to those with the lowest incomes.

Other locks are placed on gates by private individuals or organizations—by landowners, banks, manufacturers, landlords, and so on. The demands placed on access by these locks are usually market driven. Access to mortgages, for example, demands down payments and is controlled by prevailing interest rates. Steel and cement used for construction have market-regulated prices, albeit often in developing countries decided informally on the black market.

Other locks are placed on gates by public authorities. For example, in one home ownership program, buyers must make at least a 5 percent down payment plus other closing costs of 4–5 percent. Buyers must also show they can qualify for mortgages. Public locks may judge the clients' capacity to manage a program after purchase or construction. Sometimes public locks are structured (and then monitored) by international agencies, which lend money on the condition that borrowers demonstrate the capacity to recover costs, to administer public services, or to manage the acquisition and disposal of buildable land. Development options that involve international funders are often coupled with training programs and experts with their own keys, which aim to build local capability where it may be weak or nonexistent, generally to safeguard the interests of the donor.

Finally, some procedural locks are so encumbered with bureaucracy that they prevent even the most willing community from gaining access. David Walton (1984, 191), for example, counted twenty-one steps in formally obtaining a building loan in Tanzania, "which was too much for either the applicants or the administration to cope with." And in New York, which in 1965 represented "only the average in bureaucratic proliferations" for the United States, anyone wanting to construct even the simplest new building was required to conform to some thirteen codes and regulatory processes administered by nearly as many city authorities. Even then, once plans were complete, preliminary approvals were needed from each of five additional agencies, each with their own procedures, not all coordinated in their codes of practice, and even more depending on the location of the building, be it waterfront, public park, along a subway route, and so on.[5]

Inasmuch as locks measure the capacity of a client to acquire an option, so gatekeepers judge clients' eligibility against criteria set in the public interest. Gatekeepers ensure that the client is qualified to pass irrespective of their resource ability to open the gate based largely on good conduct. There are at least two kinds of gatekeepers. One kind is legal and legislative; they judge eligibility with zoning ordinances, building codes, and safety standards. They ensure that you will not block your neighbor's light, endanger his or her means of escape in case of fire, invade the other's privacy, pollute his or her air, or even threaten his or her investment in property or land. The other kind of gatekeeper is a "people" kind. There are interest groups who want to see their interests served by any proposed development. They may include abutters, mayors, neighborhood interest groups, business district committees, and school committees.

Some legal or legislative gatekeepers have a moral obligation to ensure greater equity—to facilitate or even restrict those who might not normally be eligible. In Massachusetts, for example, anyone applying for home ownership subsidies (a financial gate) through the Home Ownership Opportunities program must satisfy the guard with a number of conditions. Their project must have at least 30 percent of units affordable to low- or moderate-income families; there are resale restrictions on the affordable units; buyers must be first-time home buyers; and no more than 15 percent of the development can be for commercial or office space.

As we have seen, some gatekeepers are in place less to ensure good conduct in the interests of safety, equity, or technical efficiency and more to protect the interests of party politics—to check the intentions of clients against established or desired political ideals. Do the intentions, for example, fit the political desire to move toward privatization? Will a particular option, if acquired, help build local political constituencies that may be in opposition to the center? Will the granting of titles to squatters legitimize the illegitimate invasion of land? Even more complex, in this respect and in the context of international development, is the placing or re-

---

5. See, for example, Abraham Levitt, Bureaucracy, the regulatory agencies and the architect, *Progressive Architecture* 46(2), 1965.

moval of guards in the interest of donor nations and the mechanics of global monetary systems.

The World Bank, for example, has developed a substantial range of criteria that it uses to guard its own interests and, ostensibly, those of its borrowers. They include affordability, lack of subsidy, lower standards for plot size and infrastructure, full cost recovery, replicability of project components, and market value of land. Some of these international guards are not welcome by the borrowers. There may be squabbles among gatekeepers, their numbers may increase to the point where gaining access becomes a drawn-out and complicated process, too difficult for local groups to achieve.

Not all gatekeepers are placed or legitimized by government or international agencies. Some gatekeepers are placed informally by local self-styled community organizations—perhaps to protect their status in local politics—and others are set in place by religious or tribal laws.

Finally, some legal and legislative gatekeepers are very old and have lost much of their purpose. They represent no one's interest in particular but remain because no one has bothered to change or remove them. The trouble is that they can still interfere with access to some legitimate options.

In most cases, there are usually two ways to pass gatekeepers and acquire an option. The first is to acquire a pass—a zoning approval, a variance, an environmental impact approval, a building code approval, or something similar. Acquiring passes from people-type gatekeepers might involve a show of hands at a public meeting in favor of a particular option, a letter or a petition. The second way to pass gatekeepers is to dodge them—for example, legally by finding loopholes or through grandfather clauses. Well over 80 percent of most residential developments in developing countries are built without formal approval.

From the model, it becomes more evident whether more options (gates) should be added to the field specifically designed for the poor; whether gates placed there by private organizations (banks, developers, speculative builders) can have their locks changed, placing fewer demands for access; or whether keys are made easily available in the form of subsidies, grants, cheap loans, information, skills, experts, or land. It becomes evident that gatekeepers could be changed or eliminated or that special passes can be arranged for the poor in the interests of equity or social or political stability. Special organizations might be needed to facilitate access to money, skills, and professional help (the Community Enterprise Fund in England, the Urban Community Development in Hyderbad, India, the thrift societies in Sri Lanka, the community development corporations in the U.S.) to facilitate partnerships (another way of building resources, or acquiring keys), to channel private wealth for public good (land sharing in Bangkok, land readjustment schemes in Korea, linkage programs in Boston, land reforms in Sri Lanka).

This kind of enablement planning and design demands not only innovations in technique. It places additional demands on the services of architects and on the tools and methods of practice itself.

REFERENCES

Abt, Clark C. 1970. *Serious Games*. New York: Viking.

Argyris,Chris; Putnam, Robert; and Smith, Diana McCain. 1985. *Action Science—Concepts, Methods and Skills for Research and Interventions*. San Francisco: Jossey-Bass.

Arnstein, Sherry A. 1969. A ladder of citizen participation. *Journal of the American Institute of Planners* 45(4) (July 12).

Freind, John, and Hickling, Allen. 1987. *Planning under Pressure—The Strategic Choice Approach*. Oxford: Pergamon Press.

Gibson, Tony. 1980. Sooner done than said. *Architects Journal,* July 30, 204–5.

Gibson, Tony. n.d. *Planning for Real—Users Guide*.

Hamdi, Nabeel; Goethert, Reinhard; and Mongold,

Neil. 1989. *Planning Assistance Kit—A Planning Guide for Community-based Organizations.* Unpublished manual. Cambridge, Mass.: M.I.T., Department of Architecture.

Walton, David S. 1984. The role of international consultants. In *Low-Income Housing in the Developing World,* pp. 187–98. Edited by Geoffrey K. Payne. New York: John Wiley and Sons.

Ward, Colin. 1987. Community architecture: What a time it took for the penny to drop. *Built Environment* 13(1): 22–32.

CHAPTER 10

Architects and Housing: Changing Professional Responsibilities and Training

When I graduated from an architectural school in Bombay, I was not aware of an increasing income disparity between the rich and the poor, and that my degree was too expensive for the ordinary people. People who needed me to house themselves could not afford me, while rich people who already had houses needed me to increase their housing stock. Where to turn: money or people?

Ramesh Manandhar
(in Saini 1988)

Planners and especially architects working as supporters do much soul searching. They are torn between two sets of conflicting objectives: a social commitment to improve the lot of the poor majority living in slums and shanties and a desire to contribute something tangible and immediately useful but also a commitment to careers and to their status within their discipline. The result, says Turner, is that even the best find themselves paralyzed by guilt or ambition. Those who pursue housing find themselves without architecture, and those who pursue careers often find themselves without reason. These issues are of concern to many students of architecture who are interested in providing housing to those with low incomes, especially in poor countries.

As they search for theories, explanations, and even answers, students will read numerous books, articles, and reports describing the different ways to house the poor and deal with the complexities of urban settlements. Some of the books concentrate on the importance of institutional changes with which to lever social and political reforms and so to link more equitable housing with more efficient cost and resource saving techniques. Others take us back to basic principles and trace the legacies inherited from a market either overly dominated by public intervention or left to the free play of private entrepreneurship. Some point to technical explorations with a heavy emphasis on technology—better ways of building, designing, and utilizing land and better methods for modeling the complexities of urban life, measuring the impact of policies, making evaluations, and gathering data about people and places.

Some expound the euphoric successes of self-help, sites-and-services projects, and participatory planning and place heavy emphasis on the importance of the organizational and management components that led to these successes. Others, the behavioral determinists, try to convince us that if places are made defensible, crime rates will fall and thus improve the social fabric of projects. They will count everything from where people urinate to how many window panes are broken and will plot their data on trend lines correlating vandalism with density, entrance type and position, and security, among others. They will lay the blame firmly on poor design.

Some books set housing in the context of development (the term usually means economic rather than social development) and tell us that aid to developing countries is directed less at alleviating poverty and is instead "primarily concerned with the preservation of the existing world economic order," which itself is threatened by poverty in underdeveloped countries. We are told that international aid has compounded poverty and that modernization and then development are necessarily exploitative, systemic, and aided by imperialism. "Their astonishing accomplishments have caused and are still causing considerable social injuries" (Dube 1988, 5).

Many texts are drably descriptive and even critical of cases that may inform but fail to enlighten. Some are downright disheartening: "Ask yourself which was the period of maximum house production in British history. The answer is the 1930s when from 240,000 to 400,000 houses were completed each year. Who was building them? The answer is that they were built with no architectural aid by a myriad of tiny two-men-and-a-boy-and-a-barrow firms, largely undercapitalized, with a bankruptcy each week, operating on credit from builders merchants" (Ward 1987, 24). Ward (1983, 104) has also written that "thirteenth century churches, Tudor Cottages, Georgian squares, regency terraces and Victorian warehouses, were built without benefit of professional gentlemen, as indeed were the converted windmills, outhouses, and stables which are most sought after as residences within the architectural profession."

The best writings conclude that building houses through idealized, centralized, static, technocratic, professionally controlled, and large–in–scale means is not a good way of solving housing problems for the poor majority. This is a puzzling conclusion for architects committed to housing and to architecture.

If, students ask, building houses or designing housing projects has little to do with solving housing problems, what then is the function of architecture in housing and what is the role of architects? The answer to this age-old question, phrased as it is, probably has to be: very little.

ARCHITECTS AND HOUSING IN HISTORY

History tells us that neither architecture nor architects had much to do with the prolific building activities in housing before, during, or after the industrial revolution in the developed world or today in the developing world. And when they were a party to the evangelical interventions of public authorities in both first and third world countries, together they managed only a small dent in the context of overall supply—even then with only marginal success in producing the right numbers of houses, of the right kind, in the right place, and at the right cost.

"In the excitement of high practice," few architects and few clients in history managed to connect what architects did or what their art had to offer to the task of improving the conditions of the working class. Many architects were far too busy to notice "the humble attempts at house design" that engaged small builders and self-helpers and were appearing all over, whether in the growing industrial cities or in the plotlands of southeast England.[1] Indeed, many clients, corporate or individual dispensed with architects to save money, much as they

---

1. Plotlands are plots of varying sizes and shapes built on at first with makeshift houses and later becoming formal suburban or urban subdivisions. The term is used by Colin Ward in *Arcadia for All* (1986, London, New York: Mansell Press) and in *Housing, An Anarchist Approach* (1983, London: Freedom Press).

still do today, "preferring to muddle through with the help of a tame builder" (Tarn 1969, 17).

In Britain, Henry Roberts, architect to the Philanthropic Society for Improving the Conditions of the Laboring Class, founded in 1844, dispensed with architecture and retired from practice so that he could devote his time to housing. Roberts no doubt realized, as did Henry Derbyshire, who worked for the Peabody trust (another Victorian philanthropy that survives today), that the major issues of the time were not architectural but had more to do with sanitation, with the politics of improved standards and public intervention, with organization, and with management. These might have been the concerns of another architect, Richard Elsam, whose consideration for the welfare of the peasantry in 1816 inspired a book of model cottages for rural workers called *Hints for Improving the Condition of the Peasantry*. His explicit intention was to reward the peasantry who, he claimed, had contributed to the riches of the nation and who "constituted so considerable a portion of our wealth, it is doubtless the duty of those in whose hands providence has placed the means, to assist in promoting their welfare."[2] Other notables like George Gilbert Scott, designer of cathedrals, when he was invited to submit his design for a working-class suburb in Halifax, did so with bundles of ideology but with little practical consideration for standards, building economies, and environmental conditions. His designs, like many others of his colleagues, were viewed as esoteric and criticized as "antiquated, inconvenient, wanting in light and not adapted to modern requirements" (Akroyd in Tarn 1969, 17).

Yet others were challenged by the demands of the model cottage movement to improve sanitation, separate the sexes, and provide decent storage—all at a modest cost and all preferably in the romantic picturesque style of rural landscapes. John Nash, the architect of Regent Street in London, designed a model village at Blaise in 1809, and John

Sloane and John Wood published their plans for laborers' cottages in the 1790s. But despite the obvious improvement in sanitation and construction, they met with the kind of criticism still leveled at architects today:

Only too often are the inhabitants made to suffer from the artistic sloping of roofs and tiny windows. When one has no choice of bedrooms, gables and eaves are often a picturesque cruelty by every inch of height and light and air of which they deprive human beings.

Until Norman Shaw designed the middle-class suburb of Bedford Park in 1876, no architect [in England] found a place in the history of the nineteenth century architecture who also played any significant part in the development of the housing movement. The reason is not really difficult to discern; the housing problem was not solved in what might be called architectural terms—within the nineteenth century meaning of the word—until the end of the period. (Tarn 1969, 17)

As Ruskin put it in 1849, "Let us therefore at once confine the name to that art which, taking up and admitting, as conditions of its working, the necessities and common uses of the building impresses on its form certain characters venerable or beautiful, but otherwise unnecessary" (Ruskin 1925, 14–15).

In the United States, architects have progressively attempted to increase their involvement in the profitable business of housing in the face of an industry that has been captive to owner builders, owner sponsors, merchant builders, and manufacturers.[3] With some notable exceptions, their desire

---

2. Quoted in Bauer 1934, *Modern Housing,* pp. 67 and 68.

3. According to Gutman (1985) *owner builders* own the land and build their own homes. Some 50 percent of all housing before 1900 was built this way and some 15–20 percent is done today. *Owner sponsors* generally do not use their own labor but may assume a management role. Some 15 percent of all housing is built this way, with significant opportunities for "architectural" innovation. *Merchant builders* like Levitt, Ryan and U.S. Homes provide the entire package, sometimes from manufacture to details of equipment, mortgages and other management services. Some, such as Skyline Homes, sell 25,000 to 50,000 mobile homes annually, and function as manufactures only without land development involvement.

to experiment with style, with an alternative aesthetic based on innovations with technology and to distinguish their work and themselves from the run of the mill, to make architecture out of dwelling, meshed with the popular demand for high production and low prices. On the one hand were the ornamentalists, imbuing "even the smallest projects [Williamsburg Houses in New York City] [with] copper roofs, elaborate brickwork, and canopies over every door" and where "sculptors carved friezes of muscular 1930s style workers for doorways and entrance courts" (Wright 1981, 227). On the other hand were the futurists, who were party to the industrialization of housing and experimented with form and materials: Albert Bemis, the Boston industrialist, with his various modular housing systems; George Kech, with his prototype Home of Tomorrow, exhibited in Chicago in 1933, which featured a garage and space for a small airplane; the motohome "that was unveiled in Wanamaker's store by President Roosevelt's mother on April Fool's day in 1935" (Jackson 1976, 215). Few of these projects were commercially successful. Few of them matched American aspirations and images, which were more regional in taste than modern. Few were directed, in any case, toward alleviating poverty. And few were taken seriously enough by policy makers to make any difference.

Most architects in the United States, like their counterparts in Europe, were disdainful of those who were scoring successes—the developers, builders, and private entrepreneurs. They looked down on the Sears Roebuck mail order houses and William Levitt's model homes in which Levitt combined traditional styles with up-to-date construction techniques. Few of the innovations that architects sought could match the extraordinary capacity of Levitt and sons, who produced 17,450 houses between 1947 and 1951 and put up one four-bedroom house every 16 minutes by 1950.

Architects who did manage to have something to say about housing did so in ways that were mostly at odds with the conventions of architectural practice. Some established partnerships or retainerships with builders and earned not only a fee for designing a basic type but an additional fee for every house built. The California builder Joseph Eichler is one successful example, who with the architectural firm of Ashen and Allen constructed thousands of suburban ranch-type houses all over the state. Design magazines and architectural journals "endorsed these collaborations, proudly declaring that the influence of professional architects would be the salvation of mass building" (Wright 1981, 249).

Other architects, sometimes in collaboration with each other, captured bits of the market by emulating the Roebucks and Levitt. The Architects Small House Service Bureau, which started in 1921 in Minneapolis, offered around 250 different designs to suit all sorts of conditions, incomes, and aspirations. The bureau produced standard plans at a minimum price of $6 per room, selling these through plan books and magazines. In addition, they provided training courses for owner-builders as well as more conventional design services for houses larger than six rooms. "Robert Jones, the Bureau's technical director claimed that the architectural profession was demonstrating its sense of civic responsibility by providing a service, making a reasonable profit and offering a rational approach to the housing business" (Wright 1981,200).

The American Institute of Architects saw in the bureau profit for architects and was quick to endorse and sponsor it, although many architects disavowed this endorsement, objecting no doubt to the drab monotony of standardized designs. According to Gutman (1985) designing stock plans, which are often sold through magazines or plan shops, was until recently the dominant way in which the architects contributed to housing. Even today, about 100 stock plan services operate in the United States, providing anything from 100–2000 plans each month, depending on the size of the organization. In 1980, a single set of designs cost between $50 and $80. They are typically advertised in popular books and magazines (*Better Homes and Gardens,* for example) or in books specifically geared to sell stock plans (*America's Best Home Plans*). Some are sold through plan shops (many of which were started by architects to keep small firms solvent) open to individual families and small builders who often buy additional architectural services through those shops to tailor plans to specific sites and to pass local building regulations.

Finally, there were two other significant ways which architects in history (and now) involved themselves in housing: through competitions and sometimes with studies. In the latter case, the New York Building Congress listed over 200 pieces of ongoing research in 1933, not all, of course, conducted by architects. Some were done by the notable Housing Study Guild, established in 1933, by Lewis Mumford and the architects Clarence Stein and Henry Wright, who were known for their model suburb of Sunnyside Gardens in Queens, built in 1928 (Wright 1981).

Competitions have always been a vehicle on both sides of the Atlantic for experimentation and new ideas, although mostly relative to style or technique. Their successes in housing for the poor, however, no less in Britain than in the United States, were marginal—sometimes because of their "perennial capacity for self-deception" (Jackson 1976, 56) and sometimes because the terms of competition leave little room to succeed. One example of the latter was the competition announced by the Plumber and Sanitary Engineers Magazine in December 1878, which was sponsored by notable philanthropists of the day. Its objective was to find a solution to the 25 x 100 ft lot in New York to alleviate the appalling conditions of poorly designed and built tenements. Two types emerged that more or less satisfied the competition conditions to improve light, ventilation, and standards of space: the side courtyard and the dumbbell. No one, however, was that happy, not least the jurors, who concluded: "[the] committee emphatically declares that in their

view, it is impossible to secure the requirements of physical and moral health within these narrow and arbitrary limits" (Jackson 1976, 51) and that the real problems could be resolved only through statutory reforms to change the conditions within which design and building could best serve the poor.

But architects' lack of knowledge of housing for the poor equally prevented many from joining the bandwagon. The Model Housing Competition for New York in 1934 drew 1775 entries. Of these, only 22 showed any real knowledge of housing, according to the Housing Authority technical director of the time.

One clear lesson emerges from history and from the successes and failures of architects' interventions in housing: most who have made any difference have done so through innovations with organizations, through knowledge of policy and the conditions it places on practice, and through commitment. Few have made any difference experimenting with style, technique, or technology. Most who have made gains have done so by understanding the form of building as it fits the form of organizations most suitable for its development, as fits the form of political and social institutions that give it context. All this has very much to do with the architecture of housing.

IMPLICATIONS OF THE SUPPORT PARADIGM FOR TEACHING

Today many architects and students of architecture are still torn between the two characteristic and seemingly irreconcilable dispositions of their profession. Yves Cabannes has suggested these to be

either to act as a social catalyst, or to exert their skills in the alchemy of forms. The architect's intervention in the field of low cost housing is an expression of the former and has had some serious setbacks: the massive involvement with social issues, with architects trespassing on the preserve of other disciplines, on the one hand, and on the other, the fact of having to operate housing solutions set within very narrow technical and economic limits, have made architecture lose its specificity, which it is now trying to get back. (Cabannes 1985,103)

Others find themselves divided in their allegiances. Professional aspirations, unchecked by schools, "make it difficult for architects to remain committed to the ideals of their professions and at the same time, undertake the entrepreneurial and management functions that the house-manufacturing industry demands of its participants" (Gutman 1985, 13).

Students in the developing world will be under additional social and peer pressure to make good in a world that measures success in terms of professional status and prestige, usually counted in the amount of money earned, the size and location of their practice, the number of buildings built, and the kind of people they know. They will be under considerable peer pressure, as were their counterparts in history, to demonstrate their creative individuality and to distinguish themselves from others—whether in journals, at conferences, or in school: "There is only true prestige and glory in the eyes of the profession itself. [The student] is encouraged to look down on bureaucrats, lawyers, and technicians who invariably hamper his quest for architectural excellence and to treat his clients and users with benevolent paternalism" (Habraken 1983, 6). On top of it all, their families will have invested substantial sums of money in their education. It is unlikely that there will be much status earned, or people worth knowing, or building of architectural significance built while working within the slums of Bombay, Cairo, or Lima.

Many will have struggled to earn their architectural degrees at universities that find it difficult to connect architecture and what they should be teaching architects with housing and its multifaceted issues. While housing may be high on the list of national priorities, it remains low on their teaching agenda. These students wind up starting their careers on the fringe of their profession. Worse still, working within the public sector, as most often they will, they will be viewed by their colleagues as low on the professional status ladder.

Whether at home or abroad, most students will have been taught architecture in a climate not dissimilar to that of their predecessors in an atelier setting with ambitions and pedagogy still borrowed substantially from the days of the Beaux-Arts academy. Their teachers will feel uneasy teaching housing of the kind advocated by Turner and others, work that cannot be easily measured against strictly formal architectural criteria.

The academics may feel uneasy or worse. The work cannot be properly programmed, it doesn't fit the time table, it is chaotic, emotionally loaded, uses weird activities and suspect disciplines, isn't part of the established main stream of the profession, and creates in some teachers, a sense of loss of authority. Not everyone enjoys moving into unknown territory, or disclosing their ignorance of any ready made formulae for solving the problems. It makes demands of a teacher to get down from his podium and form a team with his students. It can release creativity, vigour and enthusiasm, but is not without risk. Finally, the school has to foresee that the project certainly has no more guarantee of success than other more conventional work, and unlike them may not have any easily evaluated project. (Lloyd 1985, 82)

Various commentaries alert us to the extraordinary time lag between architectural pedagogy development and the diversity of knowledge demanded today of architects:

I would like to make the following argument: that architecture—and especially architectural education—has not, even through stylistic and ideological attempts to repudiate Modernism, managed to improve or even grow beyond the ideals set forth in the manifestos of the early twentieth century. (Kunze 1987, 36)

No amount of research, discussions on "relevance" or compiled information can disguise one obvious fact: Architecture as taught and practiced today is but a grammatical fiction. Enough to see the gulf which separates what is taught (and how!) and what is built (and why!) to understand that somewhere a lie is being perpetrated. Only a sophistic method could mask a situation where so many spend so much to do so little—with such damaging results. (Libeskind 1987, 46)

This is but legitimate criticism from American academics and practitioners of an academy that teaches in a climate largely dominated by single clients (of whom there are few), where information is abundant, readily available, accurate, and easy to get (which it is not), where they are largely in control, or should be, of the design and building processes (which usually they are not), and where uncertainty is thought of as threatening and a sign of weakness rather than a condition of practice. To change one's mind is to seem inconsistent. Consistency is held in high esteem—a measure of rigorous inquiry and proficient design.

Students are taught that innovation in housing is the prerogative of their profession and they earn their grades for the new, the unfamiliar, the extraordinary. The ordinary is frowned upon.

Few, if any, "ordinary" or everyday examples of building had ever been featured in architectural history books (with a few exceptional cases)—the everyday and largely residential environment was not something to which students of architecture ordinarily aspired or through which architecture could be easily explained. Rather, "The history of architecture is the history of separate public monuments with occasional apologetic digressions to include the larger and richer and more isolated private houses" (Bauer 1934, 214). Even today, when housing does feature in the annals of architectural history, its concern is with the architecture of country houses, with the classic, the exotic, the post-modern and the picturesque. Habraken said,

In schools we are told to find our own voice and to do our own thing. In architectural criticism, the worst you can say of an architect's work is not that he is inept or had bad judgment, but that he did what someone else already did before. Indeed, in the course of time, the idea that architecture is the special within the ordinary has been developed in the idea that originality is the prerequisite of good architecture. The idea of the special has evolved into the cult of the new and unheard of. (Habraken 1985)

As students venture into the field, they will become frustrated by a muddled and largely unregulated world, as often will their employers. They will come to realize soon enough that most times to be original is to be divergent from the realities of ordinary people and ordinary places. They will be disappointed in various ways—notably because many will take jobs outside the mainstream of traditional architectural practice, and even fewer, in the United States at least, will practice in housing, unless they take poorly paid jobs with nonprofit organizations. (Some 15,000 to 20,000 architects out of the estimated 90,000 in the United States work for government agencies, contractors, material producers and developers, mortgage banks, and builders [Gutman 1988].) Others will work at levels below their talent and training, for example, in drafting.

Even those who do commit themselves to working within slums with community groups and in the multidisciplinary way demanded will find that what they need to know has little to do with architecture. Instead, it will be "more akin to that of the 'fixer' in East Europe, who gains a living from his knowledge of The System and how to manipulate It. It demands a certain sophisticated cunning rather than radical commitment. It also demands an old-fashioned conception of what it means to be a member of a profession, giving a direct and personal service to one's client" (Ward 1987, 29).

Students will have been told at school to bring their own values uncompromisingly to their design work, only to find that few outside architecture care much about their architectural value systems. Worse still, there will be a double disappointment, one for employers and one for employees, because employers expect their new employees to have received the kind of training that can be relied upon to respond normatively to well-known standard patterns of client demand, especially in the technical and contractual fields. The new graduate will be ill equipped in this respect and much better equipped at inventing new patterns, at challenging convention, "demonstrating the consequences of an attempt [by schools] to educate rather than train" (Meunier 1987, 47).

On the other hand, students will become disappointed with their practices, which they see as failing in their responsibilities to architecture, to experimentation, to innovations with form, style, technique, and in its representations of societal values. Most important, they will be disappointed because of the conflict they will experience in work habit between the rigorous and idealized methods of their education and the diverse, untidy, inconsistent world of practice, best summed up by Donald Schön (1984, 3):

In the geography of professional practice, there is a very dry, high ground where you can practice the techniques and use the theories on which you got your Ph.D. Down below, there is a swamp where the real problems lie. The difficulty is to decide whether to stay on the high ground, where you can be rigorous but deal with problems of lesser importance, or go down into the swamp to work on problems you really care about but in a way you see as hopelessly unrigourous. It is the dilemma of rigor or relevance. You can not have both, and the way in which people choose between them sets the course of their professional lives. One consequence is that architects who stick to the high ground become not only separate from practice, but increasingly divergent from it.

The swamp is characterized by innumerable groups of clients with competing vested interests, conflicting values, and priorities and by fragile networks of organization and relationships of people, high densities, petty economies, and often neighborhoods that are technically difficult to service or develop.

Statistical information is time-consuming and hard to get, and even when it is not, it often hides as much as it reveals about what people earn, how they earn it, or what the real housing deficits are. If the client is a government, it will want quick, visible, countable results that gain it votes and can rapidly expand the scale of its operation, but finds itself encumbered with processes and conditions that do not fit its general schema, or any general theory of planning or design. What governments confront are processes that are spontaneous, intuitive, incremental, and usually unregulated. These processes, which we now consider productive, demand assistance that is flexible, participatory and enabling. They demand a support rather than provider approach practiced with methods and attitudes that are open and dynamic.

OPERATIONAL IMPLICATIONS

There are practical operational implications here too, over and above the lack of historical precedent and the general unpreparedness of professionals. There are implications for funders, for local architects and planners, and for international consultants.

Implications for Funders

The World Bank, for example, like any other bank and like most bilateral and international development agencies, is in the business of managing money. It wants to be clear about what it will get for its money before work starts. It will want to minimize risk, protect investors, maximize its visibility and impact, and protect its own interests, and sometimes the political and economic interests of the nation it represents.

Eugene Black [Hayter 1981, 83], a former president of the World Bank, said: Our foreign aid programs constitute a distinct benefit to American business. The three major benefits are: 1) foreign aid provides a substantial and immediate market for United States goods and services. 2) foreign aid stimulates the development of new overseas markets for United States companies. 3) foreign aid orients national economies toward a free enterprise system in which United States firms can prosper.

This view was even more bluntly stated by President John F. Kennedy in 1961—"Foreign aid is a method by which the United States maintains a position of influence and control around the world, and sustains a good many countries which would definitely collapse or fall into the communist bloc"—and by President Richard Nixon in 1968—"Let us remember that the main purpose of American aid is not to help other nations, but to help ourselves (Hayter 1981, 83).

How do these broad policy views translate when it comes to the nitty gritty of practice? In order to be precise about their interventions and in view of their interests, most development agencies want control over packaging the content and details of project programs. They want to ensure that their borrowers have the kind of institutional capacities to exercise that control. The result is a process that is lengthy, arduous, and deterministic and where even small changes of mind or politics can lead to substantial delays. The result is in stark contrast to the attitudes and methods advocated under a support paradigm. It can take 6–9 months of study, including various missions dispatched for project appraisal, a feasibility study, and loan negotiations, all of which are documented in attractive appraisal reports.

When it comes to feasibility, whole ranges of procedures are set up. Hordes of local and international consultants are dispatched to explore site development alternatives, to make surveys, to undertake registration, to figure out beneficiary selection, to sort out resettlement, to set up banking facilities, and to work out cost recovery plans—all before projects can start. "A typical World Bank housing feasibility study may, for example, have a manpower input of some 50–60 man months. Half of this will go to local consultants, for junior engineers, architects, various local academics, draftsmen and support staff. Of the remainder, perhaps 15 man months may go to planning, 5 to economics, 5 to engineering and 5 to specialists support" (Walton 1984, 189). But governments that want to take advantage of international funding will accept the terms of reference as prepared in some European or U.S. capital and the practitioners who will accompany them and will spend substantial time and money implementing ideas and strategies that for them may be a low priority. It is no wonder that the real problems are often seeded outside the context in which they appear.

In view of all this, the support approach—the open-ended nature of the program, the difficulty in defining an accurate time frame, the idea that the program develops and consolidates in action and during settlement and that it is worked out with communities, and, in many cases, the difficulty in determining clear, quantifiable performance results—is problematic for most funders. In essence, the issue is one of institutional need for detailed terms of reference versus the realities of the program with its spontaneous, essentially ad hoc formulation. The position of the lenders-donors is understandable. They want to know what will be achieved with the funds, when it will be achieved, how it will be done, and who will do it.

Funders in the past have taken much deserved credit for innovations and ideas they have pioneered. The World Bank has its sites-and-services initiatives; the U.S. Agency for International Development pioneered thrift societies in Sri Lanka, and UNICEF advertises its presence in Quito, Ecuador, with large labels on newly installed pit latrines. While none of these initiatives is inherently inhibited by the support approach, there is, by implication, a reversal of trends, an onus on in country innovation and even credit. Does this represent a loss of status for funders? Does this represent a loss of control or power?

Implications for Local Professionals

For local architects and planners, whether in Colombo, Sri Lanka, Boston, Liverpool, or Santiago, all places that have experimented with support policies, various additional practical issues still need to be resolved.

First is the issue of status. To many of the staff working for the National Housing Development Authority in Sri Lanka, for example, the work lacked the prestige and the rewards they had come to expect as students of architecture or planning: money earned, buildings built, the number of buildings published. Project officers, despite their enthusiasm and commitment, viewed their work as largely unglamorous, inglorious, and unlikely to earn them a place in the annals of architectural history.

Many staff, whether in Sri Lanka or working for the Public Facilities Department in Boston, are involved in activities for which they were not trained. Their work is more diversified than their training. Few are familiar with processes of planning and design participation and with dealing with ordinary people on a day-to-day basis. Many program components that may appear after the various participatory workshops—health improvement, income generation, community development, for example—demand far greater collaboration with health workers, sanitary engineers, social workers, and others than is familiar.

Because of the intensely participatory activities of the support approach, staff complain of endless hours at endless meetings and troubleshooting squabbles among community members. Much of what they confront connects more with social science and management rather than with architecture. Often staff will work evenings and weekends because that is when people are around; they are on constant call. Remuneration is small, their working environment is far worse than that of those working in offices, transportation to and from sites is not always readily available, and some occasionally feel threatened if meetings get out of hand.

Most staff are under pressure to decide details of planning without tracing these decisions up the usual hierarchy. Their work demands the kind of autonomy that is not adequately reflected in changes to the decision-making structure of either housing authorities or funding institutions. The result is that the decision-making responsibilities of project staff are often unclear.

Project officers need ample opportunities to improvise. Like good managers, architects or planners need to come with no firm plan. They need to avoid the "orthodox view that good [design] starts with logical analysis or forethought . . . successful [design] strategy is rarely if ever thought up in advance. It comes into being for the most part by accident, and the [designer's] role is to recognize it as it emerges, and turn it to profit" (Dixon 1986, 85). The designer, especially if employed as a consultant, is probably in the pay of one funding agency or another, which will want extraordinarily precise descriptions of what he or she will propose and produce before work starts.

Given the nature of incremental programs, job satisfaction has to be sought less in quality of project achieved and more in a the quality of process enabled. Project staff who are committed to handling a number of projects, all of which were not easily scheduled with the usual "completion" dates, wind up with a backlog of projects. Unable to count completions is unhelpful to future career development; it is not easy to compile a portfolio or point to success. This is especially true where the nature of work in upgrading projects is more nitty gritty—repairing roads, adding extensions, positioning wells, extending utilities, inserting a few homes, working with elements and materials that are much finer grained. Society is unprepared to reward these activities despite the enormously challenging design constraints which they impose. Geddes (1947) once said: "The work cannot be done in the office with ruler and parallels, for the plan must be sketched out on the spot, after wearying hours of perambulation—commonly amid sights and odors which neither Brahmin nor Briton has generally schooled himself to endure, despite the moral and physical courage of which each is legitimately proud."

On top of it all, architects or planners working as supporters will have a pedagogic purpose. They will be teaching communities to cope and become proficient in their own right as "developers." The architect in this role will be a teacher. The best teachers do not tell students what to do but rather provide methods to describe how to find out what best to do and then how to find different ways of going about doing it. They will have access to resources and methods that will enable their students to discover their own line of reasoning and, in time, their own range of methods and answers.

Teachers must involve themselves through a series of interventionary measures in the interests, ideas, and thought processes of their students (community) and subsequently build on their strengths and strengthen their weaknesses. Similarly, students involve themselves with a teacher, tapping resources, questioning precedents, and challenging methods. Together they build knowledge based on mutually shared interests and on consensus of how to proceed. There will be little or no curriculum, although there will be formal ways to transfer information, and no specific agenda other than to achieve their goals as broadly set.

There will be a bank of existing resources to tap and link together as fits their purpose, to build an agenda as they go along, deliberately and incrementally. It is an intensely participatory process, looking to position the issues in ways that extend the boundaries of their understanding and therefore the basis of deciding how and where to act.

In all respects, the objective is to enable students to develop their abilities and to acquire the necessary skills to solve problems. They will need to know how to evaluate and monitor their own progress. One could call teaching a process of enablement and therefore the practice of enablement teaching. It is not surprising that many community-based architects who subscribe to the enablement principles are also teachers. It is equally unremarkable that teaching, or training, should feature so prominently in current developmental objectives and has become an integral part of the practice of housing.

Implications for International Consultants

International consultants are there either because they have been invited by the host government or because they have been appointed or recommended by their client—normally one of the funding agencies.

The best consultants bring with them what locals most lack: methodology. This includes ways of thinking and doing or ways of going about resolving issues, positioning problems, discovering locally rational responses to any given set of circumstances. Inevitably they will be working under the auspices of their employers, who will often have a very different agenda.

If consultants have been appointed, they will usually come as part of the funding package and will be under pressure to ensure that the demands set by the agency are implemented. If they are to implement the proverbial demonstration project, something that an agency may be pushing (a particular system, a scheme for privatization, a sites-and-services project), then they will be under pressure less to demonstrate an idea or teach its principles but more to prove it works. They will be inclined to define or even invent the problem to fit their client's intentions. At best, they will "cut off pieces of the problem that don't fit their general schema" (Schön 1984). They will reshuffle to find a good fit.

If the consultant is invited by a government, it will also be looking for legitimacy and sometimes reassurance. Consultants bring legitimacy to their host client, who may have already embarked upon a program but needs the endorsement of an intentionally reputable individual, firm, or university in order to receive further funding, to attract international visibility, or to endorse their national status in a wider intellectual and political community. Sometimes, however, host clients simply seek reassurance. "This is what we are doing," they say. "Are we doing it okay? Are we doing it any better or worse than anyone else? Do you have any suggestions on how we can improve things?" Consultants in this case work more in their capacity as resource rather than as engineers, architects, or planners.

In either case—whether appointed or invited—they will be party to proposals and solutions out of sheer economic necessity that come from outside in or from top down. In neither case is this strictly consistent with the three tenets of the support paradigm: flexibility, participation, and enablement.

A NEW AGENDA

We will need to shift away from making instant projects, away from sectoral programs, away from teaching housing under the compartmentalism of architecture, planning, economics, or any other discipline. We need to move toward programs that deal with systems of habitation that change and consolidate gradually and in which housing is one major component. We might rethink what Koenigsberger and Marcus put forward, without success, in 1972 (p.12): They envisaged people "who will be educated in basic physical and social sciences relevant to planning and building, and who will have some design skills, a grasp of building tech-

nology, surveying and building economics and, in addition, have management training."[4]

Whatever the model in teaching, and there will be many, we need to engage students in a multiplicity of pedagogic forms and in various cultural settings that parallel what they are likely to encounter in practice. We need short, intensive workshops with practitioners working on real problems, with minimal information, and with very little time.

We need field-based programs of working and learning from communities, located on sites where students confront real constraints with conflicts of values, priorities, and timetables, with changes of mind, with client members who appear and disappear, with no access to photocopying machines and drawing tables, inventing not only how to respond physically and intellectually but also how to communicate.

We need clinical workshops in the classroom with case studies that teach methods, where we can develop our tools, where we can demonstrate how minimum design intervention might enable alternative forms of consolidation over time. We need more field research to teach methods for story gathering and how to make quantitative surveys that emphasize the understanding of qualitative networks of relationships between formal and informal processes of production and building.

We will need to shift our attitudes out of the confines of master plans, with their singular prescriptive solutions, their reliance on consistency rather than diversity, with all the futures they envision and the guesswork they entail. We might think instead of dynamic models that are inviting of transformations and tolerate spontaneity, that are responsive to change, that are synthetic and made up

---

4. See UNESCO: Training of "barefoot" architects, Report of a working group, UNESCO Regional Office for Education in Asia and the Pacific, Bangkok, 1983. See also SAINI Balevant, Manandhar's Dilemma—Architect or activist: A professional predicament, *Architecture and Design* (India) 4(2) (January–February 1988): 82–86.

of systems rather than artifacts, structured by the values, prejudices, and actions of those who live in and near them.

We need to find good working linkages between the desired goals of people and governments and the idealized goals of disciplines or fields like architecture, planning, management, and public administration. We need to reconcile the realities we confront in any of the settlements and neighborhoods of poor people and the institutional truths of agencies, professional organizations, political parties, and even schools. And we must find better ways of linking the high ground of academia and the swamp of practice.

We must face the dilemma in education, where we confront a demand to broaden our base of knowledge in order to understand complex, dynamic systems of settlements and yet to be more specialized in applying that knowledge.

We must provide a better setting where all of the disciplines that connect to housing focus on the issues and interpret their responses, not so that we can become those other disciplines but so that we can be clear about our own.

We need to recognize that "there is no greater evil than a problem misstated," the root cause of much of the failure of housing responses both in history and now. We need to recognize that our collaboration with ordinary people, communities, and other local organizations has little to do with benevolence or patronage but more with rigorous inquiry, tainted significantly with human values. We need to improve the ways and means of securing this collaboration and conducting our inquiries and to improve the tools of practice to take advantage of its immense resourcefulness.

We have reached a watershed in the thinking and practice of housing for the poor where the only certainty we can state with confidence is the uncertainty of all our answers so far and all our ideas for what comes next. We cannot answer supply with certainty by increasing the production of houses. We cannot answer affordability by lowering standards or inventing new systems of construction. We cannot answer blight with wholesale clearance and redevelopment. We cannot answer high densities with high-rise buildings. We cannot answer crime and social deprivation by putting design utopias on trial. We cannot answer quality with better technology. We cannot answer better housing by building better houses. And yet, despite the euphemisms on the one hand and all the misleading rhetoric on the other that fill our texts, there is undoubtedly the beginning of consensus on issues of major concern, which must be cause for optimism.

REFERENCES

Bauer, Catherine. 1934. *Modern Housing.* Boston & New York: Houghton Mifflin Company. Reprinted 1974 New York: Arno Press.

Cabannes, Yves. 1985. Architects: Social catalysts or alchemists of forms? In *The Architect As Enabler,* Special issue of *Architecture and Competitions,* pp. 103–4.

Dixon, Michael, 1986. The Canadian guru of "bottom–up" theory. *Boston Globe,* August 10.

Dube, S.C. 1988. *Modernization and Development—The Search for Alternative Paradigms.* London: Zed Books.

Geddes, Patrick. 1947. *Patrick Geddes in India.* London: Lund Humphries.

Gutman, Robert. 1985. *The Design of American Housing. A Reappraisal of the Architect's Role.* New York: Publishing Centre for Cultural Resources.

Gutman, Robert. 1988. *Architectural Practice—A Critical View.* Princeton, N.J.: Princeton Architectural Press.

Habraken, John N. 1983. The general from the specific. Keynote address for the Eighth International Forum of the European Association for Architectural Education, Newcastle-upon-Tyne, England, April 13.

Hamdi, Nabeel. 1986. Training and education: Inventing a program and getting it to work. *Habitat International* 10(3):131–39.

Hayter, Teresa. 1981. *The Creation of World Poverty—An Alternative View to the Brandt Report.* London: Pluto Press in association with Third World First.

Jackson, Anthony. 1976. *A Place Called Home—A History of Low-Cost Housing in Manhattan.* Cambridge, Mass.: MIT Press.

Koenigsberger, O. H., and Markus, T. A. 1972. The structure and operations of the New School of Housing, Building and Planning at University Sains Malaysia. Penang: A Report to the Vice Chancellor.

Kunze, Donald. 1987. Commentary on architectural education. *Journal of Architectural Education* 40(2): 36.

Libeskind, Daniel. 1987. An open letter to architectural educators and students of architecture. *Journal of Architectural Education* 40(2):46.

Lloyd, Michael. 1985. Schools: The challenge of change. In *The Architect as Enabler,* Special issue of *Architecture and Competitions* pp. 80–83.

Meunier, John. 1987. Paradigms for practice: A task for architecture schools. *Journal of Architectural Education* 40(2):47–69.

Ruskin, John. 1925. *The Seven Lamps of Architecture.* London: George Allen and Unwin Ltd. (Originally published in 1880 by Allen and Unwin.)

Saini, Balevant. 1988. Manandher's dilemma—Architect or activist: A professional predicament. *Architecture and Design (India)* 4(2).

Schön, Donald A. 1984. The architectural studio as an exemplar of education for reflection-in-action. *Journal of Architectural Education* 38 (1):2–9.

Tarn, J. N. 1969. Working-class housing in 19th century Britain. Architectural Association Paper 7. London: Lund Humphries.

Ward, Colin. 1983. *Housing, An Anarchist Approach.* London: Freedom Press.

Ward, Colin. 1987. Community architecture: What a time it took for the penny to drop. *Built Environment* 13(1):22–32.

Walton, David S. 1984. The role of international consultants. In *Low-Income Housing in the Developing World,* pp. 187–98. Edited by G. K. Payne. New York: John Wiley and Sons.

Wright, Gwendolyn. 1982. *Building the Dream—A Social History of Housing in America.* Cambridge, Mass: MIT Press.

Additional Readings

GENERAL READINGS

This list provides an introduction to the housing field. The focus is on linkages between social and physical developments taken in both first and third world contexts.

Abrams, C. *Man's Struggle for Shelter in an Urbanizing World*. Cambridge, Mass.: MIT Press, 1964.

Discusses numerous aspects of the development process and highlights housing as an important component of the process. 307 p.

Achtenberg, Emily Paradise, and Marcuse, Peter. The causes of the housing problem. In *Critical Perspectives on Housing*. Philadelphia: Temple University Press, 1986.

The treatment of housing as a commodity and its subservience to the maintenance of profitability are seen as the root causes of the housing problems in the United States. 6 p.

Berry, F. *Housing: The Great British Failure*. London: C. Knight, 1974.

Discusses housing in Britain. 281 p.

Blackman, Tim, ed. *Community-based Planning and Development*. University of Ulster, 1987.

A useful collection of critical accounts of community-based projects in architecture, planning, housing, social research, health care, and economic development. Examples from Northern Ireland, Scotland, England, the Netherlands, and the United States. 137 p.

Boles, Daralice, ed. *Progressive Architecture* (October, 1988).

The entire issue is devoted to the current housing crisis in the United States. Several examples of housing projects are included.

Checkoway, Barry. Large builders, federal housing programs, and postwar suburbanization. In *Critical Perspectives on Housing*. Philadelphia: Temple University Press, 1986.

Explores the relationship between large merchant builders and the federal government. It traces how the growth of suburbs resulted from explicit needs and goals of each and rejects the popularly held belief that suburbia resulted primarily from consumer preferences. 20 p.

Coleman, Alice. *Utopia on Trial: Vision and Reality in Planned Housing*. London: Hilary Shipman, 1985.

One of the great postwar visions was of the ideal housing environment. The reality is squalor and social breakdown. This book proposes effective measures to correct past mistakes and to avoid them in the future. 219 p.

Faegan, Joe. Urban real estate speculation in the United States: Implications for social science and urban planning. In *Critical Perspectives on Housing*. Philadelphia: Temple University Press, 1986.

The private housing market consists of many actors. This chapter focuses on the role real estate speculators have played, historically and currently, in shaping urban areas and the rules by which the market system operates. 20 p.

Hamdi, Nabeel, and Robbins, Edward, eds. Special Issue: Third World Housing. *Architectural Review* (August 1985).

Critical reviews and case examples including sites and services design methods, the Fundasal in El Salvador, Bhogal in India, and housing trends in Egypt.

Hamdi, N., Goethert, R., eds. *Open House International: Design and Housing in Developing Countries* 8 (4)(1983).

This issue is devoted entirely to design and housing in developing countries. The articles cover enablement, policies, design with limited resources, and a Sri Lanka case study. 48 p.

Kemeny, Jim. A critique of homeownership. In *Critical Perspectives on Housing*. Philadelphia: Temple University Press, 1986.

The author examines the myths surrounding the superiority of home ownership versus other forms of housing tenure. 5 p.

Mathey, Kosta, ed. *Trialog*. (3 Quartal, 1988).

The entire issue is devoted to self-help housing. 59 p.

Meyerson, Ann. Deregulation and the restructuring of the housing system. In *Critical Perspectives on Housing*. Philadelphia: Temple University Press, 1986.

Efforts to rescue ailing thrifts in the early 1980s resulted in increased deregulation and homogenization of the banking system, profoundly altering the nation's housing situation and financial structure, which exacerbated the affordability problem. 30 p.

Payne, Geoffrey, ed. *Low-Income Housing in the Developing World: The Role of Sites and Services and Settlement Upgrading*. New York: John Wiley & Sons, 1984.

Sites and services and settlement upgrading are two major approaches to the massive need for low-income housing in developing countries. This is a comprehensive survey of the experience of these approaches throughout the world. It includes case studies and examines the roles of international agencies, consultants, the users, and the impact of land markets, institutional and political factors, and the options for servicing and building shelters in such projects. 271 p.

Peattie, Lisa. Some second thoughts on site-and-services. *Habitat International* 6(1–2)(1982).

When a new policy instrument is developed, promising to provide an economically feasible alternative to shanties, it can easily be seized upon as a panacea. Such may be the case with sites and services. 8 p.

Schlesinger, T., and Erlich, M. Housing: The industry capitalism didn't forget. In *Critical Perspectives on Housing*. Philadelphia: Temple University Press, 1986.

There has been great concentration of activity and control in the housing industry in recent years, substantial technological change, and vertical integration. This chapter explores the problems that result from these changes. 26 p.

Schneider, Bertrand. *The Barefoot Revolution: A Report to the Club of Rome*. London: Intermediate Technology Publications, 1988.

The "barefoot revolution" calls for a redirection of the economic strategy of the last twenty years. It identifies and measures the impact of an alternative approach through small-scale development projects run by nongovernmental organizations. 296 p.

Schumacher, E. F. *Small Is Beautiful: Economics as If People Mattered*. New York: Harper Torchbooks, 1973.

The founder of the Intermediate Technology Development Group shows how fragmentation of specialized competence, particularly that of economists, scientists, and technologists, has led to confusion of the means and ends of modern life; he stresses the need to return to wisdom in planning for the future. 290 p.

Scoffham, E.R. *The Shape of British Housing*. New York: George Godwin, 1984.

A historical documentation of postwar projects and their influences, of design and technical innovations, with critical evaluation of successes and failures. 250 p.

Stevens, William, ed. *Community Self-Help Housing Manual*. New York: ITDG North America, 1982.

Reviews the experiences of Habitat for Humanity, a U.S. nonprofit organization, in building hundreds of houses (in North America) for thousands of people, selling them at cost, with no interest. 72 p.

Stone, Michael E. Housing and the dynamics of U.S. capitalism. In *Critical Perspectives on Housing*. Philadelphia: Temple University Press, 1986.

Focuses on the mortgage lending system as a cause of the current U.S. housing problem. 27 p.

Stretton, H. *Urban Planning in Rich and Poor Countries*. New York: Oxford University Press, 1978.

A survey of urban planning around the world. 220 p.

Turnbull, Shann. *New Sources and Profit Motives*. Sydney: John Sands Pty Ltd., 1975.

Focuses on the fundamental and sometimes forgotten role of money and particularly people in the success of ventures. 99 p.

Wright, Gwendolyn. *Building the Dream: A Social History of Housing in America*. Cambridge, Mass.: MIT Press, 1981.

Wright shows the controversies surrounding thirteen different kinds of housing as each was first adopted and what happened when they were generally accepted. Topics include row housing, rural cottages, Victorian suburbs, urban tenements, and apartment life. 329 p.

HISTORY

This section illustrates historical examples of popular control over the physical environment. It traces the emergence of formal recognition for informal development and of participatory design as a legitimate professional activity.

Applebaum, Richard. Swedish housing in the postwar period: Some lessons for the American housing policy. In *Critical Perspectives on Housing*. Philadelphia: Temple University Press, 1986.

Sweden has probably gone further than any other country in the world in ensuring that all its residents are decently housed. The approaches and programs that Sweden has used so successfully may provide useful models for the United States. 23 p.

Burnett, J. *A Social History of Housing, 1815–1970*. 2d ed. New York: University Paperbacks, Methuen, 1986

The author focuses on the history of the dwelling and gives a detailed account of the standards, facilities, and amenities of rural cottages, artisan housing, bylaw terraces, council houses, suburban owner occupation, and the tower block. 344 p.

Hardy, D., and Ward, C. *Arcadia for All: The Legacy of a Makeshift Landscape*. New York: Mansell, 1984.

In southeast England during the first forty years of this century, thousands of families made their own place in the sun without the benefit of councils, planners, architects, building societies, or even builders. Were they making rural slums and seaside eyesores, or were they providing a unique example of unaided self-build housing, with lessons for us all? 307 p.

Jackson, A. *A Place Called Home—A History of Low Cost Housing in Manhattan*. Cambridge, Mass.: MIT Press, 1976.

A critical history of New York City's efforts to provide housing for its poor. The book deals with the attempt of both private and public enterprise. 359 p.

Marcuse, Peter. A useful installment of socialist work: Housing in Red Vienna in the 1920s. In *Critical Perspectives on Housing*. Philadelphia: Temple University Press, 1986.

For a brief period after World War I, the socialist-controlled municipal government of Vienna launched an all-out attack on inadequate and unaffordable housing. The approach included many of the components advocated by progressives today. 28 p.

Schifferes, Steve. The Dilemmas of British housing policy. In *Critical Perspectives on Housing*. Philadelphia: Temple University Press, 1986.

Traces the evolution of British housing policy, analyzing the factors that facilitated the coexistence of a large public housing sector with an active private sector. 21 p.

Tarn, J. N. *Working-class Housing in Nineteenth-Century Britain*. Architectural Association Paper 7. London: Lund Hampshires, 1969.

An outline of the main forces at work during the second half of the century that influenced British working-class housing. 105 p.

Ward, Colin, *Tenants Take Over*. London: Architectural Press, 1974.

Argues for tenants' control on local authority housing estates. 180 p.

Ward, Colin. *Housing: An Anarchist Approach*. London: Freedom Press, 1983.

The author advocates popular control, individual or collaborative, in existing housing or in the production of housing. 200 p.

IDEAS, APPROACHES, AND CRITIQUES

This section establishes the theoretical and practical roots of community planning and action. The titles elaborate on issues of professional responsibilities in the context of community control over housing design and building and highlight hurdles and opportunities.

Achtenberg, E. P., and Marcuse, Peter. Toward the decommodification of housing. In *Critical Perspectives on Housing*. Philadelphia: Temple University Press, 1986.

Housing must be made available on the principle of socially determined need, not profitability. The strategic implications of this proposal, in terms of their potential for political organizing, are explored. 10 p.

Alternatives in Housing—A Report of Self Build in Britain. London: A. A. Papers, 1976.

Angel, Shlomo. Instead of focusing on housing, focus on urban land development. *Open House International*. Special Issue: *Biennial International Shelter Workshop 1986* 11(4)(1986).

"Housers" would do well to abandon their emphasis on house construction and their later emphasis on sites-and-services projects and move to taking an active part in urban land development. 36 p.

Arnstein, S. A. A ladder of citizen participation. *Journal of the American Institute of Planners* 45(4)(July 1969).

Atlas, J., and Dreier, P. The Tenants' Movement in America. In *Critical Perspectives on Housing*. Philadelphia: Temple University Press, 1986.

Change in the U.S. housing system is necessary and must involve broad-based, grass-roots mass mobilization. This chapter looks at a range of questions related to this idea. 20 p.

Beheshti, M. R., and Dinjens, P. J. M., eds. *Open House International: DPC '85 International Design Participation Conference*. 10(1)(1985).

The first International Design Participation Conference hosted by the University of Eindhoven School of Architecture. The projects, workshops, and papers show the developments that have taken place over the last twenty years in the participatory housing field. 58 p.

Borgos, Seth. Low-income homeownership and the ACORN squatters campaign. In *Critical Perspectives on Housing*. Philadelphia: Temple University Press, 1986.

One organized consumer response to the housing crisis is squatting. The squatting campaign organized by ACORN in over a dozen U.S. cities has assisted hundreds of low-income families in acquiring low-cost housing. 19 p.

Comerio, M. Design and empowerment: 20 years of community architecture. *Built Environment* 13(1)(1987).

An account of the recent history of participatory design. 16 p.

Cooper-Marcus, C. *Housing as If People Mattered*. Berkeley: University of California Press, 1988.

Deals with issues of habitability of low- and moderate-income U.S. urban housing as reflected from evaluation studies largely oriented to site and massing concerns of the housing environment.

Cowley, John. The limitations and potential of housing organizing. In *Critical Perspectives on Housing*. Philadelphia: Temple University Press, 1986.

The author is sympathetic to housing organizing as a strategy for change and uses the comparison with workplace organizing as a tool with which to understand and, he hopes, remedy the problems the housing movement has encountered. 6 p.

De Carlo, G. *An Architecture of Participation*. Melbourne: Royal Australian Institute of Architects, 1972.

A paper delivered in October 1971 in Melbourne. 54 p.

Fathy, H. *Architecture for the Poor*. Chicago: University of Chicago Press, 1973.

Describes Fathy's plan for building an Egyptian village using low-cost traditional techniques and crafts and working closely with the villagers themselves. He seeks to provide for third world countries an alternative to the normally excessive cost of public housing. 224 p.

Francis, Moore, Iacofano, Klein, and Paxson, eds. *Journal of Architectural and Planning Research: Design and Democracy* 4(4)(December 1987).

A special issue devoted entirely to participatory housing. 89 p.

Grimes, Orcille, Jr. *Housing for Low-Income Urban Families.* Baltimore: Johns Hopkins University Press, 1976.

Offers guidelines for improved housing policies in many urban environments and evaluates various options for low-income housing. 175 p.

Habraken, John N. *Supports: An Alternative to Mass Housing.* New York: Praeger Publishers, 1972.

A very strong critic of mass housing, the author presents the idea of supports as an alternative to the way housing is produced. 97 p.

Habraken, John N. Involving people in the housing process. *RIBA Journal* (November 1972).

Presents his case for user involvement in design and introduces the "supports" idea.

Hackney, R. My hopes for community architecture. *Building Design,* November 21, 1986.

The author advocates community participation in architecture.

Hamdi, Nabeel. Low income housing changing approaches. *Architectural Review* (August 1985).

Discusses different approaches and different paradigms to the process of housing.

Hamdi, N., and Greenstreet, B., eds. *Theory and Implementation.* Working Paper 57: Participation in Housing: No. 1. London: Oxford Polytechnic, Department of Town Planning, October 1981.

Attempts to provide a comprehensive overview of participation in housing. 59 p.

Hamdi, N., and Greenstreet, B., eds. *Two Case Studies.* Working Paper 59: Participation in Housing: No. 3. London: Oxford Polytechnic, Department of Town Planning, January, 1982.

Features two case studies to illustrate the possible benefits of the participatory process. 71 p.

Hamdi, N., and Goethert, R. *Implementation: Theories, Strategies and Practice. Habitat International* 9(1)(1985).

Review of some of the common causes of failure of ideas when it comes to putting them into practice.

Hamdi, N.; Goethert, R.; and Casault, A., eds. *Open House International.* Special Issue: *Biennial International Shelter Workshop 1986* (4)(1986).

The entire issue is devoted to the problem of shelter.

Hatch, C. R., ed. *The Scope of Social Architecture.* New York: Van Nostrand Reinhold, 1984.

Its emphasis is on process, the involvement of users, and democratic control of the environment. 362 p.

Illich, I. *Disabling Professions.* Marion Boyars, 1977.

A devastating and influential critic of contemporary professionalism. 127 p.

Koeingsberger, Otto. *Action Planning.* London: Arch. Assoc. Quarterly, 79(882).

Discusses action planning for community health services. Includes a bibliography. 67 p.

Kolodny, Robert. The emergence of self-help as a housing strategy for the urban poor. In *Critical Perspectives on Housing.* Philadelphia: Temple University Press, 1986.

Abandonment or severe undermaintenance of privately owned rental housing and poor management in public housing developments has stimulated tenants to try to improve their living conditions in a variety of innovative ways. Management, control, and/or cooperative ownership by tenants are seen as key to these strategies. 16 p.

Lerup, Lars. *Building the Unfinished: Architecture and Human Action.* London: Sage Publications Ltd., 1977.

Lerup rejects the "behaviorism" of established architecture, which has attempted to create a perfect fit between people and their physical settings. This view, he contends, neglects the fact that people act upon their surroundings. The architectural environment is, in his view, always unfinished and open. Lerup calls his position "interactionist" and deals with it in both an exploratory and theoretical manner. 169 p.

Metselaar, A., and Hoenderdos, A. Multi story self-help. *Open House International* 11(3)(1986).

Reports on self-help in rental units. 7 p.

Mongold, Neil. Community Architecture: Myth and Reality. Master's Thesis, MIT, 1988.

Examines the origins and the claims of the community architecture movement. 70 p.

Newman, O. *Community of Interest*. Garden City, N.Y.: Anchor Press, Doubleday, 1981.

The author attempts to formulate a new concept for physical communities that reflects contemporary needs and political realities. 356 p.

Ospina, José. *Housing Ourselves*. London: Planning Bookshop, 1987.

Examines the social, administrative, and technical aspects of communities to provide their own housing. 211 p.

Peattie, L. R. Some second thoughts on sites and services. *Habitat International* 6(1–2)(1982).

A critical look at the sites-and-services approach to housing.

Plat, T., and Bosmans, E. Self-management and construction in housing. *Open House International* 11(3) (1986).

The authors discuss self-help as an attractive possibility to lessen the housing problem in developing and developed countries. 4 p.

Priemus, H. Self-help in Dutch housing. *Open House International* 9(3)(1984).

The author outlines the early development of Habraken's ideas and of the SAR. He describes some of the early problems of acceptance and support and infill in Dutch housing spheres. 8 p.

Rondinelli, Dennis. *Development Projects as Policy Experiments: An Adaptive Approach to Development Administration*. New York: Methuen, 1983.

The author offers an adaptive approach to development administration, one that relies on adjunctive and strategic planning, procedures that facilitate innovation, and processes that join learning with action to yield more appropriate and effective development projects. 178 p.

Rybczynski, W., and Vikram, B. Understanding slums: The use of public space. *Open House International* 11(1)(1986).

Looks at slums, the informal sector, and available resources. It surveys four neighborhoods in the city of Indore, India. 10 p.

Schuman, Tony. The agony and the equity: A critique of self-help housing. In *Critical Perspectives on Housing*. Philadelphia: Temple University Press, 1986.

While the self-help ethic, in housing and other areas, has a virtuous aura, applying it on a mass scale as a program to solve the low-income housing problem raises some disturbing questions, some of them explored here. 11 p.

Skinner, R. J., and Rodell, M. J., eds. *People, Poverty and Shelter: Problems of Self-Help Housing in the Third World*. New York: Methuen, 1983.

Traces the successes and failures of various self-help programs, from sites and services in Peru to cooperatives in Tanzania. 195 p.

Strassman, Paul. Industrialized Systems Building for Developing Countries: A Discouraging Prognosis.

In some European countries industrialized systems building has been appealing and sometimes appalling. This paper explores its aptness for housing in developing countries. 15 p.

Taylor, M. User needs or exploiter needs? *Architectural Design* 43(November 1973).

Has a very good bibliography.

Turner, John, and Fichter, Robert, eds. *Freedom to Build: Dweller Control of the Housing Process*. New York: Macmillan, 1972.

When housing is seen as a physical product and when dwellers lose control over their living environments, shelter becomes a commodity of reduced value to the individual and often an inordinate expense to society. 301 p.

Turner, John. *Housing by People: Towards Autonomy in Building Environments*. New York: Pantheon Books, 1977.

The author promotes self-help and argues that government should cease doing what it does badly—building and managing houses. 169 p.

Ward, Colin. *When We Build Again*. London: The Planning Bookshop, 1987.

For generations the left put its faith in council housing as the central solution to housing needs. Housing policy now lies in ruins. This is an argument for a popular and populist approach to housing. 127 p.

Ward, Colin. Community architecture: What time it took for the penny to drop! *Built Environment* 13(1)(1987).

The author asks why the simple task of housing oneself and adapting and improving one's immediate environment has been made tortuous and complicated. 12 p.

Ward, P. ed. *Self-Help Housing—A Critique*. London: Mansell Publishing Ltd., 1982.

A collection of articles that examine theories of self-help, the impact and contribution of self-help in different cities, and experiences of the application of self-help. 296 p.

Wates, Nick, and Knevitt, Charles. *Community Architecture: How People Are Creating Their Own Environment*. West Drayton: Penguin Books, 1987.

Werlin, H. Starting small on big urban problems. *Open House International* 11(3)(1986).

The author argues for small-scale pilot projects. 4 p.

Ziss, R., and Kotowsi-Ziss, J. Squatter consolidation in Mexican intermediate cities. *Open House International* 10(4)(1985).

An analysis of housing development processes within four squatter settlements in Mexico. 9 p.

PUBLIC AND PRIVATE: POLICIES AND INTERVENTIONS

The texts listed here elaborate the role of public sector housing in a historical setting versus private initiatives. This section traces public-private partnership programs that have helped improve production and lower costs. This section introduces the idea of the community sector and nongovernmental organizations and the role of mediating structures.

Angel, S. Upgrading slum infrastructure. *Third World Planning Review* 5(1)(February 1983).

Discusses approaches to and problems in upgrading the infrastructures of slums.

Bratt, Rachel. Public housing: The controversy and contribution. In *Critical Perspectives on Housing*. Philadelphia: Temple University Press, 1986.

Public housing has performed better than is widely believed. To the extent that the program has not been successful, some of the major reasons for its problems are clarified here. 27 p.

Berger, Peter, and Neuhaus, Richard. *To Empower People—The Role of Mediating Structures in Public Policy*. Washington D.C.: American Enterprise Institute for Public Policy and Research, 1977.

The authors argue that mediating structures—institutions such as church organizations or voluntary associations that are closest to the control and aspirations of most Americans—should be used, where feasible, to advance legitimate social goals. 45 p.

Gilbert, Alan. *Housing, the State and the Poor: Policy and Practice in Three Latin American Cities*. New York: Cambridge University Press, 1985.

This book is concerned with the housing and service needs of the poor in Latin America and how they are articulated and satisfied. It examines the aims and implementation of government policies toward low-income housing dwellers and tries to relate those policies to the interests of the state. 319 p.

Hartman, Chester. Housing policies under the Reagan administration. In *Critical Perspectives on Housing*. Philadelphia: Temple University Press, 1986.

The Reagan administration waged war on traditional government housing programs for the poor. It was averse to the concept that government has an obligation to provide the poor with decent, affordable housing. 15 p.

Henderson, V., and Iaonnides, Y. A model of housing tenure choice. *American Economic Review* 73(1)(1983).

Considers the issues that influence housing tenure choice.

Marcuse, Peter. Housing policy and the myth of the benevolent state. In *Critical Perspectives on Housing*. Philadelphia:Temple University Press, 1986.

The author explodes certain myths about the public sector. He reveals the role that government has played in interacting with private interests and shaping housing policy. 16 p.

FINANCE AND MANAGEMENT

Following is a selective list of titles that explore alternative models of financing low-income housing and of building equity for poor communities. Models include co-ops, land trusts, land banks, and other forms of private-public partnerships.

Bottomley, T. *Business Arithmetic for Co-operatives and Other Small Businesses*. London: Intermediate Technology Publications.

A manual for staff of cooperatives that explains business calculations and analyses. 88 p.

Bottomley, T. *An Introduction to Co-operatives*. London: Intermediate Technology Publications, 1979.

This booklet deals with the principles of cooperative organization and structure. It explains in some detail how cooperatives are financed and outlines the various types of cooperatives. 68 p.

Dean, C. F. Administration and management issues: Experiences from the Co-operative Housing Foundation.'' *Open House International* 8(4)(1983).

Reviews conventional housing management approaches and proposes various types of housing cooperatives both formal and informal. Suggests a framework for setting up both large and small cooperatives.

Hartman, C., and Stone, M. A socialist housing alternative for the United States. In *Critical Perspectives on Housing*. Philadelphia: Temple University Press, 1986.

Presents a concrete program for a socialized housing sector. The program derives from an analysis that sees as the central housing affordability problem dependence on mortgage financing and the ever-higher prices and credit needs that result from buying and selling housing for a profit. 30 p.

Launder, J. *Office Management for Co-operatives*. London: Intermediate Technology Publications, 1980.

This self-teaching text deals with office management—staffing, control, files, and accommodation required to run a cooperative efficiently. Of use to managers of both large and small cooperatives. 102 p.

Lewin, A. C. *Self-Help Housing through Co-operatives: Prospects and Problems for Urban Africa*. Cologne: Lewin, 1976.

The aim of this manual is to encourage and initiate discussion on the various questions and problems related to the promotion of certain housing cooperatives for low-income households in Africa. 313 p.

Padmanabhan, K. P. *Rural Credit: Lessons for Rural Bankers and Policymakers*. London: Intermediate Technology Publications, 1988.

Discusses what the role is and what the role should be of rural credit in developing countries. Two views are presented—the "banking school" and the "development school." 160 p.

Wheaton, W. C. Housing policies in developing countries. *Open House International* 8(4)(1983).

Reviews the role of housing in the economies of developing nations. Suggests reasons why housing should be actively assisted and the role of government.

Yeo, P. *The Work of a Co-operative Committee*. London: Intermediate Technology Publications, 1978.

Explains in detail the role of the committee in the operations of a cooperative. It is written as a learning text for the staff of cooperatives for use in group training or individual study. 88 p.

BUILDING TECHNOLOGY

The following publications examine the attempt to facilitate self-help and to deal with change in buildings through simple technologies relative to arguments for speed, scale, and cost effectiveness. They also examine attempts to modernize based on more efficient and more abundant small building organizations.

Dunn, P. D. *Appropriate Technology: Technology with a Human Face*. New York: Schocken Books, 1979.

Focuses on underdeveloped areas. 220 p.

Gamser, Matthew, ed. *Mobilizing Appropriate Technology: Papers on Planning Aid Programmes*. London: Intermediate Technology Publications, 1988.

A collection of papers presented at a conference in Norway in 1987 that cover discussions on ecology, gender, basic needs strategy, institutional aspects, and appropriateness. 160 p.

Herbert, G. *The Dream of the Factory Made House: Walter Gropius and Konrad Wachsmann*. Cambridge, Mass.: MIT Press, 1984.

Traces the story of Gropius's, and Wachsmann's attempt at and failure to develop a factory-made house. 407 p.

Herbert, G. *Pioneers of Prefabrication: The British Contribution in the Nineteenth Century*. Baltimore: Johns Hopkins University Press, 1978.

A look at the history of prefabrication and the British contribution in the nineteenth century. 219 p.

Jequier, N. *Appropriate Technology: Problems and Promises.* Paris: Development Centre of the Organization for Economic Co-operation and Development, 1976.

Looks at the appropriateness of technologies to culture and context. 344 p.

London, R. J., ed. *Introduction to Appropriate Technology: Toward a Simpler Life-Style.* Emmaus, Pa.: Rodale Press, 1977.

What is meant by appropriate technology? What might we benefit from it? 205 p.

Parry, J., and Gingold, P. Fibre concrete roofing: The Latin American experience. *Open House International* 10(4)(1985).

Gives some technical and institutional background to the development and implementation of fiber concrete roofing materials in Latin America. Several brief case studies are included. 10 p.

Rosenberg, Nathan. Economic development and the transfer of technology: Some historical perspectives. *Technology and Culture* 11(3)(July 1970).

In earlier days we believed that there was a purely technological solution to the problems of poverty and economic backwardness that beset most of the human race. We have now learned that this was an unrealistic expectation. 25 p.

Stultz, R. *Appropriate Building Materials.* London: Intermediate Technology Publications, 1988.

Updated description of low-cost and locally available materials. It covers foundations, walls, ceilings and roof construction, and brickmaking. 360 p.

METHODS AND TOOLS

The following publications examine methods of design, gaming, and negotiation that facilitate user involvement and improve communication among actors. They look at the methods and premises of community architecture and community practice and illustrate tools and techniques that help communities and local organizations craft projects and programs.

Alexander, Christopher. *The Timeless Way of Building.* New York: Oxford University Press, 1979.

Describes patterns and perception in architecture. 552 p.

Alexander, Christopher. *A Pattern Language: Towns, Buildings, Construction.* New York: Oxford University Press, 1976.

Presents patterns for architecture and city planning and discusses signs and symbols in architecture. 1171 p.

Alexander, Christopher, *The Oregon Experiment.* New York: Oxford University Press, 1975.

Describes a project undertaken in Oregon. 190 p.

Argyris, Chris; Putnam, Robert; and Smith, Diana. *Action Science: Concepts, Methods, and Skills for Research and Intervention.* San Francisco: Jossey-Bass. 1985.

Action and science are central concepts in Western thought. Action science attempts to bridge the two.

Caminos, H., and Goethert, R. *Urbanization Primer for Design of Site and Services Projects.* World Bank: Urban Projects Department, 1975.

Provides tools for decisions affecting policies as well as physical design. 214 p.

Friedman, Yona. Architecture by yourself. In *Professionals and Urban Form.* Albany: State University of New York Press, 1983.

Describes a program whereby architects and users can jointly participate in decisions and in some situations the user can make the design decisions. 10 p.

Habraken, N. J., et al. *Variations: The Systematic Design of Supports.* Cambridge, Mass.: Laboratory of Architecture and Planning at MIT, 1976.

Proposes a design method in which the dwelling is not a product that can be designed and produced like any other commodity but is a result of a process in which the user can make decisions within a larger framework of communal services and infrastructure. 216 p.

Hamdi, N., and Goethert, R. *Making Microplans: A Community Based Process in Programming and Development.* London: Intermediate Technology Publications, 1988.

Urban settlement upgrading is a complex business characterized by innumerable groups of people with competing vested interests. This is a practical guide for community groups and their leaders. 80 p.

Illich, Ivan. *Tools for Conviviality*. New York: Harper and Row, 1980.

A criticism of professions and their tendency toward monopoly. Advocates participation. 135 p.

Lewin, A. C. *Housing Co-operatives in Developing Countries: A Manual for Self-Help in Low-Cost Housing Schemes*. New York: John Wiley & Sons, 1981.

This practical manual for urban self-help housing cooperatives in developing countries emphasizes the organizational and planning aspects and looks at training participants, the construction process, and the legal framework. 170 p.

Lynch, Kevin. *The Image of the City*. Cambridge, Mass.: Technology Press and Harvard University Press, 1960.

A thorough analysis of the characteristics that make for good city form. 194 p.

Lynch, Kevin. *What Time Is This Place*. Cambridge, Mass.: MIT Press, 1972. 277 p.

Lynch, Kevin. *Managing the Sense of a Region*. Cambridge, Mass.: MIT Press, 1980.

Looks at environmental aspects of regional planning in the United States. 221 p.

McGill, M., and Horton, M., Jr. *Action Research Designs: For Training and Development*.

Examines the themes of participation and change in organizations.

Sanoff, Henry, ed. *Designing with Community Participation*. Stroudsburg Pa.: Hutchinson Ross. 1978.

A series of essays on city planning, community development, and citizen participation. 248 p.

Tenant Participation in Housing Design: A Guide for Action. London: RIBA Publications Ltd., 1988.

A guide to the participation of tenants in the design of improvements to existing housing and in the design of new housing. 56 p.

INDEX

Alexandria, Egypt, incremental growth, 35
American Institute of Architects, 171
Architects
  built form, 38
    Habraken's opinion, 45
  competitions, 172
  enablement, 39, 46–48
    defined, 88–89
    design considerations, 102–108
    example, 89–102
  flexibility, 39, 46–48
    1960s popularity, 51, 53
    defined, 41
    design principles emerging from, 73–74
    excess material, 72
    housing cycles and, 73
  future goals, 179–180
  housing history and, 169–172
  institutional form, 38
  international consultants, 178–179
  job satisfaction, 177–178
  methods, 43–46
  objectives, 39–43
  ornimentalists, 171
  participation, 39, 46–48
  professional responsibilities, 169–180
  status, 177
  students, 173–175
  studies, 172
  teachers, 178
Architects Small House Service Bureau, 171

Bauer, Catherine, on housing problem, 11
Benjamin, Solomon J., on political and social reform, 13
Bhogal, India, housing transformations, 52
Boston, growth of, 33–34
Burgess, Rod, on Turner's methods, 44

Cabannes, Yves, on architecture specificity, 172–173
Cairo, growth of, 14, 33
Cholera Act of 1832, 12
Clausen, A. W., on housing conditions, 5–6

Dandora Community Development, Nairobi, 79
Darbourne, Geoffrey, on creativity, 42
Deindustrialization, 44–46
Design reserve, 68–71

Dimensional frameworks, 63–68
Dudley recommendations of 1944, 55

Enablement. *See* Architects, enablement

Flexibility. *See* Architects, flexibility
Frank, Douglas, on Habraken's design principles, 43
FUNDASAL (El Salvador project), 80

GamePAK, 153
Gibson, Tony, Planning for Real inventor, 156–160
Greater London Council, "preferred dwelling plans," 54

Habraken, John, 38–48
  architectural criticism, 174
  design attitude, 3, 107–108
  Turner's methods compared with, 43–46
  Turner's objectives compared with, 39–43. *See also* Architects
Heath, Thomas, on building standards, 54–55
Helwan, Egypt, housing additions, 52
Hester, Randolph T., on community participation, 77–78
Homeless, 6–7
Houses for Heroes, 13
Housing
  bankers affecting, 6
  Britain's poverty and, 6–7
  building materials
    acquisition, 100
    allocation, 30–31
  bungalows, 16
  centrally planned projects, 33
  community participation, 20–21
    Britain, 76–77
    builders, 111
    building know-how, 152
    center structure, 117, 119
    cognitive mapping, 154–156
    conditions, 83–86
    cooperatives, 122
    developing countries, 78–80
    dwellers, 111
    fabric, 113
    frame, 113
    function, 113
    GamePAK, 153
    housers, 111
    ideals, 75

information examination, 126–128
international funders, 111
linkage analysis, 144–147
loans, 164
measurement procedures, 123–126
methods, 147–150
municipal engineers, 111
necessity of, 80–83
objections, 83–86
objective prioritization, 139–144, 151–152
partnership factor, 81, 129
planning methodology checklist, 132–135
Planning for Real, 156–160
politicians, 111
preliminary meetings, 130–131
problem identification, 123, 131–140
professional group reports, 114
pro forma, 160–161
project evaluation, 126
project monitoring, 149
relevance factor, 129
resident group reports, 114
resource collection, 152
time factor, 129
United States, 77–78
workshops, 82–83, 111–114, 139–144
consumption, 30–32
creativity, 56
current issues, 8–9
current problems, 3
  solutions, 3–4
debt related to, 6
demand, 4
  changes, 58
design, 21
  attitude, 107–108
  change and fit, 57–73
  checklist, 126
  dimensional frameworks, 63–68
  excess material, 72
  improvisation, 103
  income-generating activities and, 102
  incrementalism, 59–60, 94–95, 103–104
  management model, 93
  phased development, 94–95
  principles, 73–74
  reserve, 68–71
  spatial model, 91–92
  spontaneity, 103
  structure and, 106
  technology and, 72–73
  training programs, 104
  user adaptability, 98–99
differential growth, 33

disease epidemics affecting, 12–13
electrical provisions, 21
family planning, 61
first world, 6–7
fragment building industry, 31
functional changes, 58
future goals, 179–180
horticulture analogy, 47
incremental growth, 33
instant building, 33
international aid affecting, 5
land investment, 20
locally managed progressive development, 33
metaphoric model, 161–166
national versus international solutions, 18
nongovernment organizations and, 40, 130–131
obsolescence, 53
one-shot fix, 32
planning, 21
as a political reform instrument, 13, 46
privatization, 12
professional attitudes affecting, 32
professional dilemmas, 7–8
provider paradigm, 26–32
  characteristics, 28–29
public, 11–12
  additions, 52
  difficult-to-let, 56
  interventions, 12–26
questions for consideration, 9, 32, 36, 74, 128
shanties, 16–17
sites-and-services projects, 20–26
as a social reform instrument, 13
standards, 54–55, 119–121
starter homes, 97
storm drainage, 21
structure versus content, 47
suggested readings, 182–191
support paradigm, 26–32
  characteristics, 28–29
  Habraken, John, 39–43
  Sri Lanka, 109–110
  Turner, John, 39–43
technological fix, 32
third world, 4–6
transformation, 52, 53, 57
United States' poverty and, 6–7
upgrading, 16–17
  redevelopment versus, 18–19
  Sri Lanka, 17
user participation philosophy, 48
user surveys, 56
utility investment, 20
World Bank expenditures, 4, 18, 175–176

criteria for, 166
 sites-and-services projects, 24
World War I affecting, 13
World War II affecting, 13

International Monetary Fund, 5
International Union of Architects, 88

Kennedy, John F., on foreign aid, 176
Koenigsberger, Otto, on housing problem, 11
Kropotkin, Peter, on decentralization, 41

Land development, 96–97
 boundary setting, 17
 commercial potential, 118
 controlled, semipublic, 116
 history, 13, 15–16
 uncontrolled, public, 116
Lethaby, William Richard, on architecture, 51
Lloyd, Michael, on studying architecture, 173

Manhattan Institute for Policy Research, on homelessness, 7
Mexico City, growth of, 15
Morris, Parker
 on housing transformations, 53
 on spacing standards, 55

Nixon, Richard, on foreign aid, 176

Ottowa, Canada, housing transformation, 35

Party wall system, 70–71
Peattie, Lisa
 on bounds of architecture, 9
 on community participation, 82
 on land investment, 96
Peterborough Master Plan, 54
Planning for Real, 156–160
Project Assist, 1972, 77
PSSHAK project, 60, 62, 63

Ravetz, Alison, on community participation, 76
Realpolitik, 12
Redfern, Gordon, on support paradigm, 43
Richards, J. M., on professional dilemmas, 8
Robbins, E., on community participation, 84
Rogers, Richard, on design reserve, 69
Royal Institute of British Architects, 20, 42
 building standards, 55

Schön, Donald, on studying architecture, 175
Schumacher, E. F.

on appropriate technologies, 26
 on freedom and order, 40
 on support paradigm, 30
Sheffington Report, 20, 76
Shelters Neighborhood Action Project, 20
Squatters, 13, 15–16
Sri Lanka
 community participation staff, 130
 garbage collection, 115
 housing structure, 35
 planning methodology checklist, 132–135
 slum upgrading, 17
 support paradigm, 109–110
 Wanatahmulla, 101
Stonorov, O., on building standards, 53–54
Strassman, W. P., on building volume, 31
Stretton, Hugh
 on building criteria selection, 129
 on community design workshops, 111, 113
 on professional dilemmas, 8

Tarn, J. N., on criticizing architects, 170
Tenement Act of 1867, 12
Topeka, Kansas, cognitive mapping, 154–156
Tudor Walters Report of 1918, 55
Turner, John, 38–48
 Habraken's methods compared with, 43–46
 Habraken's objectives compared with, 39–43

United Nations Conference on Trade and Develop-
 ment: 1989, 5
United Nations Development Program, 18
United Nations Global Report on Human Settlements,
 107
United Nations Habitat Conference, 20

Ward, Colin
 on housing principles, 38
 on housing problem, 36
 on housing settlement process, 16
 on system management, 152
Water supply, inadequate, 124–125
Woolley, Thomas, on community participation, 85
World Bank expenditures, 4, 18, 175–176
 criteria for, 166
 sites-and-services projects, 24
Worthington, John, on building standards, 54, 55
Wright, Frank Lloyd
 on individualism, 53
 on support paradigm, 41

Year of Shelter: 1987, 4